A Red Pine Sunday

A Red Pine Sunday

Lex Larson

New York
2014

First Printing: 2014

ISBN 978-0-9904252-0-5

Lex Larson
995 Jefferson Ave, #1
Brooklyn, NY, 11221

www.aredpinesunday.com

Ordering Information:
Special discounts are available on quantity purchases by corporations, associations, educators, and others. For details, contact the publisher at the above listed address.

U.S. trade bookstores and wholesalers:

Please contact Lex Larson Tel: (715) 781-7278; or email LexLarson08@gmail.com

Acknowledgments

A Huge Thanks to all those who made this book possible:

Julie and Keith Larson

Sally and Rick Torgerson

Julie and Jack Heller

Eric Stiller and Susan Basu

Sarah Sweeney

David and Cecilia Steingard

Chris, Faith, and Karly

Liam Dempsey

Brittney Bartolini

The Chrest Family

Joann FWDS

Clark Lampen

.

Grandpa and Grandma Noreen

Andrew's Martinson

Mitch Bompey

RichieFox

Javier Alejandro Chavez

Aunt Judy and Uncle Bill Snoeyenbos

Matthew Wolf

Gene and Cynthia Larson

Gary and Penny Butler

Tony and Lori Jurek

1

The winters were always so fucking cold.

That's what predominantly occupied Sam's mind for six or seven months of the year. It was about a ninety/ten split: ninety lamenting the cold and what he knew was not frostbite on his toes and fingers, but he couldn't help but imagine that numb cold turning them all black and purple and maybe that deadly splash of green that without treatment with a bit of penicillin would groove right on up his bloodstream leaving purple tracks spidering up his legs (or arms of course, but he usually imagined it going up his legs as the side venture down his cock was always a terrifying highlight,) and making its way to his heart which would seize and then poof, no more thinking of the other ten percent. Which was just not dying, horribly or otherwise. People may have called it living, but Sam was too preoccupied with getting together the next meal or firewood or fixing up his cabin to give himself time to think about semantics like that. And anyway, there weren't really people anymore.

"This is how it happens you shit-heel," he said as he knocked snow off his boots and closed the pine-board door to his cabin. Sam often imagined ways he could die out here. Here being the absolute middle of nowhere. He saw his frostbitten toes falling off, and watched himself trying to limp his way the forty odd miles to the nearest... anything. He imagined stepping into a cave to eat his lunch, and having a family of bears steal the lunch and most of his flesh for good measure. His fantasies usually lingered past his death, and he'd see the bears string up his guts all around their little cave, and have a drunken cartoon-fiesta feasting on his blood and skin. He even dreamt past his own death, which kids growing up had assured him meant he would die in real life. Well, as far as he knew, he wasn't dead yet. Sam sure had showed those dead little bastards.

He took some pleasure in these fantasies. Not because he craved death, certainly not, he would have killed himself or gotten killed long ago if that were the case. No, it was more about the knowledge; the knowledge that these things could happen, and especially the knowledge that Sam knew how to prevent them. He had this insatiable urge to know things, he had decided once. He needed to know things; he craved the knowledge, he wanted to be smart and knowledgeable and only ignorant on the things he wanted to be ignorant about. But right now there was only one thing he was sure he knew.

"No more morbid thinking," he said to himself, out loud like a crazy person.

It's not novel to have been living on your own in the middle of nowhere for close to eight years and have the tendrils of doubt creep in around your sanity, but some spooky shit was happening out in the woods, and Sam, for the first time since he had absconded from civilization, wondered if he hadn't dropped a few marbles along the way. It had to do with his traps, which he had always figured had helped to keep him saner if anything. Certainly more fed anyway.

Sam loved trapping. It was as simple as that; heart all aflutter, infatuation love, not even just as a turn of phrase. It was his favorite thing to do from the start, and that love hadn't diminished at all in these eight long years. Of course he had taught himself a slew of tricks living out in the woods like he did. He could make a bow and arrow and fire it with reasonable accuracy from almost 100 feet. He'd made slingshots and could throw an axe, and he could find edible plants, not that that was a helpful skill in the middle of an intense winter, but hey, he could do it. Hell, anything you needed to survive alone in the wilderness, Sam had taught himself.

But trapping, trapping was something special. It involved so many different ideas, so many different skills, it felt like such an achievement every time he trudged through the snow along his game route and found a trap full and set. To see a fat rabbit hanging from a snare and a fiery haired fox speared below it. 'Two dinners with one stone,' he always thought with a chuckle. Those were moments of real pride, something more valuable than even the meat he collected from these kills. One day he was going to figure out a way to trap a rabbit or squirrel, get a fox or coyote, and then catch maybe a bear or a mountain lion on top of that. Each bigger predator enticed into his mechanisms and ropes and spikes by the last. The ultimate in top-of-the-foodchain technology. Or at least as close as he could get in these woods.

This used to be his challenge. He'd walk with his sled or cart, depending on the season, hopefully piled with freshly cleaned rabbit or squirrel or coyote or fox and even the occasional lynx, which he felt bad about because they looked so damn cute with their little tufted ears. But a meal is a meal, especially in the winter. It got him so excited he would almost get a little skip in his step seeing a splash of blood in the snow. But that was before all the animals started killing themselves.

He had read somewhere, probably the Internet in a bygone time, that animals were much more in-tune with nature and the universe in general than humans. Birds could sense a storm coming, cows would lay down before the rain, deer and other forest creatures would dash away from a fire or a flood something like days before the danger was anywhere close. Sam envied this but didn't exactly believe it. He had learned, after repeated embarrassment in his younger years, that some people knew more than he, and trusting everything you heard or read was dangerous.

But he could usually believe his eyes, and he'd be damned if this wasn't reality. But apparently not his reality, which is where the question of sanity came into play. This like many things in life had started not slowly but all at once.

About a week before, Sam had walked his trapping route and found every last one of his traps full. He was elated. His tired face wrinkled with a smile that for the first time in months traveled all the way to his eyes, and he turned to the nearest pine tree, his only real friends out here that didn't shrivel up and abandon him in the winter, and gloated, "Look at that! You like that? I won't need to trap for another month with a haul like this! I bet you're sorry ya ain't got teeth, huh?"

He coughed out a laugh and took a manic bite from the rabbit's leg, smiling widely at the tree as the blood dripped down his face. Sam imagined the trees to be females and a pang of embarrassment flipped his stomach as he regretted his display.

He meant it though when he said he wouldn't need to trap for another month, but assuming it was a fluke and just to be safe, he set his traps again. Finding them full like this was too fun, too exhilarating to pass up in his world of gentle boredom. Not that he expected another haul like this.

Winter was generally better for trapping for him. It snowed often at his altitude, which helped to conceal Sam's presence around traps. In the summer he had to squeeze an old kill's bladder all around to mask his own scent. Which even after all these years still made him want to puke. But even with the best of covers, this sort of catch must have been a miracle or at the very least a fluke. Lucky break at best.

Except it wasn't.

The next day he stepped outside, stretching his too-full stomach out in front of him and his sore arms out behind him, and he breathed in the thin mountain air. He looked out across what he thought of as his domain. The pine and birch forest stretching as far as he could see, or at least as far as the next set of mountains to the north, the frozen river that stayed fresh and cold even in the heat of summer to his west, and his own little cabin behind him, nestled in what during the summer months was a beautiful open field and now was just a white plane.

He strapped on his skis and set out. He reached the first trap and found two rabbits snared together, something he'd never seen before, and below was what looked like the rest of their family speared in his pungi pit. He checked the bodies, and it was exactly how it looked.

"What the hell," he asked a nearby lady-pine with a distressing amount of red needles, "happened here?"

The pine tree shivered in the breeze, coating the snow with a bit more of her red hair as a response.

"Oh, so everyone's dying on me, huh?"

He cleaned the rabbits, using their entrails to create a snare trap for bigger game, and loaded the small carcasses onto his sled. Then he walked down to the frozen river and found all his traps there full as well. He wasn't doing anything differently. These weren't special new traps; nothing unique or extraordinary, or even interesting. They were just his usual snares and pits and snap traps. But something about them was apparently incredibly enticing because otherwise why would all these animals be so dead? He marveled at the amount of beaver he had caught; knowing he'd decimated the population.

He didn't set most of the traps after that. He had enough meat now to last him the rest of the winter or longer. He was usually happy if one, two, hell five was the most traps he'd ever had full on any given day, and that had become like a holiday to him. He'd wake up late on its anniversary, eat a large meal, he'd double stoke the fire, and just walk around naked the whole day. The only way someone so alone knew how to cut loose and enjoy himself.

He got home and didn't even finish cleaning the meat; he just packed it deep into his freezer and went to bed. The day had stressed him out, and stress tended to make Sam tired.

He skipped going outside the next day. It was too cold. It was a day that deceived you into thinking it was nice, with yawning blue skies and not even a wind to make the trees dance. But those clouds hold in all the heat, and when it's beautiful and clear out that's when nature draws you into *her* snare and freezes you solid, then comes along and dumps a few feet of snow on your corpse so people thousands of years in the future could find your stupid, frozen corpse and fail to reanimate you. But that's not what happened to Sam because Sam was smart and stayed inside, mostly whittling new arrows, as this whole trap thing had him spooked, and he wanted to be prepared for any eventuality.

Aliens ran through his head. Maybe the animals were being brainwashed by aliens. Or maybe there was some bull about star alignments? He tried to sit down and read his survivalist books, tried to shake the mystical thoughts, which were not at all like him, but it was difficult to focus on leaf shapes when the back of his head was rolling with monsters and shadows.

He set his book down in his lap and leaned back in his rocking chair, trying to focus on the texture of the fraying fabric against his fingers, the feel of the blanket draped over the chair, trying its best to mold itself to the curves of his back. The monsters melted away for a moment as he concentrated on breathing, something his mother had taught him to do when he had trouble sleeping all those years ago. It felt like he was aware of each rib expanding out with his diaphragm, and all his organs squishing together as he exhaled as much as he could. He started to drift off and he was back in his childhood home.

He didn't remember it as it actually was, he just flowed between memories of sights and sounds and scents and repeated actions. He thought of playing with his mother's hair as he tried to fall asleep, looking into a mirror during a time-out locked in the bathroom and wondering who he really was, who he might be. He saw his kitchen from the perspective of opening the freezer searching for treats and finding nothing but old bags of vegetables, digging through the under-stair closet searching for lost treasures of his parent's past. He saw blonde hair, he saw snowy mornings, the empty fireplace. The form seeped away from the images and melted into feelings as he drifted further into sleep. He had just slipped far enough under to lose him-self, when a loud THUMP startled him awake. He fell out of his chair and scrambled toward the middle of the cabin, away from the shut-tered and insulated windows, which were as strong as any wall he had, yet still caused him anxiety when his mind was on monsters.

The thump was singular, and slowly Sam convinced himself it was just snow falling from one of the two white oaks that stretched over his cabin, which is what it had been. Finally Sam made himself peek outside and he found darkness had taken hold, and the clouds had retaken the sky. It was warming, and the danger seemed less in-tense. And Sam relaxed some and slept again as the sky dumped three feet of snow all over his domain.

He woke the next morning and got to work clearing out his path to the river, and thus water, of the snow.

"Three more goddamn feet," he said to himself with a small laugh, "What a fucking winter."

At least he had a shovel. And enough food. There were a couple winters where he'd gotten snowed in far worse than this and had to live off meager dried meats and canned fruits and vegetables for the better part of a month before he was able to get out and hunt anything. It had gotten so bad he'd almost considered eating the leather off some of his books. The things hunger brings out in a man.

As he worked, Sam's head drifted between how cold it still was and ways to stop the sneaky snow from packing in between his socks and his boots. The anxieties of the past couple days seemed to seep out with his sweat, being all but forgotten when his shovel hit some-thing solid that shouldn't have been there. He was already exhausted as shoveling was miserably hard work, so he used his hands to dig out whatever it was.

He scooped away large handfuls, tossing it back into the path he had just created, until he hit the large, hard pile again. He wiped away the last bit of snow and a brown eye, surrounded by downy fur stared out at him.

Sam screamed, and strangely no flock of startled birds took to the sky. He flew backwards and his embarrassment stung as he thought of the trees, but his back stung worse as he slammed into more frozen mysteries. He dug these out too and found a pair of frozen rabbits and a crow staring at his cabin.

"Holy hell. It must have really been cold yesterday if you guys froze waiting to get into my door," he said to the frozen corpses, as he tried to catch his breath. They rudely responded with silence, so Sam tapped at their bodies to see if he could salvage any of the meat. Unfortunately they were frozen through and wouldn't budge, and Sam couldn't imagine crow tasted good anyhow, so he went back to check on the eye that had sent him sprawling.

It was a fawn, small and mottled, adorable and dead. 'First winters are the hardest, you little fucker,' he thought with a bitterness he couldn't source. He tested the fawn's skin and found some give, so he tore the critter from her icy grave and happily walked back to his shed, an enclosed space he used as his butcher shop. He did his best to clean her, although the frozen hide was unforgiving and he lost a good deal of the meat. He added what he could to his food stores, and thought that altogether it hadn't been too bad of a morning. He changed out of his snow drenched clothes and set them to dry over his roaring stove; careful to keep them just far enough away that the clothes wouldn't start a fire and burn the cabin to the ground, another scenario he often considered, especially when he was away on his routes. He put on some dry clothes and his boots and headed out again.

He picked up his shovel, took a deep breath of the crisp mountain air and slammed it into the snow and into a whole herd of deer. With every swing of his shovel he hit more deer, rabbits, and he even found he was even stepping on some mice, which never showed their faces around his house. An uneasy panic started to set in that accompanies a mystery, and his unearthing of these frozen, staring beasts became frantic as he flew from mound to mound, finding them all with docile looks, most with tongues just peeking out from beneath their frozen lips, and all staring, wide eyed and dead at his cabin.

Sam threw his legs into motion, but his feet slipped right out from underneath him, and he banged his head on another rabbit. He clawed his way forward, on hands and knees because to stand would take much too much time, right to his front door, and he slammed home the bolt that he unnecessarily locked every night.

Why hadn't they hid from the cold like he had? Why were they all just throwing their lives away in his traps? If they had just stuck to the woods, under cover, they'd have been fine. Was this a warning? What was this?

Sam's mind reeled with his biggest enemy: the unknown. His happy, simple existence, where he had needed and wanted for nothing more than he could find for himself, suddenly became a dreadful burden. He was out in the middle of nowhere, everything was killing itself around him, and was it for a reason? Did they know something he didn't? What the fuck was going on? He felt his head, and his fingers came back red with blood. That was going to leave a nasty goose-egg, which sent another irrational wave of fear through his body, causing him to shiver slightly.

He had a bottle of pills he kept for situations like this, when his mind started to spin, and he couldn't wrap his head around anything. He popped two in his mouth, and washed them down with a gulp of snow-water. He had found he'd needed them after the incident 8 years ago, an incident that changed the whole world. He'd mostly blocked it out though because it had killed his whole family and everything he loved and especially this beautiful blonde girl who lived next door who used to sunbathe nude by her pool, and with his father's binoculars he would hide behind the curtain and- except his thoughts were cut short as he passed out on his bed.

2

Sam stepped through his dark cabin.

The furniture he still always smashed his shins into seemed to move out of his way tonight, making a straight path for him toward the door. He was dressed in his sleeping clothes, a ratty one-piece number you'd expect to see on an old cartoon prospector, but he didn't have any desire or make any move to put on a coat or boots as the door to his cabin, strangely unbolted, creaked itself open, and he stepped outside into the winter world. The mountains rose, higher than he remembered, and the snow banks and drifts seemed more menacing and tall.

But the sky was clear, the moon bright, as Sam, not feeling any of winter's bite, took a few steps outside. As his feet touched the ground the snow spreading away from him began to melt, revealing the hunched carcasses of what seemed like a hundred creatures. The snow left them to fester and boil as their skin and hair rolled away and only their empty moon-bleached skeletons were left, pointing at Sam and his doorway. The last of the snow disappeared into the ground and spring took hold in an instant.

Plants grew quickly up through the pelvises of the creatures and filled in their ribcages. Vines and leaves wrapped themselves around bones in a cheap, green imitation of muscle. Winter took hold of Sam though as a chill ran through his body, and his feet seemed frozen in place, his eyes frozen open to watch the first of the skeletons shake to life. The moon dimmed as the dark recesses of the skeletons' eyes flickered into life with a dull, even white, shining out from the hundreds of sockets, all desperate for eye contact with Sam. The tiny rabbit skeletons, the shaky deer ones, the multitudes of menacing bone-piles that Sam realized he couldn't place as any animal that lived around him, or that he had ever seen or imagined even, all crawled toward him in a sinister parody of walking.

Sam tried his best to scream, to run, to do anything, but his body had become encased in an ice that while not cold, forced him to watch this parade of horrors create a semicircle of white, staring orbs and implied shapes around him. The eyes slowly turned from Sam to the middle, where a giant shape lumbered its way forward from the shadows. It was a great pile of bones, cobbled together with moss and bark, shambling toward Sam. It shuddered to a halt at the edge of the circle of bones, and opened its eyes, which were shining, white beacons, electric almost. At the feet was a body, a human body. Sam couldn't make out the face, but he instinctively knew who it was. Horror gripped him, and the ice squeezed his heart even tighter.

Sam's face turned up, and the creature looked right into what Sam assumed was his soul and raised its neck revealing a grisly wound that opened from the moss and vines with a waterfall of blood which crashed out over the other skeletons. The thing managed to spit out, "Again," in a deep growl, before eclipsing the moon and all light as it fell to envelop Sam in blood and darkness and-

Sam woke up, drenched in blood. No it was sweat. Not blood, it was his own sweat. He had the briefest flash of a human body smashed by the waterfall of blood as he lit a candle with a flourish of a match and checked his own body. No snow on his feet, no blood on his clothes, with a panicked heart his eyes flew to his door, which was still safely bolted shut. He almost didn't have the courage to check, but he inched his way forward, certain there'd be a skeletal beast waiting to eat him whole the moment he opened that fucking door. But he knew that was ridiculous. Nightmares were nothing new to him. It had just been a nightmare. Except the pills were supposed to protect against nightmares. He shouldn't have remembered a thing. He should have been waking up nice and late feeling refreshed, feeling like his moment of panic from the day before was just a silly little trifle, something crazy thought up by his lonely mind.

Except he was awake and panicking worse than ever as his hands, against his mind's intense objection undid the bolt. He slipped boots on, put a large coat over his pajamas, and slowly pushed the door open, his eyes closed. A wave of cold snuck over him and inside, which helped to clear his mind. He opened his eyes. A bear loomed in front of him and raised his hand in a wave.

"Geaahh!" Sam screeched, as if he'd just taken a punch to the stomach, and he reeled backwards, into the warmth of his cabin.

It's interesting to see how people react to incredibly stressful, surprising situations because they're just so varied. Some people flee gracefully like a springing whitetail, and, for some, adrenaline kicks in, and they fight back like a mountain lion or a wolverine, and some people just freeze up and can't move like a opossum or one of those broken goats people pay to tease at county fairs.

Sam threw up. All over himself. Much worse than any broken goat, he just covered himself with chunks of rabbit liver and bits of harvested roots and other assorted meat and stomach juices all staining his onesie. The bear looked surprised, and Sam scrambled up, dripping vomit, slammed the door shut, and locked the bolt again. Hard. He grabbed his axe and sat on the floor shivering as he had let his fire go out, and he was dripping with vomit. There were a couple knocks on the door, and Sam could have sworn the bear was asking him questions. Sam plugged his ears as tight as he could, shutting out the insanity of it.

When the sun finally rose, Sam cautiously stretched out his legs, rubbing a bit of life back into them, chasing away those horrible pins and needles. He got to his feet, and with white knuckles on the handle of his axe, cautiously approached the door. He reconsidered when he saw his bow with the quiver of new arrows he'd just carved, and he switched weapons, readying the bow. With one hand he kept the arrow tight in place, and used his other to open the bolt. He drew the bow, pulled open the door with his boot, and let loose, but his arrow flew through space and lodged itself firmly in a birch tree at the edge of his clearing. Sam felt bad about that. She was a beauty, and that would leave a scar.

He loaded another arrow and cautiously stepped outside, head on a swivel, even checking the roof as if that bear had crawled up there in order to ambush him. No bear. Lots of snow. He slowly crept forward, jumping at every little creature he had unearthed yesterday, but no talking bear. No bears at all.

"Well god damn it. I spent so long not being crazy!" he yelled to the mountains and trees. A couple spare chickadees, thankfully alive, took off from a nearby pine and mocked him with their song.

CHICKA-DEE-DEE-DEE-DEE-DEE!   CHICKA-DEE-DEE-DEE-DEE! CHICKEN-HEE-HEE-HEE-HEE!

Sam, enraged because he was crazy now, fired arrow after arrow after the birds, easily missing every single one, and losing a good dozen arrows in the process. He calmed down and walked back inside, spitting some of the taste of his crazy vomit into the snow bank as he went.

Well if he was going to be crazy he was going to make the most of it. He stripped off his clothes, partially because he assumed that's how crazy people tended to like to exist, but mostly because his clothes were still covered in stomach acid and smelled like how he imagined a bar floor might taste. Not that he'd tasted a bar floor. It was just a thought that occurred to him. Maybe since he was crazy now he'd try it.

He might walk, naked as sin, down the mountains to the spooky ghost town he raided for supplies he needed, like new cookware, and canned food when he was desperate, and find the bar there and just run his tongue across those dark boards. Because fuck it. A dam had burst inside his head, and all this pent up loneliness and anger at the universe and confusion just poured right on out of him. He began to scream nonsense, swears he knew, and whatever came into his head.

"CUM-DUMPING HANDLE JOCKEY PUSSY-FUCK CUNT LAWNMOWER HANDJOB, WHOREHOPPING ASS-MUNCHING PIECE OF FUCKING SHIT-LIFE!" he took a moment to be proud of his swear-smithing and catch his breath before he tossed open his meat cellar and started taking huge, manic bites of the raw, frozen meat.

3

Sam walked out of his cabin, naked, his front covered in blood. Sam's mind had slipped just a little maybe. All this fun stuff with the animals had driven him toward an edge. He didn't think he'd fallen over the edge yet, but he definitely was teetering somewhere near it. He didn't think he could stay here with everything that was happening, so he set off west, his crazy on his back, his axe at his side, and the suicide animals crunching under his heavy winter boots.

The trees greeted him like old friends, swaying ever so slightly in the winter chill.

"At least we don't think you're crazy," they whispered to him softly as he passed through. Sam gave a nearby birch tree a gentle hug and whispered back, "Thank you," knowing full well they were just saying that to be nice.

Sam trudged on, away from his home... did he leave the door open? Shit, that would be bad. Thankfully he was only a few hundred feet out, and spun around and headed back toward the cabin. Maybe he didn't have to be crazy. Maybe he could just wait it out here.

He looked at the dead little critters and knew he couldn't just stare at them forever, but he should close the door first off. And probably bring some supplies. Maybe put on his hat. He looked down at his naked wet body, and suddenly he felt the cold, which shocked him back to his senses. His cock went from erect to a shriveled nothing as he sprinted back toward his door. "Shit, fuck cold, cold, cold! Wuz- I thinkin'!"

He wasn't. That was the problem. He sprinted through the front door, slamming it behind him.

"Hey there!" The Bear said with a slightly Canadian accent.

"AHHHHHHHHHH!" replied Sam when he saw the Bear digging through his cabinets, Sam's special occasion whiskey emptied and cradled between the Bear's paws. Sam brandished the axe at him.

"Oh woah! Hey hey there! I come in peace here!" the Bear said as he put his hands up, the bottle smashing to the floor. Sam chopped at the air with shaking, terrified hands, and the Bear stood up tall.

Sam lobbed the axe at the Bear, hoping to hell it would connect. It didn't. It bounced harmlessly off the wooden floor and skittered to a halt against his stove.

"Woah! Hey that was close! Enough!" the Bear yelled. He had to stoop in the cabin, being a bit too tall, and this fact wasn't lost on Sam when the Bear reached him: a veritable tower, "Please."

"Where in da heck do ya get off throwing a darn axe at me?"

"You broke in."

"The door was open. You should be thankin' me. I was guarding yer," the Bear stepped back and gave a sweeping gesture at the rusting cookware, the shabby piles of blankets and old puzzles, "stuff."

"Yeah well, you're a bear. You're a…"

"Bear, yup, and you're a heck of a sleuth. Hey, I got a question."

Eye contact. Silence.

"Ok, well shoot I guess." Sam said, if he was going to be talking to a bear, he might as well just go for it.

"Doncha think ya oughtta put on some pants there first?"

Sam looked down at his naked body and had a moment of panic. Like that dream everyone talks about where they are at school or church and they've forgotten their pants. Sam had never had that dream, but he had to imagine this is what it felt like. Sam cupped his hands around himself as his manhood tried even harder to force its way up inside his body, and he waddled over to his dresser. He used a ratty old towel to wipe the blood from his face and chest and then tossed on some clothes.

"Sorry about that, I wasn't expecting company. You had a question?"

The Bear laughed heartily as he walked over to Sam and put a hairy arm around his shoulder, "What have ya got to *eat* 'round this place?"

Sam gave some thought to this as he coolly shirked the Bear's surprisingly realistic embrace and walked over to his makeshift refrigerator. What the hell was happening to him? Pleasant enough surprise anyway. Sam never had company over. He was dying to show off his venison steak recipe with steamed tubers. Despite containing foods called 'tubers' which sounded gross but always turned out delicious.

"I have these nonstick pans I picked up from the city on my way up here," Sam explained to the Bear, "and they're a real life saver. I ran out of olive oil just about forever ago, and you animals out here just aren't fatty enough for me to use you as a... what do you call that? What do you call something that makes a food not stick to stuff?"

"Not glue?" suggested the Bear.

"Ha. Ha. Ha. Good one. Well anyway, it doesn't matter, how do you feel about venison steak with steamed tubers?"

"I'll pass on the deer, I'm actually tryin' to watch my weight there. When you said 'you animals' was all thin ya obviously didn't take this gut here into account," the Bear said as he jiggled his belly, "but those tubers sound delicious, thank ya kindly!"

Sam was a little disappointed by this turn of events. The steak was the best part in his opinion. The tubers were just there to make it a 'meal.' But that's ok, he'd make the shit out of the tubers and the Bear would have no choice but to be impressed.

"Yeah, of course. I mean it's not every day I get to have company. I'm Sam by the way."

"I know," replied the Bear, "It's written on everything in here. You worried you're going to confuse your stuff with the all the other folk living up on this mountain? Sorry that was mean. I wasn't trying to be mean. Heck, listen to me here, shooting my mouth off to the guy feeding me. I'm sorry. Dang, where are my manners at?"

Sam couldn't think of what to say to that, so he just smiled and nodded, letting the Bear know in an odd, nonverbal way that he wasn't offended.

Sam stepped outside for a moment and filled a pot with snow. Wait... since when did he treat an imaginary bear as a guest? A stand had to be made for his sanity he decided. Sam stepped back inside.

"Listen. I know you're not real; you're a figment of my imagination. I had some trouble processing why all you animals were out there trying to-"

"Kill ourselves?"

"I mean, yeah. What's with that? It's got me pretty spooked."

"Ditto. I wouldn't be in here hanging out with you if it didn't probably. Can we save the heavy talk for after dinner though? I always eat more when I've got depression."

Sam put the pot on the stove to melt the ice. He gave the Bear an incredulous look. He wasn't real.

"Can I touch you?"

"Wow, frisky so fast, little Jack? You must be real lonely," the Bear said with a chuckle to himself, "Hey, I'm just joshin' with you kid. Go on ahead, give this luxurious coat a good rub down if it'll help ease your mind there."

Sam tentatively walked over, arm outstretched. He closed his eyes for a moment before making contact with what still felt like real fur. Well shit. Why was this all so hard? What was real, what was not? How long had he been standing here? Were those little zombie critters going to bust in soon and stare at him some more?

The Bear, as if reading his mind said, "Ya looked spooked kid. I ain't gonna hurt ya. Seems to me we're all in a similar boat now that everything's dead and dyin'."

Sam smiled but was too distracted by the fur.

It felt so real. He could feel the warmth of the Bear's body beneath, and each fiber of the hair seemed to leave its own impression on his nerves. He watched the light dance across the coat as his hand broke it up, like ripples on water.

Sam had been standing there thinking for much longer than he realized and shook his head, suddenly angry. Probably at having just lost the last 8 or so minutes of his life.

"You can't be real. There's no such thing as a talking bear. There's just fucking not," Sam said with desperation welling up. He was still petting the Bear's coat, trying to convince himself it wasn't real. The Bear, with a tenderness not often seen in animals his size, took Sam's hand into his own and gave it a little pat.

"Da water is boilin' Sam."

So it was.

Sam went over to the pot and put his dented, metal colander with the tubers over the boiling water, and he threw in a good dash of rosemary he had harvested and dried in the summer. A secret weapon that was sure to impress his guest.

"So how long have you been- ah, a bear then?"

"Oh come on, we can make better conversation than that," the Bear said as he sat down on the old, ratty armchair. The bottom of which creaked under his weight. When he was settled in he started going through Sam's books.

"A while anyhow. In fact, I'd say mosta my life, to answer yer question. A bang-up lot a survivalist stuff here. Hoofda, these look real boring," he said as he threw books onto the floor, "You never hearda enjoying reading? Ya know, uh, a fun adventure novel, or a steamy romance? I bet you've got some romance novels tucked away 'round here somewhere huh? Tucked under the bed maybe for them lonelier nights? Or maybe you're jerking her to this Canadian Arboreal Guidebook: British Columbia and Beyond? Mmmmm sweet, sweet maple bark!"

"Enough!" Sam spat as he wheeled around, brandishing a large, wooden spoon, "Leave the trees out of this."

A chunk of tuber that had been stuck to the spoon fell to the floor.

"I've hit a nerve then have I?"

"I- it's a weird- I have an active imagination. I mean, clearly. I'm talking to an imaginary bear-"

"Hey now. I thought we was all through with dat, eh? What the heck'd I let you pet me for so long for if it didn't convince you of nothing?"

"Alright whatever. Tubers are almost done. Are you sure I can't offer you a nice piece of rabbit? Bobcat even? Shit, I have some lynx if you're… you know, inclined."

"I am not, but thank you. The tubers smell delicious."

"Hopefully, yeah. So you were- you're from these woods then?" Sam asked as he drained the pot and added a bit more rosemary, some pepper, and even a dash of salt, which had become a rare commodity what with how much of it the dried meats he made called for.

"Oh yah. Born and raised. My ma raised us cubs up in an old maple hollow. It was small, but it was home. Mmmm, mmmm, mmm! My stomach is growlin'."

"Well come and eat up then. And I have some frozen raspberries for dessert too," Sam said with a smile, knowing he was certainly making this figment's night.

The two sat down at the dining table, Sam in his chair, the Bear on the ground, a big heap of tubers for him and the same plus choice venison steak for Sam.

"Well dig in," Sam said. And they both did. Sam ate quickly, rationalizing that being crazy was a tiring job, and a bit of hunger was deserved. The Bear ate more slowly, methodically. Savoring every bite.

"Now that's the problem with being a bear! Cooked food is so much harder to come by. Unless you want to reduce yourself to garbage cruising like a raccoon. My god, is that rosemary I detect?"

"It sure is," Sam said, just barely masking his delight that his guest had noticed.

"Well I'll be danged. This might be the best darn meal I've ever had."

Sam felt some happiness rise up in him. Pride too. He liked this bear. He didn't even care that his presence was trying to rip Sam's mind into pieces.

"So did-"

"There used to be this taco shell factory outside ah the town there," the Bear interrupted, mouth full of tubers, gesturing at the air, "They'd ship the things down to California from here. Authentic Mexican food my butt, eh?"

Sam nodded, his mouth too full of food to respond.

"So," the Bear swallowed, continued, "They used to put the extras and ones they'd dropped and misfits out on these old wire spools for us bears to eat. Now at first, the bears I knew were like 'hey, no way there!' but pretty soon we all got a hunger, and the curious got to us, and we went for a taste. And yah know what? They were gosh darn amazin'! We'd go there for special occasions, and whenever we'd been real good, according to my ma. People'd drive up just to watch us eat, and I'd put on a little show."

The Bear rocked a bit with his hands up in the air.

"You know, do the cute thing and make people like us bears. But one day a guy got too close to an older, meaner Bear. Samson was his name. Ol' salmon-breath. Anyhow this guy gets up close, darn tourist, and starts snappin' pictures ah ol' Samson with this big flash there."

The Bear splayed his paws, and made the noise of a flash, as if Sam wasn't aware of how the whole process worked.

"Anywho, Samson didn't like that all too much and he gets up and takes a chunk outta the guy in front of a bunch a children, human children, so the taco factory was forced to stop putting out the tacos for us."

The Bear stopped talking and started to eat again. Sam swallowed a huge bite of meat and said, "What?"

"Well, I guess the point a' that was: ya wouldn't happen to have any taco shells would ya?"

This conversation had taken an odd turn.

"Well, no. What? Are you sure you're real?"

Sam reached across the table once more to feel the Bear's fur. It was still there. Fuck. This was all so confusing but at the same time kind of great. Having no one to talk to for so many years was not everything Sam had hoped for. Fuck it right? Hadn't he already decided to be off his rocker for a bit? This was better than what he was on track for when he first lost it. I mean, eating raw, frozen meat? Running around, out in the cold, half naked? That's like day one suicidal crap. At least now he was just talking and not freaking out. Even if his talking partner did happen to be a seven foot tall Canadian grizzly.

"Have you always been able to talk?"

"Yeah."

"Why wasn't I able to talk to you before?"

"'Cause we only just met."

"No, like before just now I'd never talked to an animal."

"Did ya ever try?"

Sam guessed he hadn't. He'd just trapped them and ate them.

"We were never big on talking to humans."

"Why not?"

"Because you're mostly jerks. No offense, you're a good host, but I can tell ya when all the air ran out there was some celebratin'."

"Air?"

"Yeah, when all ya'll died?"

"What did that have to do with air?"

"All the air just kinda disappeared for a while. I was pretty young then, but that's definitely what happened. Killed most of your kind, far as I know."

"Most," Sam said, a little excited now. He had truly thought he was the last human. He sort of thought the whole apocalypse might have been his fault even, "Did others survive?"

"I dunno, probably. I've heard there are maybe some a bit south."

"How'd they live?"

"I don't know, Sam. This is all hypothetical. Probably something with the water. There was still air in the water. That's how most of us animals lived.

"Wait, you knew it was coming?"

"Sure. You're a dummy if you can't sense something like that coming."

This bear sure knew a lot of interesting information for a figment of his imagination.

"Well then I'm going to go south."

"Can I come?"

"Uh, no."

"I'm going to come."

"You're not."

The Bear just smiled and wiggled what would have been his eyebrows at Sam.

9

The Bear was taking a dump.

"Somethin's happenin' I think," he said.

I don't need to hear a play by play of your poop, Bear," Sam said with a good deal of disgust.

"No not that. Somethin' else. A sort of trouble like before. Remember, we animals can sense things like that."

"I've read that. I think it's a lot of baloney."

"Explain hurricanes then, huh?"

"Well there's a build up of atmospheric pressure near a-"

"Very funny. Jerk," the Bear said cutting him off. The Bear had finished his bowel movement and had sauntered back over to Sam. He had insisted on wearing a hat out, which Sam thought was ridiculous, but the Bear had taken it anyway, saying he looked dashing in the wool-knit.

Sam had had to change into his winter gear: long johns covered by jeans, tucked the flannel, snowpants on, followed by sweater, scarf, heavy coat, hat, and then of course his thick gloves. There was a protocol you had to follow if you wanted to survive in negative 40-degree weather. And most of it had to do with layers, layers, layers.

He had also had to finish packing his winter travel bag: 1 LED flashlight, extra batteries; 1 length of nylon rope, 40 feet; 1 compass, conveniently pinned to the front of his coat, a little floating bobble of plastic; 1 extra pair of gloves; 1 extra pair of woolen socks, both secure in a ziplock bag; 1 fire starting kit, flint, steel, tinder, matches, and a butane lighter (just in case;) 1 buck knife, strapped to his belt; 1 roll of toilet paper; 1 first aid kit; 2 pounds of jerky; 1 pound granola, his own special mix; 3 quarts of water, contained in a thermos to prevent freezing; topographical map, of course, with relevant and important locations highlighted in a very visible red; 1 trusty axe and whet stone for sharpening said axe, the latter strapped to the back of the now bulging pack along with; 1 bow and 1 quiver of arrows, both homemade; and lastly, for his boots, not his back, skis he'd crafted himself from a big chunk of oak. He kept a checklist of all these things he needed, just in case, and ticked them off as he went.

Sam skied along, and the Bear ran along behind him, his travel buddy now whether Sam liked it or not. Sam looked up at the trees as they went along.

"You know, I've never killed a bear before," Sam said.

"Well ya certainly tried earlier," the Bear replied with a touch of bitterness.

"Not my fault really. You were in my house. I was spooked already. I have my axe, I'm gonna use it, you know? And anyway I missed, so it's sort of a moot point."

"Yeah well ya scared the berries outta me."

"I always dreamed about killing a bear. Not in a like," Sam contorted his face to look like a little gremlin and put his hands up like he was pretending to be a T-Rex, "I will murder you all, sort of a way."

"Disconcertin'."

"I mean, you guys are huge. The amount of meat I'd get, and the kickass rug I could make from your fur, and I would totally make a necklace from your claws and wear it around like a fucking badass…" Sam's words drifted off as he stared at the Bear's claws.

"Man, them trees sure make you nuts friend. You ain't tearing off my claws," the Bear said as he pushed Sam down into the snow.

"Oh now you've done it," Sam said with an equal mix of anger and mischief as he grabbed a chunk of snow. He whipped it at the Bear and hit him square in the face.

"Hey!"

The Bear got down and tried to grab the snow, but his bear hands didn't work like that, and Sam pelted him with another chunk of hardened snow.

"Not fair! I can't do that!"

Sam stuck out his tongue and started to ski quickly down the mountain, dipping down to pick up ice chunks as he went, and lobbing them behind him. None hit the Bear as he ran on all fours after Sam, a murderous look in his eyes. Sam laughed with delight at the little game they were playing; he hadn't played a game that wasn't with himself in about forever, and he was really enjoying it.

'Just like the good ol' days,' he thought, as he turned around, a big doofy grin plastered across his face. He was having so much fun until he saw the Bear right behind him, his eyes manic, homicidal.

Sam screamed as the Bear caught him in a tackle and brought him down in the snow again.

"Don't kill me!" Sam begged.

The Bear licked Sam's cheek, stood up, and said, "I win."

They continued on in silence for a while, as Sam was still concerned the Bear was planning on killing him. If that was even possible. The tackle had definitely hurt some, and he was a pretty realistic figment. Eventually, when the snow in his boots stopped bothering him, and he'd more or less forgotten his anger toward the Bear, he got bored of the silence and struck up conversation.

"So you were saying something about something before?"

"What?"

"You keep starting to say something about something happening and then we get off track. I'm sorry, I don't mean to keep cutting you off; it's just…"

"Jeeze, ya know I don't think I remember," the Bear said.

"Well don't do that," said Sam, "I'm trying to be civil here, what were you trying to say?"

"I'm not tryin' to say anythin'. Figments of your imagination can't tell you nothin' you don't already know, right? That's still all I am to you, inn'it? A figment a' your imagination. I thought we'd grown closer than that. We've shared meals, we've shared laughs; we've shared a toothbrush."

"Oh come on," Sam said as he spit into the snow.

"Relax. They say bears' mouths are somethin' like ten times cleaner than a human's mouth anyhow."

"No they say that about dogs you fucking animal, and yeah, so what if I think you're a figment of my imagination? And that thing about dogs isn't even really true. Dudes spend all day licking their own buttholes. Does that bother you? The figment thing, not the butthole thing. I mean, I bet you've never just struck up a relationship with a human before, this whole thing doesn't strike you as strange?"

"What strikes me as strange is dat you humans aren't able to see what's right in front a'yer eyes. It killed ya'll once, and it's threatenin' to do it again."

"What do you mean? The air thing again?"

"I don't know. I don't think it's that. Seems worse. Less managable," the Bear said. Not manageable, huh? Well that wasn't helpful. Sam squinted and looked around. He pointed to a valley just to the east and said, "That's where camp is."

Sam had this trip so worked out, having made it so many times, that he hardly had to consult his maps anymore as he moved between cabin to cabin. He had different cabins and camps set up at intervals along the way, each with their own cache of supplies so he would never be caught unprepared. So far none of them had been messed with too badly by animals, a couple break-ins by curious critters, but nothing that had set him back in any serious manner, and it wasn't like there were a lot of people up here to ransack his shit. They arrived at what was one of Sam's favorite campsites.

It wasn't so much a camp as just another cabin he had found, and he liked that in a resting spot. Very little extra work was a huge bonus. It was small and lacked some of the creature comforts he had come to know at his regular cabin, but it beat the hell out of spending the night in a cave or something. He wouldn't want to run into a bear, he thought as he let himself in. The Bear followed, unaware of why Sam was giggling, and took a good look around.

"Nice place ya got here," he said as he ran his paw across the thick dust covering the stove. What a prissy ninny, thought Sam, then felt strange for even having thought the phrase 'prissy ninny.'

"Seriously though, I'm excited to sleep with a roof over my head," the Bear said after seeing Sam's odd expression.

"Well it's not like I'm here all that often to clean up, you know, so cut me some damn slack. But I have canned food stores here, and it's stocked with firewood, so at least we'll be fed and warm. It gives me something to do during the summers. I like to walk this trail and make sure I don't get trapped up in my cabin with some sort of emergency or something in the winter. Make sure I have places to go. Make sure they're ready for me. They're my safe houses I call them. I've got some other stashes of gear and tents and things along the way, but if I can make the time I like to stay in my cabins. They're much nicer."

"Especially in the winter I suppose," the Bear said, "I mean, look at'ya. Hardly any fur at all, eh?"

Sam stroked his laughably small amount of facial hair wistfully before adding, "I have some fur…"

The Bear had another good laugh at this and started rummaging through the stacks of canned foods. Sam got to work building a fire in the stove, and soon enough it was crackling away. Not producing any real heat yet, but in a half-hour or an hour's time this frigid little space would be toasty warm.

Sam often made the mistake of over-stoking the fire when it was this sort of cold outside. Moderation wasn't necessarily his strong suit, and it always seemed like, well hey, it'll be warmer sooner, so why not? But he'd get all hot and sweaty, and that would be a royal pain in and of itself. And then when the fire started to go down all that sweat would freeze up, and he'd be colder than he started. It was back and forth like that all night some nights because he couldn't get his shit together. He was careful to not do that this time though. One look at the Bear, and he knew the big, hairy son-of-a-bitch wouldn't fare well with overheating. Which drew up a very funny mental image for Sam. He saw the Bear sitting out on a beach somewhere wearing a floppy straw hat and sweating into his bouquet of a tropical drink. Sam gave a little laugh.

"That fire tellin' ya some jokes now?" the Bear asked, halfway through reading the back of a can of baked beans.

"Something like that," Sam said, trying to sound enigmatic to shove it back into the Bear's face. It worked, sort of. The Bear was finally interested. He put down the can of beans and faced Sam.

"Are you laughin' at me?" The Bear looked at the cans he'd separated into piles, "Is it… because… because I'm… fat?"

Sam couldn't help but laugh. This was a *bear* he was talking to. Bears shouldn't care about weight, and even so, this one didn't look like he was too chunky. He had another image flash through his brain of the Bear, but now just morbidly obese, with cheeks the size of milk gallons and a stomach like a wrecking ball and just sweating like he was on the Sun. Sam doubled over with laughter and the Bear pouted as he put the cans away.

"Oh stop," Sam said, "You're not fat, you're… you're just a bear. And it's winter. You're supposed to be hibernating right now, and you naturally would have put on a winter's coat of fur and fat. It's not bad, it's just nature."

"You...ya really mean that?" the Bear said, as if these were truly touching words.

"Well yeah, why not?"

The Bear dashed up to Sam and gave him a big bear-hug, lifting him up into the air and spinning him around. Sam was a bit light headed by the time he was set back down, but he didn't mind. It was a nice hug.

"So ya won't judge me if I have a couplea cans a beans 'n franks for dinner? I always wanted franks, I just didn't know it 'til today," the Bear said timidly.

With another laugh, Sam said, "You can have all the franks you want buddy."

And he meant it because that was the kind of guy Sam was.

So they ate some dinner of pork franks and beans heated on the stove and washed down with a can of grainy pear. They were hungry from walking and fighting through the snowdrifts all day, and they scarfed their food down like someone was about to steal it away. They didn't even talk. The fire crackling and the horrible smacking sounds that accompany a pair of people who aren't worried about impressing each other at a dinner were the only sounds that filled the room. The meal ended, and Sam belched loudly. The Bear nodded approvingly. Not too bad.

Sam stepped outside, filled a big pot with snow, and brought it back to the stovetop.

"To refill our canteens," he explained, "Have you figured out any more specifics on what's happening?"

"Oh, well, no. It's nothing specific, just another bad feeling."

"That is not helpful at all. You've got a bad feeling? I have those all the time. I would say ninety percent of all of my feelings are bad."

"Well that's depressing."

"Right but I mean... we're living in a world that's depressing. Everyone's dead. I'll never have a girlfriend, or you know, kiss a girl, or even probably get to talk to a real girl again, or feel her breast..."

"You think about that a lot, eh?" the Bear said as he motioned for Sam to sit next to him on the bed, "But listen, ya spent yer whole life now runnin' away from the world, or what's left a it, and there's a whole heck of a lot ya don't know. There could be a bunch of wonderful surprises for you out there."

"There's so much I can never know," Sam said with rising anger, "There is so goddamn fucking much that was taken away from me, and I don't know why. I don't know why I'm here, and everyone else I knew is dead, why I had to wake up from... from what I went through. I just walked home, and there were my parents dead on the couch. Do you know what that is like for someone who's 15? All I wanted was for someone to comfort me, protect me, and they were all dead. All I want in the world is to have a peaceful life, one I can understand, and you're ruining that for me!"

"I-" the Bear started.

"You," Sam cut him off, "are trying to rip me away from that whether you like it or not! I knew how the woods worked; I knew everything about it until you and the rest of the animals started killing yourselves. Fucking why? It doesn't make sense to off yourselves. I could tell you the name of every tree in this woods, tell you what berries are poisonous, which are delicious, which mushrooms will get you high, what leaves will soothe burns, and I could cut a mosquito in half with an axe at thirty feet if I really felt like it!"

Sam took a moment to breathe.

"I don't think you could cut a mosquito in half with an axe at any distance. I saw you throw that thing," the Bear said without making eye contact.

"Well maybe I exaggerated, but I've got a talking bear following me around telling me everyone is going to die again. Or I'm going to die, so excuse me if I indulge in a little fucking exaggeration."

Sam punched the rolled up sleeping bag.

"Listen," the Bear said, "I know all about how life is tough. I watched my own ma die. Oh yah. No joke. You wanna talk traumatizing, hey? Some bull moose charged her one day while we were out blueberrying. It came outta nowhere, and just took her right off a doggon cliff with it. She fell down 'round twenty-five meters, and you wanna know the worst part? That ol' moose lived. I was just a sprout then, but I was old enough to get mad, and in my mind, big enough to get even, ya know? So I climbed on down ta where that moose, who'd landed on my ma's body, crushin' the life outta her, was trying to shake off that fall. He had a busted ankle, but that was about the worst of it. He had no idea what hit him. I tore him apart, tore his dang ol' throat out. I try to live my life enjoyin' every day, and just, ya know, appreciating the good times my ma gave my brothers and me. But every now 'an then I think of that moose and... Sam I really hate mooses... Meese? Moose? What da hell is da plural on 'moose?'"

"Wow," Sam said, "I'm sorry, but at least you got revenge. And it's 'moose.' Just 'moose.' But at least you know what happened."

"Sam, you're on yer way toward revenge. You don't know it yet, but steppin' out that door with me today, you're starting somethin' huge, like mountain huge. There are forces in this world that you as a human'll never feel, never get, but you can help because ya'got opposable thumbs and those things are just about useful as all get out."

"They are nice, huh?" Sam said, admiring his own, "I went away to try to pretend like humans never existed at all. I figured I could trick myself into believing I was the only one in the world, and deep down I kinda knew that might be true, so it seemed better to, you know, make it into a game."

"Yah," the Bear said.

"I just really want to kiss a girl. That's all I want. Just to kiss her. Not even anything else. Just a fucking... goddamn... kiss. Hey, I have an idea!"

"Y'ain't kissin' me."

"What? No. You're a dude. And a bear."

"Good 'cause it ain't happening."

"Let's get drunk. That's my idea."

"I'm not gonna letcha face-slobber me even if we're drunk."

"I'm not going to kiss you damn it!"

"Ok then, whacha got?"

Sam pulled out a bottle of Johnny Walker Blue from one of the cabinets.

"Stars and garters! Is that a bottle of Blue?" the Bear asked, excited.

"Oh yeah, let's crack this baby open!"

Which he did. Sam took two dented tin cups and poured generous amounts into both. He then raised a finger with a smile, ran outside and tore some icicles off the roof and tossed them into the drinks.

"I hear ice really opens up the flavor or something," Sam said.

"Makes it easier to drink fer a baby maybe," the Bear replied.

"Cheers," Sam said as he clinked glasses with the Bear's cup. Sam let the burning liquid all rush down his throat at once as the Bear dove in licking and slurping greedily at his own glass with a tongue that seemed impossibly long. Sam came up for air with a terrible hacking cough which made the Bear pause and smile.

"New to this, eh?" the Bear said as he went back to lapping up the whiskey, "When ya said 'drunk' I half expected you to pull oot some bottle a' Apple Pie liqueur or something real girly, eh? You're alright, ya know that Sam?"

Sam was still coughing and trying his best to keep his meal down, but he nodded anyway and gave a half-hearted thumbs up.

"Pour us another, barkeep," the Bear said as he finished licking the inside of his glass. 'His tongue is so fucking long,' thought Sam. He imagined the Bear used it to get just all the honey from the bees. Sam was already getting drunk. For a man of his size, an inch or two over six feet probably, he was a true grade light-weight, but he poured two more tall drinks anyhow, this time resolving to take it a little more slowly. He stepped outside, broke off a couple more icicles and tossed them into his drink.

Oh shit! He'd forgotten the water on the stove. It was at a rolling boil. Well, it'll be clean, he thought as he dumped more snow in. They were going to need a good bit of water for the next day. It was a long section of the hike.

"Where'd ya get this anyway, and why do ya have it here of all places?" the Bear asked with a hiccup.

"It was here when I found the place. Had a ribbon on it. Blue one I think. Not sure where the owner of this place ever got to, but I assumed it must be nice if it was a gift."

"You kiddin' me? This is some grade A gall-darn whiskey. Like a two hundred dollar bottle amazing if I'm not mistaken."

"Shiiiiiiit," Sam said, his mind actually reeling with that figure and whiskey, "How do you even know that?"

"I know some things, hey?" the Bear said.

"Yeah."

Sam was starting to nod off; he wasn't a good drunk.

"So what do ya wanna talk about?"

"Man, I don't know, but that whiskey's got a kick like a mountain goat sniffin' pepper. I am feelin' it. You?"

"What?" Sam seemed caught off-guard by this. Feeling?

"Are ya feelin' drunk?" the Bear said.

"Wha- man, I think I gotta go to bed. I gotta."

"Are you kiddin' me? We're just gettin' goin' here. Stay up an play some cards with me."

"But I don't know any card games."

"Not a problem, I'll teach ya."

And he did. The Bear managed to teach Sam cribbage, and they played for a couple hours, just gushing about the woods and their favorite spots and what were the best bends to catch fish and things like that. They slowly worked their way through the whiskey, and when they finally killed it they were both proper drunk, really tired, and terrible at cribbage.

"You 'boot ready fer bed?" the Bear asked with a yawn.

"Yeah, shit, but there's only one bed…"

"Ya min' if I get it? I ne'ereally slept in a bed before, and I 'zerve it fer kickin' yer butt so many times in cribbage" the Bear said, pleading with his eyes, "Please?"

Sam wasn't too psyched on the idea, but he didn't see what it could hurt.

"Ok, but since you got all fur, I get the sleeping bag," he reasoned drunkenly.

"Deal."

"Deal."

So the Bear laid out on the mattress with a huge sigh and a great squeaking and protesting of bed springs, and Sam threw a little more snow into the pot and removed it from the stovetop. He stoked the fire, not too much, but enough so that it'd stay lit until he got up to pee. He was proud of himself, controlling his drunk self like this. He was being so goddamned responsible. He drank three full cups of water before bed, so that, at the right time in the night he would wake up and have to pee like a pregnant infant. It would remind him he had to restoke the fire so he wouldn't freeze to death in the night. He thought it was a pretty ingenious trick, and it made sure he stayed hydrated, which is important to just about every aspect of your health. When you're alone for so long with nothing to think about except surviving, eventually you start to wonder what you're surviving for.

Sam, for the first time in eight odd years, felt like he was living, not just surviving. And that felt good to him. He had that smile on his face again.

"G'night," he said to the Bear as he shimmied into the sleeping bag.

"'Night buddy," the Bear replied. And they both passed the fuck out.

12

Sam woke up.

His head hurt like he'd been hit with a cartoon mallet, and his mouth was dryer than a desert. And he had to pee so badly he could taste it. He looked over and saw the Bear was still sleeping soundly curled up on his side, facing the wall. What a peaceful creature, thought Sam as he put his boots and coat and hat on, dancing back and forth to keep the piss at bay. He may have overzealously drunk too much water, he thought. No blame went to the whiskey of course. The only problems whiskey had ever been blamed on were those that were not yours. But Sam ran outside, where the bright moon had punched a hole through the clouds and had lit up the snow like some half-assed daylight.

The blue, winter world was beautiful and peaceful until Sam unzipped and started the equivalent of projectile vomiting piss into the snow bank. Halfway through he decided to spell his name and got almost all the way through the 'M.' San, he read, contemplatively. Goddamn his head hurt. He closed his eyes, held his fingers to his temples, and rocked back and forth. He opened his eyes again and looked at the beauty that surrounded him. The trees were dense and blue and black and white in the night, and the snow banks that ebbed and flowed around them seemed alive with a strange, blue luminescence. It was majestic, but what was that taste in his mouth?

It was horrible, it was… familiar. Oh right, he'd thrown up again. He remembered now: he'd gotten up from playing cards and taken a piss and thrown up some too. Right over… there.

Three mangy-coated coyotes were crouched over the spot he'd lost his dinner. Sam made a small noise and they looked up at him, mouths full of Sam's vomit. They showed their teeth and growled.

Fuck.

Sam's head hurt. Sam couldn't think; all he could think of were all the mistakes he had made. He'd gotten drunk. If this had been home he would have had his bow or his axe. If he had been fully prepared now he would have had it with him. Where was his head? That fucking bear. None of this would be happening if it weren't for him.

The coyotes circled Sam carefully in the deep snow, sizing him up, figuring if they could take him down. They sensed a weakness in him, and they were a little drunk and a little loose from eating Sam's whiskey soaked bean-vomit. Sam tried to make a move toward the door, but one of the coyotes barred his way, grinning at him through black lips. Fuck, shit, fuck. Coyotes aren't too bad are they? They're just… they were hungry, they were desperate. It had been a tough, cold winter, and apparently these ones hadn't found all the dead animals to snack on. Or maybe they had, and they were just mean fuckers. Sam didn't know; he didn't care. He just wanted his axe. But it was inside.

"Hey, uh, you guys wouldn't happen to speak English too?"

"Shhh," said one of the coyotes.

A coyote lunged for Sam, and he managed to kick it away using his heavy boot but slipped and fell into the snow bank. The thing yelped in pain, and he could hear the other two coming for him. He could smell the vomit on their breath, and he closed his eyes, accepting that maybe this was it. He'd been careful up until now; he deserved this.

Except the coyotes stopped dead in their tracks when they heard the Bear roar. They tried to scatter, but he was too fast. He picked the first one up and tore through its neck, raining black blood onto the blue snow. He caught the other one with his claws and tore its stomach open.

"No!" it yelled, as it tried to run away. But its guts got caught on the winter-dead branch of a small tree, and it strung its own intestines and vital organs up like Christmas lights across the forest.

The Bear caught the third in his teeth as it tried to bound its way out of a deep snow bank it was trapped in. He bit down and shook his head, which sent blood and a leg flying off. He tossed his head again and threw the howling coyote into the forest to die. The leg landed near Sam's pee signature, and it almost looked like he'd finished his name.

Sam, Sam thought.

He still hadn't processed much of what had just happened by the time the Bear picked him up by his coat.

"Holy shit," he managed.

"You're welcome. Now come on. I got a doozy of a hangover, and I need my beauty rest."

And, with a last, bewildered glance at the carnage, the Bear pushed Sam back inside.

16

It was a pretty miserable morning. Sam didn't talk about the coyotes; his head was too full of noise from his hangover, and the Bear didn't seem to be faring much better. They packed up the gear, reprepared the cabin, filled their canteens, put out the fire, and headed outside. SAM was written in big yellow and red letters in the snowbank out front. It had actually happened. There was the coyote leg. Sam's head hurt even worse.

Until now Sam had been convinced, truly convinced, that the Bear was a figment of his imagination, but Sam hadn't done this. Sam couldn't have done this. There wasn't even much blood on his clothes, and there was blood everywhere, a common theme in his life these days. Sam looked at the Bear who didn't seem ready to acknowledge anything and was already marching away.

"Did you see? I wrote my name in the snow. In pee," Sam said.

The Bear turned, gave a polite chuckle and said, "Oh yah. Good one."

And they walked. Well, the Bear walked and Sam skied. All goddamn day. Sam went from hot to cold to wanting to throw up to wanting to die, and the whole time he wanted to strangle the throat of every little songbird that wouldn't shut it's fucking little mouth.

Was the Bear mad at him? Did he do something else last night to embarrass himself, other than almost die? He didn't try to kiss the Bear or anything, did he? He didn't think he had. He didn't have any desire to, not while sober at least, but the Bear had made that joke last night about him kissing him, and there's a chance that... I mean, he kept making that fucking joke about Sam kissing trees. Sam didn't kiss trees. He never had and never would. No way no how. And he didn't kiss bears. Alcohol made him paranoid.

They were going to reach the city tomorrow though. He was glad for the snow. He wouldn't see most of the bodies. That would be a nice change. His biggest reason for not coming down more, because let's face it, it'd be convenient to be closer, it'd be convenient to be near where all the good, free stuff was, but Sam couldn't stand finding the decaying ruins of humanity every day.

They were skeletons now, and a lot of them had up and fully disintegrated, gone back to mother nature, and he was glad for that too.

But the ones indoors? They were still there, and Sam was terrified he would walk by one and it would grab his leg. He'd had nightmares about that. Especially in the beginning. And anyway, they reminded him of too much, and he was not interested in that sort of nostalgia.

But he was better now. Time had made him good and sane. Alright, ok. Not true. He had no idea if he was crazy or not. He sure hoped not. It'd be great if he were allowed to keep his new friend and not have it be a crazy thing. The Bear was nice, and last night he very well may have saved his life. He liked that in a friend. He liked sentience in a friend really. He wasn't overly picky when it came to friendship he realized. Hell, most of his friends for as long as he could remember had been inanimate, so even the sentient thing was stretchable. As they walked they found more animals frozen in the fields, crumpled at the bottom of cliffs, death basically everywhere. It was unsettling.

"You wanna stop for some lunch," Sam asked, his voice devoid of any desire to do so. The Bear groaned in response. Sam took that as a no. The thought of eating was fully horrible. Life felt fully horrible at the moment.

"I think there's a Denny's around here some place," Sam said, gesturing at the thick forest. He was lying of course. He definitely didn't think there was a Denny's around. This was Perkin's territory.

"Why don't you have a gun or something? I thought all humans had guns," Bare asked as they continued along. Sam felt the pit of his stomach drop out. The thought of a gun filled him with dread.

"I hate them," Sam said, emotion pushing through his colossal hangover.

"Oh yah?"

"Yeah."

"Well muck a truck, my head feels like a gosh darn beehive took up shelter between my ears," the Bear said miserably. Sam felt just about the same way, and told the Bear that. It made him feel better, and he was glad the gun thing was dropped. At least they were kindred spirits. Sam watched silently as a crow flew from the crisp cold of the atmosphere and speared the snow head first.

They reached the next camp later than Sam usually would have. It turned out they were moving a little more slowly today. This, since it was closer, wasn't even a cabin anymore, simply a home built in the country, presumably as a summer home for a wealthy family who had lived a distance away. Now it was Sam's outside the city house. There was a really nice old four-wheeler in the garage that Sam, in the summers, would use to speed his commute. The Bear seemed impressed by the whole place.

"Holy Hannah! Why don't you live here?" the Bear said as he patted one of the huge log pillars that framed the door.

"Too close to town... I just, I don't know. I didn't want civilization. I wanted nature. I wanted what I had."

Out of nowhere, Sam remembered aspirin existed and ran to the bathroom. Yes! It was here. He grabbed the bottle and twisted it open. He looked up, and the Bear was silently staring at him in the mirror. Sam, startled, jumped back and bumped into the Bear, and the little white pills popped and scattered across the floor like hail.

"Woah!"

"What's that?" the Bear asked.

"Th-this? This is aspirin. For my head. You want some?" he asked as he struggled to corral them from the tiles back into the bottle.

The Bear looked past Sam and into the cabinet.

"That, ah, Vicatin in there?" he asked as he grabbed the bottle, "Oh yah! We can get proper messed up on this stuff! Open that for me?"

Sam did and handed it back up to the Bear who took a handful. Sam figured he'd come this far, what the hell, and took a couple himself.

Halfway through making dinner in the beautiful marble and stained wood kitchen, the Vicatin kicked in, and Sam felt as if he had melted along with the mixed vegetables and canned pasta. Oh woaaaaah. He felt weird. And... and was he even feeling anymore? This was fucked up.

"This was fucked up," Sam said aloud.

"But it's sooooo good, eh?" the Bear said, evidently riding the same high.

"I don't feel... anything. Not even my hands. This is canned..." he trailed off.

The Bear was a bad influence, Sam thought. He'd seen videos warning him about people like the Bear when he was in school. Don't do drugs videos and stay away from bad apple videos.

An egg cracked open into a frying pan.

He was hungry again.

Apples.

The Bear must have been a bad apple.

Sam didn't get high. He couldn't afford it. Not monetary-wise, that system was gone, but in survival terms. Sam didn't want to have to depend on anything but himself. But the Bear didn't give a fuck. He just loved getting high. His brain was probably that egg in the movies, frying, sizzling in that pan. The things Sam would do for a chicken egg right now. He should keep chickens. Chickens wouldn't like Vicatin. They'd just choke to death on the pills and become delicious, delicious dinner.

Sam watched as the Bear rolled around on the rug, feeling the fibers. Sam had the urge to go over and touch it too. He wanted to be a part of that rug. This was ridiculous. But it did feel good. Sam couldn't argue that. Maybe there were things in life he was missing out on. Maybe his cabin wasn't the only, oh my GOD! 'This chair is so comfortable,' Sam thought. Maybe he could drag the chair up to his cabin next round. Put it in right next to the fire, maybe drag it outside on warm summer nights, and watch the stars from it. He should build a porch. That would be great. He could... he could sit out there... maybe get a grill. He should make a grill.

"Do you remember cookouts?" Sam asked the Bear.

"I'm a bear," the Bear reasoned.

"Man they were the best. Something about grilling meat just makes it so much tastier. I was thinking about building a grill. Or maybe a smoker. Or a barbeque pit..."

The Bear scooped some more pills into his yawning mouth, and Sam fell asleep in the chair and didn't wake up until morning.

He woke in a panic with a crick in his neck. His panic didn't come from having gotten high, he felt fine today, other than a little groggy, but that probably came from sleeping in a chair and not a bed. He was panicked because today was the day they'd reach the city. And that always intimidated the shit out of him.

"Good morning," said the Bear as he gave a great big yawn. Sam looked at all those teeth, and, even though he and the Bear were friends now, he couldn't help but feel a wave of intimidation travel through his chest and down into his balls.

"Morning. What the hell did we take last night?"

"Vicatin. It's a pain reliever, but fer a lotta folks, apparently to both of us, it can give ya some real good vibes and stuff like that. Fun, eh?"

"Yeah, I guess. I just passed out," said Sam, "You want some breakfast?"

"Oh yes, yes, yes," the Bear said as he got to his feet, "More than anything."

So Sam made pancakes, sort of. He was missing some key ingredients, but there were some flour stores left, and he used that and some baking powder he found, and he crushed all that up in a big mortar and pestle to get it into a powder form again instead of the giant white brick it had become. And he found some powdered egg and did the same with that. Then he added water, and it looked just about right. The real kicker was that he had honey, and that would make a fine syrup.

Somehow honey was ageless. How did it not go bad? How did it not dry up or crystallize or something? He dipped his finger into the amber liquid and tasted from it. It was good. It was really good! Maybe honey was the ultimate food. Bees, the key to it all, and that's why all the bad things happened in the winter, because that's when the bees slept. It all started to make sense until he managed to convince himself again that what he was thinking was nonsense. Cooking always made his mind wander.

He looked down on the patties he'd made and felt pretty good about them. They weren't burnt, and they looked pretty much like pancakes. He brought it over to the imitation vintage dining table, and it seemed fitting: the very image of false decadence.

The Bear's wet nose twitched, and he spun around, his eyes excited and wild.

"What in the name of the tree spirits is that heavenly smell? Is that… honey?"

"You fucking stereotype," Sam replied with a laugh as he set the two plates piled with the sloppy pancakes on the table, "they're pancakes, or the best I could do with what I had, and there's honey on them as syrup. Enjoy."

The Bear took a tentative bite, and his eyes widened with surprise and delight.

"Ohhh my gawd," he said, his mouth full, "is this da sorta thing you humans always eat? Why wasn't I born human. Pan cakes…"

"It's pancakes. One word. And you're lucky you weren't born human. You'd be dead now if you had."

"Pan cakes would make it totally worth it. And drenched in honey…"

"Just pancakes, and usually we'd put maple syrup on it, but I'm out even at my place. The only time you can get maple sap is a couple weeks in the spring."

"Why only then? The trees don't have sap in them all year round?"

"No they do, it's just like, it needs to freeze over night and then heat up during the day for it to run. That's a big reason why I think trees are so interesting. It's like when you walk into a warm place from a cold one and you get a runny nose… trees do that too. Just like people."

"Except instead of snot its delicious maple syrup?"

"No, it's actually sap. You have to boil it down to get the syrup."

"Oh. Well I like honey just as much anyway. I don't know how much I'd like tree boogers."

"It's not tree boogers it's…"

But the Bear just nodded as if saying, 'ok whatever dude,' and went back to eating his breakfast. Sam started in too now. It wasn't the best thing he'd ever made, but for using mummified ingredients they didn't taste too bad.

After breakfast they cleaned up and put everything back into working order, and they got their supplies together once again. Putting the house back in order, as if he were definitely planning on returning, felt good. It was reassuring, it was normal. Except he had a talking bear helping him.

"You ready for another good walk buddy?" asked the Bear, punctuating Sam's thought.

Sam smiled and said, "Not quite. Follow me."

Sam led him into the garage where two snowmobiles were parked. There was a small trailer attached to one that Sam threw his packs into.

"This is our ride," said Sam proudly.

"Why don't we take the truck?" asked the Bear as he pointed to the large, black pickup parked beside it.

"The road's are all snowy. And there are cars and stuff scattered. I need maneuverability."

"Fine. But I'm not excited about this. I can't drive one of these, and that trailer doesn't look too comfortable," the Bear said, gesturing with his lack of thumbs.

"It'll be a blast, I promise."

So Sam secured his gear and ran the sled out of the garage into the snowdrifts. He put a helmet on and helped the Bear get into the trailer.

"Comfortable?" he asked. The Bear sneered back at him and wrapped himself tight in a blanket, "Here we go!"

Sam pulled the starter cord a few times, and the engine roared to life. Nice. He twisted the handle, and with a jarring hop, they started off toward the city, the mountains looming behind them.

17

Sam couldn't remember the last time he'd had this much fun. The cold wind bit into his face, but it had gone numb long ago. He was enjoying the feeling of being awake and alive too much to put his facemask down. The cold air rushing in was at first tough for his lungs to take, but he found himself used to that as well after a time and now breathed easily through a smile as he flew between abandoned cars and trucks on the snow-laden street.

Sam couldn't remember the last time he felt like this. This was better than any drug. Actually it turned out he wasn't psyched on drugs. They mostly just made him woozy. The trees whizzed by on all sides. He was tired of dodging cars. This was a high-end sled, and he wanted to really push it into gear. Even with the Bear on the back he figured he could go 70 or 75 if he really pressed it. The snow was fresh, and the powder whipped up behind him as he pulled off the road and into the woods.

Now this was adventure. The area was perfect for this. The trees weren't incredibly close together; he imagined there was a mess of rock and moss underneath him if he were to dig under that blanket of white, but as it was, he was cruising easily above it. He swerved between trees and twisted the accelerator all the way to its stopping point.

"FUCK YEAH!" his words muffled by the helmet and the rush of the wind. His words were swallowed up by the cold and whisked away, never making it to even the Bear's sensitive ears.

He spotted a frozen-over lake to his left, and he swerved again and thumped out onto the ice. This was what he had been waiting for. It was perfect, it was smooth, it was beautiful. He cranked the accelerator as far as it would go, and the speedometer needle smoothly climbed up and up. He topped out around 65 miles per hour.

Two hours later, two hours of cold, brilliantly fast lake riding, a herd of elk, knobbly knees pushing through the snow, crowded in around Sam. He couldn't tell if he had spooked them or if they were trying to race, but Sam grinned and revved up the engine again. He smiled as he swerved through the snow, keeping up with the hooves that were flinging their own snow to the wind. He was still smiling when the elk swerved off the lake and up a small hill and then plunged down out of sight. Sam was disappointed he'd lost them, so he pulled the craft toward the hill where his new friends had disappeared. It wasn't a hill though, it was a cliff. He pulled up as close as possible and peered over the edge. A beautiful cascade of ice, in sunnier climes a small waterfall, worked its way down into the white snow below where a small lake must have formed in the summer. But right now it was a pool of writhing and dead elk. Sam could see red, and limbs twisted at aggressive angles, antlers snapped and pierced through flesh. He shuddered and turned away.

The Bear was standing right over him, baring his teeth, and panting as if he were out of breath.

Sam fell back, terrified and confused, almost to the cliff's edge.

"I-" he started.

The Bear stared at him, into his soul maybe, his eyes burning like a grease-fire. The Bear was just too angry to speak yet. So many words were dancing in his head, most of them unspeakable in front of one's grandma, and his mouth was working like a dam: keeping them all bottled up inside his head, poised to explode.

Sam watched this dance across the Bear's face, and winced, terrified and waiting for death. But like a light switching off, the Bear's face melted, and the rage drained out.

"That was... horrible," was all he managed before he fell back into the snow and just rested. Sam sat down next to him.

"Hey buddy, you all right?" Sam asked, honestly concerned.

"Yeah. I'm fine. That was horrible though. Turns out I don't like traveling like that. I was... I was so miserable," the Bear said, surprising himself by being close to tears.

Sam gave him a hug and felt legitimately sorry. He had let the trail get the better of him, and he hadn't even thought to check on his passenger. The Bear looked wet, he looked cold. All the snow from behind the sled had covered him as they went. That fresh powder Sam had been so excited about had all blown right back into the Bear's face.

"I am never riding in that thing again. There is literally no way. I will run beside it before I get in that trailer again."

"Ok, sure, I'm sorry man. Really. I guess I got carried away. It's just... I haven't felt myself lately, what with the whole... maybe being crazy thing and..."

"It's whatever."

"Well don't be that way."

"What way?"

"All like, 'I'm so sad and a victim.' Do you realize how much shit you've put me through? You got me drunk, you're making me a crazy person, and you practically drugged me."

"I did what? I don't seem to remember me forcing you to do anything!"

"You-"

"I did nothing but offer stuff because I thought we were friends, and last time I checked, friends shared! You didn't have to take that stuff, and anyway it was your idea to get drunk in the first place. I saved your life back there too."

Sam knew the Bear was right, but he was mad at this point, and his face was numb, and that made him madder. He was just looking for a fight now.

"Well fuck you and your life saving! I'm a badass you know that? I can take care of my fucking self! I know how to throw fucking axes? Can you throw a fucking axe?"

"No, I can't you little runt, and stop saying that. I don't have your gosh darn god-given opposable thumbs, but I do have giant claws, sharp teeth, and it looks like now I have a mean grudge against you!"

"Oh whatever, YOU'RE. IN. MY. HEAD. You've been in my head since the start! I'm just imagining the things that make me think otherwise. You're just a fucking figment!"

"Oh yeah? Is this imaginary?" the Bear said as he shoved Sam into the snow again, precariously close to the cliff's edge. The snow didn't feel all that imaginary, the vertigo either, but Sam was still all hopped up. He dragged himself up and tried to push the Bear back. It didn't work. The Bear didn't move, but he did throw Sam off his feet with a good backhand. Sam grasped at snow and stood again.

"You fucking asshole!" Sam yelled as he charged the Bear again. The Bear just swatted him once more. A little payback.

"Had enough yet?" the Bear asked. Apparently not. Sam tried to kick at the Bear's balls. The Bear was faster though and swatted

Sam's legs out from under him, sending him down into the snow once again, that cliff and the jumble of elk, menacingly close.

"You never, *never* go for another man's berries," the Bear said with just enough reason to snap Sam out of his rage. He shook his head as if coming out of a daze.

"Woah. That hurt. Look, I didn't mean- I'm not myself lately," Sam said, trying to apologize, sort of.

"Alright. I'm sick of these outbursts. I know you're having a difficult time with this here, but look around. I know you don't notice because you're a dummy, but there are frozen animals everywhere."

Sam felt hurt. He had noticed. He'd felt all the bumps in the road. And Sam was about to point out the blob of elk at the bottom of the cliff they were still too close to.

"I know it's hard for you because you're selfish and an idiot, but there's a lot happening right now. The animals aren't killing themselves fer no good reason, and you know it. I wouldn't be here if it wasn't important, hey?"

"Are you saying you actually don't exist? Are you a ghost? Are you an angel?"

"What? No. I just wouldn't be hanging out with a douchebag like you if it wasn't for a good reason."

"I suppose I probably deserve that."

"Yeah ya dirty ball kicker."

"I didn't actually kick you in the balls."

"Yeah, but you meant to."

"I guess I did. I'm sorry, ok? Can we put it behind us?"

The Bear thought for a moment, and apparently decided 'what the heck' because he nodded and gave a big bear-smile.

"I'm hungry again, we got food?"

"Yeah man, check in the pack," Sam said as he twisted the cap off the fuel tank.

The Bear rummaged around in the pack as Sam hefted a gas canister out of the trailer.

"So where are we exactly?" asked the Bear as he opened a can of lima beans with his claw. And it dawned on Sam that he had no idea. In his excitement at being on the road again he had totally forgotten to follow his usual path.

"Hmm, shit," Sam said.

"What?" the Bear said as he swallowed the last of the lima beans with a grimace.

"I'm not sure."

"You're not sure why you cussed?"

"No, I'm not sure where we are."

"I'm not going to get riled right now, but just know I have all the right to."

"You don't even care where we're going. You just wanted to go on an adventure."

"I have reasons and stuff. Mostly like, where will we sleep when it gets dark, huh? I have no intentions of freezing to death with you. Especially not way the heck out here."

Sam peered around, trying to get his bearings. The sun was hidden by the clouds, so he was pretty well lost. But he was glad he was moving at least. He wasn't about to sit up in the middle of a cabin that had become a frozen animal vigil. It was too spooky, and he just didn't fucking get it.

And that, *that* was the theme of this whole thing. What the fuck was happening to Sam's head? Had he secretly died and this was the world's way of telling him so? Did it actually happen that solitude rots your mind away? That couldn't be true. There were plenty of people who lived alone. Or who had lived alone before. Obviously, right?

That frozen fawn's eye flashed through his head, and he thought about the sparse amount of meat he'd carved from her bones. He thought about it sitting up there in his cabin, and the whole place take on the dressings of a tomb.

"Yo, space cadet," the Bear said, interrupting Sam's thought process and shaking him back to reality.

"Yeah, sup?" Sam said, still on his way out of reverie.

"What's the scoop?"

"Vanilla with a chocolate twist."

"What?"

"Sorry, nothing. Well we're on a body of water, towns are usually built around water, so I figure all we have to do is follow the lake," Sam said, pointing toward the horizon, "But you're not gonna like this."

"What?"

"We're not going to make it unless we ride."

"Not happening," the Bear said, crossing his arms, " No way."

"If we don't then we're stuck in the middle of nothing and no-where without a place to sleep."

The Bear thought it through.

"How do I know you're not just saying that?"

"I don't know what I'd have to gain by lying to you."

"I'm not doing it."

"You have to."

"Well then I get to drive."

"You can't. You don't even know how."

"I could learn."

"Without thumbs?"

"Oh, sure, throw that in my face again why don't you? You know I'm sensitive about my bear-hands."

"Well you're not going to be able to use the throttle without thumbs, big guy, which means you're in back. I'll make sure the blanket is tighter over you this time, ok?"

"Fine," the Bear said with an angry growl.

He climbed into the trailer and begrudgingly let Sam cover him with the blanket. Sam used the barrels of gas to make sure the blanket would stay in place, and when he was satisfied, he gave the Bear a small reassuring pat.

"You'll be alright buddy. I'll get us there quick."

And with that he hopped on the snowmobile, pulled the starter cord, marveled at how catastrophically the engine broke the silence, and then twisted the throttle.

Sam was back to feeling great. The sense of adventure welled up in him, from his balls into his stomach, through his chest, and out his mouth in a primal scream that took on an edge of fear toward the end, which surprised Sam, and made him sit back down as he headed toward what he hoped would be civilization.

19

This was it.

The sun was going down, and they had just ridden into the outskirts of town. It started slowly with a few homes visible from the lake, working its way toward the smaller suburban communities. Then they reached the billboards, and Sam knew they were going to be ok.

"Drink More Molson's," the billboard read. Molson's. That was beer. Canadian beer. This was definitely still Canada then. He wasn't sure if that was a relief or not, but at least this city wasn't some insane figment of his imagination. He would never imagine a Molson's sign.

On the second leg of their journey the air didn't clear his mind so much, and his thoughts were a swirling mess that kept draining right down to: this is what crazy feels like. He wasn't ready for the feeling of such total isolation that came with the idea that you were going crazy. He had lived in isolation for eight years technically, but he'd always had himself. So now what did he have? A talking Bear shoved into a trailer behind a snowmobile. Sam wondered if the Bear was ok. He was probably still miserable, Sam reasoned. Well, they were almost there. In fact, Sam pulled up to a ruinous old lodge. Caribou Lodge. This seemed to be a fine enough place to camp for the night.

It wasn't the largest city in the world, the highest building he could see was this hotel, and it was one, two, three, only four stories high. A nice roof though. He wondered if the log decorations were real timber or if they were plastic designed to look like giant timbers. Maybe he'd find out tonight.

"Hey, a little help here," the Bear said from beneath the cloth.

"Oop, sorry about that."

Sam lifted the gasoline off the blanket and threw the cloth onto the snowmobile seat. The Bear wasn't happy, but that murderous glint had left his eye, and he seemed content now that the whole ordeal was over with.

He rolled out of the cart and landed with a thud in the snow. As he stood and brushed himself off, Sam noticed the hundreds of animal tracks crisscrossing the otherwise untouched snow.

Well, at least the animals here weren't just killing themselves. 'City animals got sense,' Sam thought as he helped the Bear brush the snow off his coat.

"So how'd the second leg treat you?" Sam asked.

"I'm never doing that again."

"Noted."

"Even if that means we have to teach you to drive."

"I know how to drive, I'm just not overly confident."

"Coulda fooled me."

"Let's just go inside."

Sam walked up to the glass-paned front door. The automatic door slid open, which should have been a surprise or at least a red flag.

Sam and the Bear walked in to the Caribou Lodge. The lights were on inside, and a fox in a vest stood on hind legs behind the counter. His cute fox face lit up with surprise when he saw Sam, and he let out a small yelp. He ducked under the counter, and all the lights went out.

"Hello?" the Bear called, "I thought this was Canada, how about some polite service, hey?"

Slowly the lights of the lodge, as if by magic, flickered their way back on. Then came the unmistakable sound of nails clicking on hardwood floor, and the animals began to appear. The fox slowly drew his head back up from behind the counter.

"We-welcome," the fox said, "My name is… is Craig, how may I, uh, help you today- this evening."

"We'd like a room, no two rooms, adjoining if you've got it, if not at least next to each other. Also do you have a pool?"

"Room?" Craig seemed bewildered by the request.

"Where'd you get that vest?" Sam asked when he realized he'd been staring at the comfortable red cloth since he came in. Craig looked down at his vest and then up at Sam, his eyes squinted as if he were missing something.

"Can you hold on a minute? I need to talk with my manager," Craig said with all the confidence of a pubescent boy at a dance.

Craig slipped out again, and now Sam saw other animals poking their heads around corners, trying to catch a glimpse of what had made Craig so nervous. There was a family of rabbits standing by a doorway, the smallest of which were literally shaking with fear or excitement. An old dog lifted his head from a couch in the lounge, gave a halfhearted glance and put his head back down. And Sam was strangely ok with this. What else was he expecting? Why not this? This made sense right? A hotel full of animals that could talk and think?

Sam's head hit the ground hard as he passed out.

Sam was awake but refused to open his eyes.

He could tell it was bright where he was, the back of his eyelids were almost translucent minus the blood that reddened and obscured his vision. The tender bulbs of his eyes moved back and forth behind the closed lids, searching for an explanation for what he had seen without having to engage with it. He quickly became aware that someone or something might be watching, that they might be seeing his eyes twitch back and forth. There's no way they'd be imagining his mind was in dreams. Not even nightmares. No, this movement was too calculated. First up to the left as he thought of that old dog's boredom with his presence and then up to the right as he tried to forget it. No way.

A chair scraped nearby, and the sharp break to the silence forced Sam's eye's open. The ceiling was white. It had those little bumps on it like some ceilings used to. What was that? What was it for? Insulation? Did it soundproof? He remembered jumping on a bunk bed when he was younger and smacking his head on the ceiling. Those bumps bit into his skull, which had scared him so bad he jerked away and fell the five or so feet down onto his floor. He was mostly fine. No blood even, but he remembered his Mom giving him a great big hug. Enveloping him and-

"Hey! You're up. All that fresh air tired you out, eh?" the Bear said.

Sam reluctantly turned and faced the Bear who was wrapped in a blanket on a tall-backed chair.

"You look warm," Sam said without feeling.

"Getting there."

"Good."

"You hit your head on the way down," a shaggy, grey wolf said as she put her paws up on the bed and looked over Sam.

Sam screamed, and she winced.

"I have sensitive ears. Please be mindful of that," she said calmly.

"This is Tess! She's the Manager of the Caribou Lodge," said the Bear.

"Tess," said Sam as he stared straight into her eyes. He was intimidated by how blue they were. And pretty. They had the flame of intelligence behind them.

"How... how is this all happening? What happened that you all can talk and wear vests?"

"Wearing vests isn't all that hard."

"But I don't get it. I've never been able to talk to animals before this. And there are all these animals out there killing themselves, but you guys aren't."

"Killing themselves? That's awful. I can't explain that to you," Tess said.

"Do you know anyone who could?"

"Personally? No."

"What does that mean? Does that mean someone might?"

"Maybe. I've heard some rumors, but I can't really speak to them."

Sam was excited now. He knew all about rumors. They usually had *some* basis in fact. Bare was just staring at Tess, as if enchanted.

"What sort of rumors?" Sam asked, sitting up now.

"I'm not totally sure, but I can try to ask around for you. I do have some work to do though. So for the moment make yourself at home, and I'll see you both later tonight," Tess said before she sauntered out the door.

Sam adjusted the pillows behind his back. The Bear was still staring at the open door where she'd just been.

"You like her," Sam said to him.

"What? Are you crazy? Shut up."

Sam smiled and felt the bump on his head. It was raised a bit, but it would heal fine. He doubted he'd have any permanent brain damage or anything. Probably. And someone here might have some answers for him. Things were looking up.

"Pool?" asked the Bear.

"They have a pool?" said Sam. Even better!

They walked in to the pool area, and Sam had flashbacks to young girl's birthday parties at the Motel 8: trick candles lit on plastic furniture near the hot tub, gifts growing soggy in the salted, acrid humidity, frilly little swimsuits.

Boys had their birthdays at the bowling alley where there were racing video games and bumpers to keep their gutter balls in play, a key to any young man's bowling game, but the girls, so young and so old at the same time, knew more fun could be had in a pool. Even without an overt sexuality in them yet, the thought of different parts and soft skin and maybe a peek of something, well... Sam remembered hours of staying in the water even though his skin had long shirked its way into watered-down wrinkles because despite his best efforts his shorts were hanging in exactly the wrong way...

This pool however, and the overbearing scent of chlorine lingering didn't conjure thoughts of cleanliness or young love but somehow the opposite. The old, clean smell reminded him of something in decay, of the entirety of humanity and everything it had accomplished, rotting away. He could see all those little girls and boys, so unsure in their budding sexuality now fully eaten up by time. Just chlorine-bleached white skeletons huddled awkwardly on the white plastic furniture, any parts that had once given these spaces their magic, long since rotted off.

That bump to the head must have really thrown him for a loop. He hadn't been this negative in a long time. His hand moved to the back of his skull again, and he fingered the tacky bump. His digits came back clean, and when he put them to his nostrils, he only caught the slightest hint of iron. He'd be ok.

"How 'bout that? A winter watering hole!" the Bear said, shaggy paws on his hips.

"This was your idea. You know what a pool is," said Sam, and the Bear cocked his eyebrow and showed off his yellowed teeth with a smile.

The Bear gave a, 'Whoop!' and, limbs splayed, jumped into the pool with a loud KERPLUNK! A spray of water attacked Sam, and he put his arms up over his head in a useless attempt to protect himself. Little bits of dirt and grime radiated from the Bear into the clear water, and Sam wondered how on earth these animals, with their complete lack of thumbs and nets, managed to keep this water so clean.

"You comin' in?" asked the Bear, his yell echoing wildly through the room.

Sam clumsily removed his shirt and folded it on a table. Even though he was used to being nude alone, the lingering apprehension brought on by the chlorine smell made him peer around the empty pool. With a deep breath, he stripped down to his underwear, buried the thoughts of girls in swimsuits and death, and jumped wildly into the pool.

The world was swallowed up as his head went under, and the huge quietness of the open room was replaced with a much more intimate silence, a silence that seemed alive and vibrant. He watched an elm leaf float by his hands and watched for a moment the Bear's brown fur dancing along with the water before his head broke above, and he took a huge gasp of air.

"Wow!" Sam said with the end of his breath, "It's warm!"

"Hey, don't look at me, man," the Bear said, raising his paws in the air. Sam gleefully ignored him as he started to do a backstroke toward the deep end. The Bear followed, looking to prove that he too could swim with the best of them. They stayed like this, talking very little but for quick comments on the other's technique, as they swam and dove and goofed and simply forgot the world.

Eventually their energy waned, and they swam down to the shallow end to rest. Sam put his hand up for a high five and said, "Hey, you're pretty damn good in the water, man."

The Bear, who didn't know what a high five was, looked at the hand and looked quickly at Sam and said, "Well thank you, sir, you're not too shabby yourself."

The Bear looked at the hand again and went to try to shake it.

"No, no!" Sam said laughing, "It's a high five! See? Put your hand up. Okay, your paw."

Sam grabbed the Bear's arm and dragged the dripping mess out of the water.

"How do you know what a pool is but not what a high five is? Here you put your paw out like this and the other guy," Sam slapped the Bear's padded mitt with his own, making a dull, wet noise, "He slaps you a five. Get it?"

The Bear nodded doubtfully.

"Now try it out," Sam said, excited to be teaching something new.

The Bear stuck his paw out and said, "High five?" as if it were a question.

Sam wound up and slapped him another five, and with that sound they fell into a silence and listened to the small waves lap at the sides of the pool.

Eventually the Bear made a little noise, to which Sam anxiously asked, "What?"

The Bear had to think about his wording before he said, "Do you feel this buzz in the air? It's like a humming thing, but it's hitting me just right where I can't for the darn life of me remember what was so important that I let you take me on a snowmobile. Don't you hate that? Like when you walk from one bend of the stream to the other and you totally forgot why you made the trip in the first place?"

"Yeah...that's-"

"How's that water boys?" Tess interrupted. Sam hadn't even heard her come in. His forest-mind noted how stealthy this predator was.

"Perfect, miss!" the Bear responded cheerily, "Absolute perfection."

The Bear clumsily worked his way up and out of the pool, and Sam more than expected him to shake off the water like a big dog. But he didn't; he just sauntered up to Tess with a goofy grin, the water falling from his coat leaving a trail behind him like a slug. He gave her a little bow, sending more water splashing down onto the tiles. Sam hopped out of the pool and searched for a towel. Finding none, he decided, 'what the hell,' and shook himself off like a dog, which did very little for him. His T-shirt still stuck to his wet body as he pulled it down over his lean torso.

"We here at the Caribou Lodge would like to cordially invite you to dinner tonight," said Tess, taking on the voice and mannerisms of an upscale hostess.

"And we cord-ally accept, too, I'm five shades past famished for sure."

Sam just nodded his head as he struggled to force his jeans up his wet legs.

"I'll tell you one thing, do not try to put jeans on over wet underwear folks! Echk," Sam said as he walked bowlegged over to the animals.

Dinner was in a large dining hall, and all the food was simply laid out on the floor. Sam hated to think of how it'd gotten there, and he tried desperately to imagine the little bunnies hopping in unison with a big bowl of salad between them, but then his imagination sent in the foxes and dogs, their mouths heavy with carrots and radishes, and bunches of bananas, which was much closer to the truth he imagined. Except maybe the bananas. Where'd they even find bananas? Especially in this climate.

Around the room several families of animals scurried about for no purpose that Sam could discern. They looked like they had some place to go, but he had a feeling they were all right where they were meant to be. There was the family of rabbits again, and they moved quickly and determinedly around the outer rim of the room. The old dog apparently had some friends because three or four of them lounged near the food, their tails wagging lazily and out of sync. Craig the fox was still in his vest and grinned as he had a staring contest with a particularly expressive potato. The largest animal there was a moose that must have really struggled being inside, Sam thought as he watched the poor thing work his huge antlers sideways through the door. There were also a few deer in a corner with a fawn, and the moose, once inside, sauntered over to them.

The predators had their own corner. There was a single bobcat with that adorable, kitten-like face, and a lynx with his little, tufted ears. The Bear was the only of his kind, and Sam could see disappointment cross his face as he too surveyed the crowd. Sam could also see the anger when the Bear spotted the moose. Sam took note He steer them away from each other.

"Well, this is the whole gang," Tess said, using her large grey head to gesture around the room. Speaking up now she continued, "Everyone, I'd like you to meet our new guests. This is Sam, and yes he's a human, but I don't want you to treat him any differently than if he were one of our own."

Sam gave a wave and a fake smile as these creatures, all of which he had killed and eaten in his eight years in the woods, looked at him with years of mistrust and, for some, outright hatred. Sam for a moment considered pretending to have been a vegetarian, but then he remembered the Bear knew his dark secret. He hoped it wouldn't come up.

"And this is Bare," Tess finished, with a little nod toward the Bear. Sam, his ears burning with embarrassment, realized he hadn't even asked if the Bear had had a name.

"Wait. Your name is Bear," Sam asked incredulously, despite his own embarrassment.

"Well, it's Barry, but yeah, everyone just calls me Bare."

"So you're a bear named Bare? What were your parents named? Bearina and Bearnstein?"

"No ya jerk. I didn't know my father, and my ma's name was Michelle. She just liked the name Barry."

Someone in the crowd called out, "Hey leave him alone!" and Sam blushed again, and mumbled, "Sorry," to Bare and the yeller and to everyone.

"Hey, it's ok buddy. I don't blame you for not asking my name. This has all been a bit of an odd situation for you I'm sure. I blame you way more for the snowmobile. And for letting me eat lima beans. Yech."

Sam nodded, watching his bare feet kick at the floor.

"So what's to eat? And please don't say lima beans. I would be really embarrassed after what I just said," Bare said jovially, breaking the tension in the room.

There was another flurry of motion as all the animals came toward the middle to show off the food they'd prepared. Sam was surprised to see some meat on one side of the piles, but he supposed that although these animals were somehow taking on the speech and mannerisms of humans, they were still driven by their more carnal, instinctual desires. Although he did wonder if all these animals were sentient now, what meat was that? Who had they deemed appropriate to eat? Some of the guilt he'd been having slipped away, and he was grateful for that. He didn't deal with guilt well. Never had.

When he was a boy, and everyone was still alive and well, he and his brother Rodney would play out in their backyard. It wasn't a large backyard by his current standards, but at the time it seemed like the whole world. The property wasn't fenced in, but there were medium-sized fir trees planted around the perimeter that gave that suburban illusion of seclusion. Sam's father had built them a sandbox that they'd build whole cities in, pretending their action figures were in charge of the sloppy, anthill world, or at the very least the protectors and destroyers of the world. Everything was so important in those days.

Their home was on the corner of a small development, so there was nothing but a field to their left where Sam's father, during hunting season, would trudge out like an orange beacon and sit statue-still in the dying weeds waiting for any sign of deer.

But Sam and Rodney had their own uses for the great prairie-field: catching tadpoles in the small ditches of dirty water that formed, searching for golf balls their mother and the neighbors had lost out in the thick summer grass and weeds, and of course Hide-and-Go-Seek, one of Sam's favorite games.

Sam considered himself a bit of a hide-and-seek expert. He'd high step through the field, find a spot with particularly long grass, and lay out as flat as possible. Most of the time Rodney, though older, didn't stand a chance. Sam would lay there, letting the minutes tick by, suppressing the almost overwhelming urge to giggle or brush away the tickling bugs that wandered across his naked legs. But he resisted; he was just that good.

Rodney didn't like the fact that Sam won these contests so often, as their sibling rivalry had bred a deep hated for just about everything the other did. So one day, to teach Sam a lesson, Rodney wagered a whole week of chores on one round of hide-and-go-seek. Or best two out of three, or whatever he conceded after Sam pressed about the fair amount of hides versus seeks. Now, with overwhelming excitement, Sam let his brother's counting voice fade as he high-tailed it into the field.

Careful to disguise his movement, Sam found what he knew to be the perfect spot under a fallen tree branch, fenced in by high grass, and took to hiding, pleased as peaches to know for sure he wouldn't have to do chores for a whole week! But of course Rodney had turned around and snuck inside the moment he saw Sam lay down. Rodney was giggling in front of the TV as Sam giggled at the thought of his brother doing all those awful chores all week long.

His mind showed a cartoon version of Rodney, sad beyond reason, and moping and crying as he washed the dishes. In the fantasy Rodney dropped a dish that crashed to pieces on the floor and then exploded into flames for good measure, and in came Mom, screamin' and lookin' like a demon. Sam let out a small burst of laughter, and his hand flew to his mouth, trying to keep it in, and his heart somehow dropped and raced at the same time, as he was certain his brother was about to find him.

That certainty diminished as the sun began to set, and Sam realized he had accidently fallen asleep out in that field.

He walked inside to find Rodney casually eating the last of the good yellow flavored freeze pops (not the banana flavored one but a more tropical flavor,) and watching whatever nonsense was on the television. As Sam scratched violently at his bug-bite covered legs, he still felt he had the upper hand, and he said, "Ha ha. Now you have to do all my chores for the whole week!"

"No I don't," Rodney replied with practiced nonchalance.

"Yes you do."

"No, I don't," again as if this were the most obvious fact in the world.

"Yes you do."

"Nope."

"YES YOU DO!"

"MOM! Sam's yelling in the house!"

And of course from somewhere distant in the small house the voice of their mother yelled, "Sam! No yelling in the house! Now get ready for bed! It's past your bedtime!"

"But Mom! Rodney bet me-"

"And no betting! You're too young for any of that nonsense, now get ready for bed!"

"But why do I have to go to bed at eight, and Rodney gets to stay up until nine?" Sam yelled with the nasally whine one can only get away with in childhood.

Sam's mother had marched into the room at this point and put her hands on her cocked hips; she meant business. Rodney tried his best to conceal the freezie, and Sam took a brief pause from his violent scratching.

"You'll get to stay up until nine when you're his age. Now get to it."

She led Sam to the bathroom where she muttered her disappointment in him at how he'd let himself get this 'torn up by bugs,' while completely ignoring his attempts to explain how it was all Rodney's fault.

"Now brush your teeth and get in bed. I'll read you a story, but then that's it," she said, the routine and her obvious love for him overriding her annoyance with the pettiness of her children.

Sam put a huge glob of bubblegum flavored toothpaste on his dinosaur themed toothbrush and listened to his mother question his father on why he was always so damn quiet during the boys' goddamn temper tantrums.

Sam was mad. There was anger in this house, and it coursed through him. It was that white-hot anger of childhood, where you haven't learned to not suppress your own self-centeredness, but you're also too confined by the rules your parents have governed to you; it was an anger that seethed from everywhere, but was also achingly contained within Sam's small body. He wanted to lash out, he wanted to break something, to hurt something, to make it all fair, but he just didn't have the life experience or the knowledge to really be ruinous yet.

So he just rubbed his brother's toothbrush all over his butt. He really got it in there too. Just scrubbed away at his small anus until he'd siphoned all that shaking-rage through his butt directly into the bristles of his brother's more mature, dinosaur-free blue and white toothbrush.

And he never told him. Rodney used that toothbrush for forever. Until the bristles were curved beyond recognition, and the whole handle had lost its true colors with the caked layers of a thousand brushings gone by. And Sam had been so eaten up with guilt by that act, by the ongoing act of revenge that occurred twice a day even after the anger had long been forgotten, that he couldn't bear to fight with his brother anymore. He just couldn't do it knowing that every single day his brother put Sam's butt in his mouth. And so through that guilt they became actual friends, and they ended up liking each other a lot. But underneath all the fun times that little worm of guilt wriggled around in Sam's brain.

And even now, as Sam stared at the food these animals had laid out, and couldn't help but think of them as food still, he felt a pang of guilt for the flakes of poop on his brother's toothbrush, and every other moment of guilt he had in his life. It was shocking how much guilt he had, and the thought of his brother brought waves of the stuff crashing over him. He started to feel nauseous again as guilt blanketed him. He could never possibly redeem himself. He shouldn't even be alive right now, his guilt told him.

And then he did it, he went ahead and embarrassed himself in front of everybody and staggered between eating animals to Bare's feet and started sobbing.

"I-" the sound of snot and sadness already sending shockwaves and shivers through his voice, "-am SO sorry I didn't ask your name. You're already like just the best friend I've ever had, and I really like you, and I think you're great, and you don't even swear, and I'm just so sorry!"

Sam felt the dizzying lifetime of guilts settle a little, and a new anxiety set in as he realized a few dozen eyes from half as many species were trained on him, most of them leering as if some theory had just been proven.

Sam looked up at Bare, who looked down with the sympathy of a friend. That did it. He just couldn't take another moment and ran through the first door he could.

Sam breathed slowly and deeply as he leaned over an industrial oven that had caked on bits of egg that dated back decades. He opened his eyes and little black fireworks of light traced the lines in the tiles on the floor. He'd always seen these when his head was spinning or he was dehydrated, and he always wondered if they were a symptom of something sinister. Did everyone see these, or was his mind just more broken than most?

Deep breath in. Hold, one, two. Deep breath out. Feel your lungs empty out. Feel your anxieties breathed out with them. Feel the calm, and deep breath in. He'd learned this from a guidance councilor in grade school who wore his hair in a long ponytail. Sam had forgotten the man's name but remembered that he'd killed himself when Sam was a freshman in high school. Sam hadn't gone to the funeral, but he'd heard the councilor had tried hanging himself with a string of Christmas lights, but when that failed he'd taken a large handful of sleeping pills, a fifth of vodka, and some Dramamine to keep it all down.

Someone had made the joke at the time, 'why didn't he just try to hang himself with that pony tail,' and everyone had had a good little laugh at the dead man's expense. But that breathing exercise really did help Sam calm down when his mind was on edge, and it was one of the small tricks he carried with him through life. Remembering that man's suicide made Sam feel a bit better about his own situation. At least he wasn't ready to consider hanging himself with any sort rope, festive or otherwise.

"You okay there buddy?" Bare asked from behind him. Sam turned to face him, and the shame from a moment ago came rushing back. His cheeks burned red.

"Hey, Bare. I'm sorry again. I... I hope we can still be friends..."

"Why wouldn't we still be friends?"

"Well because I didn't remember to ask your name, or I assumed you didn't have one, and, well, I don't know exactly. It's been a while since I've had a friend, and to be completely honest, I've forgotten how a lot of it works. Ok, I probably never really knew how it worked. I never had a whole lot of friends."

Bare walked over to a large bay of cupboards and opened one. It was stocked with the giant cans of goods that you only find in commercial kitchens. Three gallons of tomatoes, a six-gallon vat of Heinz Mustard, and 64 oz. cans of pickled beets for whatever reason.

"You must be starving. Let's get you some people food," Bare said thoughtfully eyeing the cans. He pointed to a large can of mixed fruit in 'sauce,' and said, "Maybe a little fruit? They're in saaauce."

Sam looked at his new friend, and the little black bugs in his vision, those little fireworks, slowed and then stopped, and Sam managed a smile.

"What does that even mean? Sauce. What kind of sauce do you keep fruit in?"

Bare's big black lips, glistening with his saliva, split into a smile, and he shrugged.

"Hey," Sam said, "I heard this once: 'if tomatoes are a fruit, does that make Ketchup a smoothie?'"

"What's a Ketchup?" asked Bare.

Bare led Sam back into the dining room where all the heads turned at the sound of the opening door. Tess walked over cautiously.

"Hey, everything alright with you?" she asked, her posture indicating she could either pounce or run at any given moment.

"Yeah, sorry about that," Sam said and then raising his voice again, "Sorry everyone. I'm just still getting used to the whole 'animals talking' thing. As a human it's pretty difficult to get past. I sort of think I'm crazy, or dying, or you know, that whole thing."

A couple of the rabbits nodded as if they knew exactly what he was going through, and the bobcat eyed him like he was garbage, even though the bobcat had some blood left on his chin. The idiot.

"So, I hope we can start over. I'd like to be friends. Would anyone like to try some of this mixed fruit? I found a can opener. It's in a sauce. The fruit is… not the opener of course, haha. It's like a sugary fruit sauce though. Not like a pasta one," Sam finished lamely, hefting the gallons of fruit up like an offering.

There was a silence as the animals considered how they were going to deal with this high maintenance new arrival.

"I'll try a bit," said a female deer.

"Great!" Sam said, excited now.

He poured the deer a bowl of the fruit and set it on the ground. She walked up, her hooves loud in the large, quiet room, all eyes now trained steadfastly on her.

"I'm Sam, by the way," Sam said to her, making sure he didn't have another Bare situation on his hands.

"I'm Hannah," she said, "Thank you for the fruit Sam. It smells great."

Sam held out the bowl for her, realized she wouldn't be able to take it from him, so he glanced around quickly, and then set the bowl on the ground. Hannah the deer stepped forward and gave a tentative lick at the bowl. Then another, and another, and then the bowl was empty.

"That was delicious. My goodness," she said.

"Can-can I try some?" asked a small rabbit, timidly.

"Sure," Sam said excitedly. He looked up at Bare who gave him the slightest nod of approval, "Mixed fruit for everybody."

Sam ran to the kitchen and came back with a whole stack of bowls. He set them out in a line and walked his way around, filling them almost to the top with sugary, false-tasting fruit. Even though this was his peace offering, he still felt the desire to steal every single one of the red cherries that swam like maraschino roses amidst the rest of the orange and yellow cubed-mess. The dogs, the rabbits, the deer, and the moose all came up right away to eat from the bowls.

"Delicious!" said an old labrador, "I always wondered what was in those big vats."

Sam's smile faded as he looked at the predators who shifted in the back, Craig the fox having joined them. He kept looking up at the others, trying to match his expressions to theirs.

"Would you guys like some?" Sam asked, preempting their negativity or murder. Their tough exteriors diminished slightly in the face of friendliness (this was Canada after all,) and the bobcat walked over, sniffed first at the spongy fruit, then took a taste. It was clear he liked it, and the rest followed and did the same. The lynx even gave Sam what looked like a smile. It occurred to Sam that for the first time in his life, he might have not only had a friend but a whole group of them. He smiled as he listened to the sloppy sounds of the slurping animals.

35

Later in the evening, after the clean-up which Sam was dismayed to see was originally done with animal tongues but now was done with a bleach solution and a mop, the animals who weren't too tuckered out from the day gathered in the lounge around an electric fire. Sam sat close to Bare and Tess on a couch, and the lynx named Jean-Christopher, who would not abide being called just 'Jean' or 'Chris' lounged on a chair near them. The father rabbit, inexplicably named Cheese, took up a whole love seat to himself with his continuous, nervous search for that perfectly comfortable spot. And on the nice faux-native rug lay Hank, one of the dogs.

Hank was a mutt, but he looked to be mostly German shepherd, or at least his pointed ears seemed to tell that story. And the deer, Gabby, Zeke, and Hannah, were all there, except for Gabby and Zeke's daughter Farrah, who was already asleep and being watched by Jared the moose. The rest had scurried off to whatever hotel room den they'd created for themselves, leaving these few to trade stories and wait for that inexplicable darkness of sleep to come for them.

Sam and Bare had just recounted their trip into the city, leaving out some of the major details like Sam offering Bare lynx meat when they first met, and the coyotes, and the drug use; the story had actually been very much about Sam recounting their meeting, and Bare taking over as Sam got bogged down in details.

Bare focused on how much he hated, hated, hated snowmobiles. No one else in the lounge had ever ridden one, so they couldn't speak to hating them, but Jean-Christopher said in his vaguely French accent that he hated the noise very much.

"So none of you want to kill yourselves?" Sam asked at the end of the tale.

Cheese burrowed around a little faster at this, and Gabby the deer tut-tutted.

"I for one have never wanted to kill myself," Jean-Christopher said resolutely, "And I can't honestly imagine why all those mountain beasts did that."

"Yea-yeah!" piped up Cheese.

"Well there were those awkward den moments…" Bare said with a tone that clearly worked to break some of the tension Sam had again created. Bare was getting to be quite good at cleaning up Sam's messes. Except Hank said, "There was a time I was ready to die."

Everyone was silent; no one expected that. The atmosphere suddenly ballooned in weight.

"I was just a pup then, not maybe more than a year, a year and a half," Hank started after a bit of prompting that came across as more obligation than actual interest.

"Now is that one year in dog-years or people-years?" Sam asked quickly, just to make sure he could follow the story correctly.

"Is there a difference?" asked Tess.

"Yeah," Sam said, "Seven dog years is equal to one people year. Everybody knows that."

"Wait a second though there," Bare said, "Why the heck would that make any sense? It's not like dogs see time faster than you do. Are there different bear years too? What is it like one-in-three?"

"No, stop. I thought that was just how it went. Is that not a thing?"

"No," Hank said again, "That's just a thing humans said to make themselves feel better when their dogs died before they did. 'Oh, it's only natural. He was somethin' such as 112 years old in dog years.' I much hated that shit."

"Sorry," Sam muttered as he stared into the cushions of the couch. These moments were not the ones he missed while lonely in the woods.

"Hey, no, don't be upset, Sam. You've got no reason to feel down just because you haven't got knowledge. I bet this is the first time a dog ever talked back at you, yes?"

"Yes. At least with English anyway. I've had them bark when I say speak."

"Huh, ok."

"I'd be-be very excit- hey, what about your story, Hank?" Cheese asked as he displaced himself again from the spot he'd temporarily been lodged.

"Oh, ok. Sure. I guess I was young and happy mostly. We all got took away from our Ma at an early age, and that was rough on me at the time, but I don't actually remember too much about that stage of my life. Mostly just flashes of images that are more emotion than anything and ones I ain't fully sure are from my own life anyhow. I do clearly see the sides of an old tub with all my brothers and sisters cuddling and wandering around me though, licking nervously at old soap stains, and I see a sky more grey than any grey I can remember. The most beautiful shade I'd ever seen, with hardly a wisp of white running through. I remember feeling content, having just so much good feelings toward my brothers and sisters and that tub and everything. Life is so simple when you haven't seen much you know? Well you can't hardly tell it now, but back then I was the pick of the litter. I was a good count bigger than my smallest brother, and I had opened my eyes earlier than most, which at the time was an achievement."

Jean-Christopher nodded solemnly.

"So some of my siblings were still laying down blind as I watched the humans come and lean over us, their hands covered in sugars and flavors they let me lick as long as I liked. Once or twice someone was taken, but for the most part it was quiet. And it was quiet as I watched the clouds come together, and darken up to black. And as the rain started to come down. And it was quiet as the tub started to slowly fill up with water."

The whole lounge was quiet as well.

"The smallest of us drowned pretty quick. They hadn't yet learned to swim or nothing a'course. The rain was loud, so we couldn't much hear any of the struggling either. Since I was big I managed to crawl up on the backs of the littler ones, the ones that had stopped moving. I was young still and I was scared and I didn't do anything to help anybody but myself. It's my biggest regret, I imagine. It was just me and one of my sisters that made it. We probably wouldn't have had it rained any longer, but as it was the whole thing let up around morning. When the humans came again we was just shivering on a pile of all our dead siblings."

Hannah the deer let out a small gasp at the word dead, but otherwise the room was hardly breathing.

Sam took a selfish moment to wish he could command an audience like this. Hank's voice shrunk in importance as he remembered how in school everyone would stand around in the hallways between classes and talk and tell jokes, and some of the people, Henry Mindelton, a handsome and clever boy cursed with the laziness brought on by being both in middleclass-Midwest, always seemed to steal the limelight. Sam could be halfway through telling a joke or a story he believed to be quite decent, and Henry would make a quick joke off some innocuous mistake, a mispronounced word, a phrase that could somehow, vaguely be construed as sexual, and all the attention would just flow away and into the waiting arms of the Hen-man. People had even given him a nickname they liked him so much. No one had ever given Sam a nickname. Unless you counted 'Fag' or 'fuck-head' as nicknames. Sam didn't.

Sam hated the feeling of people not taking him seriously, not listening. He hated the feeling of wanting to be heard, he hated the feeling of life's sheer unfairness, and he hated the idea that people were just drawn to some, and that maybe by the simple mistake of his birth as himself, as Sam, he could never achieve what the Hen-man seemed to just have. It was a lot to deal with for a fourteen year old.

"They only hit me a few times."

And Sam was back in the story. He wondered briefly how he'd managed to even stray from it.

"Not that it was nothin' like a violent home, but being away from my sister, ya gotta know that was hard on a pup like me. And I could smell what these folks had done. They cooked food to gristle, they had a dozen small critters buried out back, and they had me and Trip, who was a hound with only three legs. Seemed cruel to call him Trip, I always thought, but my people thought it was a fine joke. So every now and again, when they were gone too long I'd have an accident on their rug. It was their dang fault for staying away so long. We got needs, you know? And they'd come home and they'd just smell it and out came the paper. And just WHACK WHACK WHACK," he really emphasized these, that pain right on the surface, even so many years later. This dog really knew how to hold a grudge. Sam was surprised; he had imagined dogs forgot things pretty quickly.

"My people would leave Trip outside when they went away. Another joke, as they weren't worried *he'd* run away. And I'd watch him pace out on the lawn, his head bobbing significantly as he hobbled. We didn't speak much at that point, except for every once and again we'd smell each other, just get to know where the other's day had taken them. But I'd watch him. I'd watch him limp around the yard, afraid of certain corners of the lawn that had many years before been an electric fence. They hadn't even bothered to train me for that. I think after one dog they'd had their fill.

"But I'd watch Trip slowly work his way up toward the road. Our People's house was right on a road at the top of a hill, you see. There was a junkyard across the street where people would cart all sorts of wonderful smelling treasures. And once Trip was sure that our people were gone he would go stand on the corner by the street, and then eventually he was standing in the street. I thought for a while that he was just attracted to the garbage. I know I was. I'd catch a whiff of that place, and it would just made my bones shake.

"I don't know what went through his head, I just watched him stand in the middle of that road, and stare down that hill, as if he was waitin' on something. Trucks and cars would cruise up the hill and stop quickly, making a terrible beeping noise, and folks would lean out and yell at Trip. They'd call him a dumb dog, tell him to get the hell outta the road. And maybe he was dumb, but he never struck me like that. But anyway, one day a big, meaty truck came racing up the hill and Trip…"

Hank paused for a second here, and his audience waited impatiently for what they knew was coming.

"He just about exploded when the thing hit him. I can't say much more, but I saw that happen, and I was hit with the image of all my little brothers and sisters drowned underneath me, and I thought of all the shits I'd left on the rug. It was one of those moments where all the bad just hits you at once, and you can't even breathe. And Trip's out there, shakin' away on the pavement. Down to… down to nothin' but two legs, and they weren't even on the same side, and he's just a puddle now. Nothin' but a puddle and fur, and this truck don't even come back. It doesn't even stop really. It just slows, sees it's a dog and not some other person I imagine, and then speeds off down the road like nothin' happened. Like Trip wasn't… hey, good golly, I'm sorry ya'll. Listen to me, bringin' down the whole place here. I didn't mean to… hell, I'm sorry. I just haven't never told this tale to anyone, and it's been eatin' at me some. Jeeze, look at me bein' just selfish."

"I'm sorry," he repeated.

"Th-then what happened?" Cheese asked urgently.

"I'm invested now," said Tess, "If it's not too painful for ya, I'd like to hear the rest of your story."

"Sounds like you've had quite the gall darn life," Bare chimed in.

"Yeah, I 'spect I have," Hank said quietly, "You sure I'm not just dampenin' everyone's moods? I mean, ya'll are new here, I don't want you to think we're just a bunch of sad sacks."

A chorus of enthusiasm urged him on.

"Ok, well, so I guess Trip was gone, and the family was left to me. And they were mad; mad at the driver, mad at the hill, mad at Trip even, but you know, they were also busy, and I don't know if they cared as much as they talked like they did. That's what I was try-ing to say before. They'd had small pets and all of them was buried shallow out back, and they couldn't even pay attention enough to their meals to make 'em decent from what I could smell, and they didn't seem to much care that their dog was gone after the first few days, or that they still had one there with 'em. They certainly didn't seem to give a mind to that. And then one day they didn't come home. And the next day and for as many days after that as there are until now they didn't come home. Now I know what happened to 'em, you know, what happened to all of them, but at the time I was just mad. And sad. When your world's that small it starts to come across like it might all be your fault, you know?

"Shit, I am really sounding like a sad sack of shit on a Sunday just now. Am I just whinin' like a toy pup?"

"Not at all," Tess said, "You're among friends remember?"

"Ha, what is this AA?" Sam asked, looking for a laugh or two. He tucked himself back away once he realized he wasn't going to get any.

"Alright, well, I got back at them. I... I shit all over every damn rug. I shit on the bed. I shit in the kitchen. The whole damn place was just covered in my shit. But I knew the moment they got back they'd hit me so damn hard. It was that satisfaction mixed with fear and self-loathing for not being able to control myself. But I think I was look-ing for the punishment, you know?

"Then I ran out of food. I had torn apart the garbages and gotten into the cupboards and eaten just about everything I could get my teeth into, and then I had to leave. I chewed my way out of a screen door and I was outside with no supervision for maybe the first time.

And I hated it. I felt lost, I felt sad. I missed my sister. I hated myself for killing all my siblings. I hated my people for leaving me, but I blamed myself for them leaving. I missed Trip, and I decided I'd just join him. That seemed right. So I went out, all cautious-like, because when you're sure your life is about to end you have a thought or two that makes you want to save some moments, and I crawled out into the center of the street and stood there and waited.

The room was silent, the tension palpable. The crowd was somehow wondering how this dog had gotten out of this tight situation, how he wasn't dead. Come on guys! Sam wanted to yell, it's so obvious!

"I waited until my legs were shaking weak, and my eyes were blurring, and my body hurt with hunger. I waited for those lights I'd watch fly over the hill to come and take me with them, to get me like they'd got Trip. I thought I knew what he'd been up to. That he'd actually been much smarter than me the whole time. Trip knew about escape, and he did it. But that truck never came for me.

Sam nodded. Duh.

"Eventually my hunger got too much, and I crawled to the junkyard and ate the rotting gunk I found. I had some energy back, but all I could think about, all I could see was those lights comin' to take me. I wanted it bad, so I started walking down the road. I kept walking and walking and not a single truck. None came for me. And then I started finding towns. And there wasn't a single truck moving there. It made me mad. I wanted it. I knew what I wanted finally and I couldn't find the damn thing. Death, I mean. But in the towns I did find people. They were all dead. So I guess I found death, just not the one I wanted. Don't laugh, but in some of those towns I'd find trucks sitting there, not moving, and I'd lay down with my belly draped across the tires, just hopin' something might happen. Never did of course. I had some better luck than that I suppose."

Hank paused, heavy thought written across his canine brow.

"Did you meet anybody on your way up? Any people?" Sam asked excited the story was wrapping up, and he was back on track figuring out how these animals had gotten to be here and be so sentient.

"What? Yeah, one maybe. I didn't see him, but a cat I met said she had one. That cat was amazing. Told me some things that made me want to live. She really got it, got me connected to nature as opposed to my old life."

"You met a talking cat? Wait, I thought dogs hated cats. When did you learn to speak?"

"Sam," said Tess, irritated.

"What do you mean?" Zeke the deer said.

"You know, it was my understanding that most animals didn't have the right parts, I mean in the voice box and all that, to achieve human speech," Sam said, trying to sound bookish, trying to win them over that way.

"Maybe we don't. Maybe you've just learned to listen. Maybe you've learned how to speak *our* language," Tess said, trying to punish Sam for cutting off the sympathy she meant to come to Hank. It's not like he wanted to kill himself now. The big baby.

"Stop," Sam said, "I'm definitely speaking English."

"Maybe," Tess said, "So how'd you end up here, Hank?"

"I walked," he said simply. His story time was finished.

"Ok, but now you don't want to kill yourself? It hasn't come back or anything?" Sam asked, the brazen rudeness of the question making the rest of the group glare at him, especially Tess.

"No."

"No?"

"No. I don't. I found some people. I have a home I'm wanted in, and I'm useful. My friend, the cat, told me about my deep connection to nature, to everyone, and how I was important. I was one of Nature's chosen creatures. That cat seemed to know everything. I can't make up for the fact that I mighta killed my own, but now that I've got a place where I'm wanted, I don't mind not being dead."

Tess got up off the seat and walked over to Hank as Bare readjusted to make it clear he didn't miss her closeness. She rested her head across Hank's shoulder and whispered something to him. She backed away, and he looked at her and smiled. Sam wanted desperately to know what she had said, and, from the look on his face, Bare did too.

"Thank you," Hank said quietly, and then to the rest of the group: "For listening to my story. It feels awful good to have that old weight off my chest. I'm sorry I'm asking ya'll to carry it for me, but I do appreciate it."

"Not at all," Gabby said.

"You've got quite the tale," Bare said as he reached his long body across the floor and tussled Hank's tail.

"Do you think that cat would still be there? You said she was connected to nature…do you think she'd know what was happening maybe? Do you remember where she was?" Sam asked, killing any moment that might have been forged through the common experience of a good life-confession.

"Give it a rest," Jean-Christopher said coldly.

"Ok, sorry. I just, I don't know if you knew this but I had this friend back when I was in grade school. I guess you don't know what grade school is, but it's like when you're between… what age do you even start grade school at? Anyway, it's when you're younger, and it was fun because you had recess and that was… oh, well recess was when you went outside. Except you were still in school, so it was like a break, but you could play and-"

Jean-Christopher yawned loudly. It distracted Sam, who was already fumbling from this new feeling of species related exclusion. Hank's story had made him feel like everyone in the room thought of humans as the bad guys, and he wanted desperately to prove he wasn't a bad guy.

"So my friend, he had a dog too. Not like you Hank, but he was like a bigger dog, with more brownish fur, I guess."

Cheese yawned this time and tried to cuddle his way under an arm of the chair he was on. When that failed he perked up briefly but then yawned again.

"I think it might be time for bed," Tess said, Cheese's yawn infecting her too.

"Yeah, I feel drained. In a good way, of course, I think," Hank said as he stretched his old limbs across the rug with a shiver.

"See you all tomorrow?" Hannah asked.

Jean-Christopher had slunk out of the room before Hannah had even finished her question. Sam felt the rest of his story burning in his lungs, dying for escape, and he saw his chances to tell it shriveling away. He needed these animals to know that he didn't hate dogs, that not all people were abusive. And he needed the attention. That his friend had let him watch his dog that time, and every time Sam went over to his friend's house he brought the dog a treat. He'd never felt so close to an animal. Why couldn't they just wait and hear that story? He found himself wishing for a moment that Hank *had* managed to kill himself, and that quickly morphed itself into self-hatred for letting himself think something so incredibly selfish.

"Yeah, let's all get to bed. It's been quite a day," Sam said, trying to make up for his internal dialogue by jumping on the bandwagon.

The lounge emptied, and Tess, after a bit more hushed talk with Hank, led Bare and Sam back to their room. Room 212.

Sam's exhaustion hit him the moment he walked inside the darkened room, and he collapsed theatrically on the bed closest to the door. He was going to treat himself today. No brushing or flossing: that dull, dull task. He was going to start taking some risks here. He was already kicking himself for not getting the answers to the questions that were really bothering him today. What happened, why are you all here, how do you have electricity, what's happening now, are there other people still alive, how did you survive when most people did not, why in the hell can you talk… as the questions raced around in his tired mind, Bare said his goodnights.

"Goodnight to you too Bare. Sorry about the snowmobile again."

"Past is past and let's leave it there. Hank sure had a story, eh?"

"Yeah, what a whiner, huh?"

Bare's laugh filled the room, and soon Sam joined in as well, the laughter, while loud, was surprisingly infectious, and Sam couldn't help himself. After a bit Sam forgot what they were laughing about, and it petered out into silence.

"Goodnight buddy," Sam said, but Bare was already asleep.

40

Sam awoke and was back in the woods. Trees caged him in on every side, and he looked up. The sky was absent of stars. The trees formed a shivering tunnel of bone white and greens that verged on blacks, and the imperfect opening led out into perfect nothingness. Sam started to float up into the nothing, into the void, and felt terror frost his insides. He knew if he made it to the top of the trees he would be lost forever. So he tried to swim against his rising current, reaching desperately for the trees. But they only seemed to drift further away from him. The tunnel was opening up, and Sam felt the desperation well up almost into a calm, when one of the trees reached out a branch to him. He grabbed on, and the tree pulled Sam to her trunk.

Gratitude moved through his body like a poison, infecting every inch of him, and swirling in his groin. As he clutched to the tree he realized he was grabbing flesh, breast and nipple and supple hip, and the delicate protrusion of bone covered lightly in soft skin. He felt himself caressing and exploring, his desire now extinguishing any other thoughts or feelings he had once or ever had. His entire world was this body now. This perfect and clean specimen, with areola's exactly shaped like quarters and the wondrous, hard nubs of the nipples playing easily between his fingers. His hands ventured down through what felt like miles of skin, hundreds of years of caresses, until the flesh broke off in two directions. He was drawn, just like he had been to the void in the trees, toward the break in this skin, this space that was beautiful, and alien, and irresistible. But this time he was not afraid. He wanted to be pulled into this void. He wanted to stay there forever. And he was almost there when-

Fuck! He'd woken up. Nothing specific woke him, it wasn't dramatic; he was just up now. That always seemed to happen in dreams. Every time he was about to get to the good part it would cut out, and he was left wanting.

'Shit,' he thought, without opening his eyes. He tried to get back to sleep, to find himself in that space he so desired, but even that desire, which had consumed him a moment ago, was slipping away with the cold, morning light. He knew to open his eyes might be to lose the dream forever, to crawl further from the realization he seemed bound toward, but it had found its way further into abstract now, and Sam couldn't really see the point in feigning sleep any longer.

The room hadn't changed much during the night. Bare slept peacefully on the bed near the window, Sam's socks and boots were strewn exactly where he'd kicked them off the night before, and Sam was still desperately and overwhelmingly horny. He laid on his side in order to hide the bulge that was working to displace his covers, lest someone walk in, or Bare wake up and try to talk to him about how he 'totally gets it.' Sam was used to his erections being not proud but deeply private.

As much as he craved sex, and he did, he was also terrified of it. He just didn't know anything about it. How did it even work? He had a general idea, obviously. Mrs. Moore had taught Sex-Ed to him and his classmates all the way back in sixth grade, and then again in Sam's freshman, and only, year of high school.

Mrs. Moore hadn't been an attractive woman. She was tall, but her body was oddly proportioned. She was about sixty percent torso. It was as if her torso had dripped down and made her legs into little stubs, and when she walked she would swing those tiny little things out to the side and fall heavily forward on them. It didn't look like she was handicapped, her walk, but rather like she took pleasure in abusing her shoes. Her face was bland like it had been carved from a reasonable looking potato, but Sam couldn't specifically remember what she looked like, just the things she had said and the perverse swinging of her tiny legs.

'-You can say no-' (Not that he'd ever worked up the courage to ask,) '-can be contacted even through kissing-' (Every lip became a disease trap,) '-squeeze the tip-' (For God's sake, why?! Could he remember to do that in the moment?!), '-abstinence is still the safest and best option-' (all the girls nod solemnly as Sam's libido shrivels like Mrs. Moore's legs.) Sex-Ed was the beast that killed any irresponsible sexual misadventures/mistakes for Sam, he figured.

All the movies showed that kids were playing Spin the Bottle, they were playing 7 Minutes in Heaven, they were playing Let's Fuck While My Parents are Out of Town. Sam hadn't been invited to those parties. He hadn't even heard a whisper about kids playing them in real life, but there were rumblings for a while about some experimentation at a sleepover involving a couple cute girls, whipped cream, and a morning filled with awkward non-eye contact and regret. Sam had catalogued that little story along with some of the late night programming he had snuck while up at his grandparent's house and the magazines featuring triplets, that's right triplets! who were celebrating Christmas in the buff in the back of the medicine cabinet in Marcus Cudd's parent's bathroom.

And the ultimate moment: a class field trip to the Zoo at the end of Seventh Grade when Zoe Hart's puffy, brown nipple snuck its way out of her daisy yellow, baby-top tank and yes that little bra and right into Sam's waiting eye line as she leaned over to pick up the wrapper from her fruit and cereal bar. That moment, Sam was sure, would be etched into his memory for the rest of forever as his greatest visual achievement. No high art could ever match the perfection of that first sight of real, human girl nipple framed by the golden sunlight of a late afternoon in the almost-summer. It didn't even seem to matter that this had been a 13 year old girl… should he feel weird about that now?

This line of thinking wasn't helping Sam's problem, and Bare had started his slow, murmur-filled ascent into wakefulness. The clock was running.

'Ok,' Sam thought, 'Count numbers. Nothing sexy about numbers.' Until he hit six, and nine followed shortly after causing his problem to jump with excitement. Herpes, genital warts (HPV), Chlamydia, boils and sores and cauliflower blossoms from pink, horrifying flesh. There he went, a reaction downstairs, but his attention drew him right back. He hated this game. Everyone he knew was dead. Everyone he had ever wanted to fuck, or love, or shit even kiss was quite and irreversibly dead.

There it went.

Sam got up, depressed now, and stretched toward the cold sun.

"G'd Mern…" Bare tried.

"Morning," Sam said as he pulled his same dirty jeans on over his same dirty boxers. Today might be a good day to go out and do some shopping, Sam thought, still a trained consumer despite years of non-practice.

"How'd you sleep?" asked Bare.

"Pretty good," Sam said, except he felt completely unrested with the unresolved dream still swirling in the back of his head. At least it was starting to get pulled down that drain in the mind where all dreams seem to go. Except for the horrifying ones. Those always seemed to get filed away in a spot where they could be accessed at moment's notice, or pick up again in another night's unconscious battles. The giant white skeleton from his dream loomed over him again briefly. "And you?" Sam asked back, escaping from the bones back into reality.

"Slept like an ol' baby. Cozy place they've got here. I could hibernate in this bed no problem. Not even a problem."

What Sam wouldn't give to be as totally content with the most simple and banal things like Bare. Sam doubted Bare even dreamt, let alone had nightmares. He was the most even-keel guy, or bear, that Sam had ever met.

Sam slid out of bed and adjusted his shorts, his back to Bare. He stretched and walked into the bathroom.

Four and one half minutes later he discovered there was no running water. Of course not. How would animals maintain the water? How did the water even work? Sam felt panic replace the space he'd just voided. His feet felt cold like the tiles, but his face and chest burned red. He got up off the toilet and looked at the brown lumped on the side of the dry bowl, partially blanketed by toilet paper.

How had he decided it was a reasonable idea to go into a dry bowl? How did the animals do it? Was there a corner or something that was like the 'shitting corner?'

The smell was starting to really take a hold of the room. Sam tried the taps, nothing, he tried the shower, nothing. Wait... how had the pool worked? How had they maintained that? How were animals doing any of this? And if the pool worked, why the hell didn't his room?

Sam found a stack of hotel towels with the Caribou Lodge's insignia etched into the corners, and used one to scoop his voided bowels out of the porcelain bowl. He used another to wipe the bowl as clean as possible, then wrapped those two into a third.

He walked out of the foul smelling bathroom with purpose, opened the window, and dropped the wad of towels outside.

"What the heck are ya doin'?" Bare asked, "You tryin' to freeze us both to death here?"

"Nothing."

"Woah!"

Sam didn't respond.

"Woah. Did you do that? What the hell did you eat?"

"Fruit. In sauce."

"Ha, oh yeah… Let's go get some breakfast."

Sam walked Bare down to breakfast where they were both greeted cheerfully, and then he took it alone in the kitchen. The sinks in the kitchen, aside from spewing some brown water for the first minute or so, worked just fine. Sam wished he understood how building and civic infrastructure worked. All his wilderness knowledge was useless here, and it made him feel naked. Also he still needed to find new clothes. Mental note. Noted.

He mixed some of the water with a healthy dose of powder from a plastic container marked '15lbs Egg White Powder.' It looked like sugar or cocaine, but when he mixed it with the water it started to take on that glossy look of egg whites. The burners worked, magically, and Sam heated a cast iron pan the size of a dinner tray on one. The only oil he could find he couldn't lift, it was somehow glued to the floor, so after seriously considering jabbing a hole in it and trying to catch run off, he just poured the egg whites in and hoped that constant mixing would do the trick.

It sort of did. He ate his heaping plate of white with black flecks quickly, trying to ignore the flavor, and washed it down with a glass of water, which thankfully tasted good and normal. He walked back out into the dining room to find a few of the more responsible animals cleaning up. Hannah was there, licking the floor like Sam had taught her not to, and Sam figured she was too dumb to not be honest with him.

"How do you keep the electricity on?" Sam interrogated her once he'd strode up, "How do you do it?"

Hannah looked up, confused, tongue peeking from her mouth, and it dawned on Sam that she probably didn't know. This was probably about as smart as asking Cheese something. And there was

Cheese and his family, dragging their butts along the floor, letting their little cottontails help the cleaning process.

SOAP AND WATER, PEOPLE! Sam wanted to shout.

"Haha, just a joke! Sorry, nevermind, you didn't get it maybe? This is how humans used to joke around. You know I, uh… sorry Hannah."

"If you have any questions about the Caribou Lodge I'd suggest you bring them up to Miss Tess," Hannah said, formality suddenly controlling her voice.

"Yeah, I'm going to go find her, thanks," Sam said, failing to imitate her formality. He ended up more in the realm of lame.

The hallway had charmingly spaced prints of wooded mallards and deer grazing near sunsets, and as Sam walked he suddenly knew he was being watched. Or stalked. He wished Bare was with him as he peered around. Two days ago he was completely free of this dependency. Three days ago he was comfortable and happy, if not the slightest bit lonely, but he at least knew where he was and what he was doing. Now he was just confused and paranoid.

He took a few more steps down the hall and spun around. A little red fox in a little vest disappeared down a hallway.

"Craig. I know that's you," Sam yelled.

Craig popped his little triangle head out from inside the hallway.

"Why are you following me, Craig? You freaked me out," Sam said.

"Fo-following you? I'm not following you," Craig replied.

"Then what are you doing?"

"Exercises," Craig said quickly as he started to stretch out, "Just doing my exercises. These office jobs really kill the back. Oooo doggy!"

"Do you know where Tess is?"

"No."

"Are you sure?"

"Yes."

"I thought she was your boss."

"So I have to know where she is at all times? Come on, I just work here man. And now I gotta do my exercises. Gotta stay fit!" Craig yelled as he blasted away back down the hallway.

That was incredibly strange, Sam thought as he walked again down the hall. He wondered where the manager's room was. He figured he'd probably find it near the front desk, so he followed the little rustic arrows that led him back there.

It was colder in the front entry. The large double doors, even with the small buffer entry, leaked winter air. No dogs lounged out here today, and Craig was off doing his 'exercises.' Sam looked around at the faux caribou-antler chandelier, at the ancient telephone and computer monitor, both of which were dead of even the smallest blinking light. He listened closely for the sound of nails on tile or any sound that would give away someone nearby, but none came, so je walked around behind the counter. There was a nice little stool carpeted in red hairs, presumably Craig's, and a door, which Sam opened; it led to a hallway where the carpeting was bleak and clearly not intended for the eyes of customers.

Sam walked down the hallway, feeling strangely cinematic. Every step he took felt important, and every door seemed intriguing, even though each was cheap and the same. Toward the end of the hall he heard a noise. It was an animal sound, possibly two, but he couldn't quite place it. He heard a dog whine behind the closed door.

'This is it! This is how I win them over! I'm going to stop Hank from killing himself!' Which is what automatically came into his head as the obvious explanation.

Sam threw open the doors and immediately wished he hadn't. Hank wasn't in there but the old lab and the other grayish dog were. They turned wide-eyed toward the door, the grayish one's red penis still halfway in to the lab's behind.

"Get out!" barked the lab.

"Oh god sorry!" Sam was already back in the hallway, and instantly it had been transformed back into the ugly, unfortunate hallway it was. He didn't know if he should hang around, wait for them to compose themselves so he could apologize, or just leave and pretend like it had never happened. What would make him feel better if he were them? Never having stepped foot in that room probably.

Another door down the hall opened, and Bare shuffled his way out, Tess following slightly behind.

"Do you think we could move down a floor then? Are there any free rooms?"

"Sure," said Tess, "There are some great rooms near mine."

"Sam!" Bare said, seeing Sam plastered against the beige wall.

"What are you doing back here?" Tess asked sternly, "This area is not for guests."

"Guests?" Sam asked, his mind elsewhere.

"Yes. Now let's get back to the main lodge," she said, nipping at Sam's pant leg as she passed.

Sam followed the two, glancing back at the door, which stayed shut. He sure hoped he'd just hallucinated that because he already didn't have too many points with the folk at the Caribou Lounge.

Craig was back at his post, apparently his exercising all finished, and Sam couldn't bring himself to make eye contact. Craig knows what I've seen, he thought.

"Hey, you shouldn't have been back there," Craig said and then looked nervously to Tess.

"I know," said Sam, solemnly. Yup, Craig knew. That was why he was off running. He hadn't wanted to hear two dogs fucking. How had Sam not put that together? It was so obvious.

"Did you have a good breakfast?" Bare asked, once they were headed down the lodge hallway.

"I had eggs," Sam said.

"Eggs are good," said Bare, "Tess here says they shut off all the water on the higher floors, just for conservation purposes, by the way."

"Sorry, I'd forgotten we'd done that to be frank, but it'll be pretty easy to put you in a room downstairs," Tess said, "Unfortunately we only have singles left on the first floor, so I'm going to have to split you two up."

Her voice was full of sweetness and winks now, but Sam felt there was something ominous happening here. He didn't want to be split up; he didn't want to see gay dogs with their red wieners in action. None of this is what he wanted in his life. He wanted his cabin. Why weren't these animals killing themselves? He rather preferred the dead animals in his woods at the moment.

"As long as we can have rooms near each other," Bare said, seeing Sam's face.

"Of course," said Tess, brushing up against Bare with what Sam knew to be bad intentions. Wolves and bears fucking? This temptress was trying to seduce his friend into… into…

He saw red, dog penis sliding in to slimy, dog anus again, and he felt the bile in his stomach turn. He wondered if Bare had told Tess about what he'd done this morning, about the mess in the bathroom. So far this had been an all around awful day for Sam.

"I mean, we could bring another bed into a room, couldn't we?" Sam asked, trying not to lose his friend to this predator.

"That seems like a lot of work," Bare said, "We can sleep in other rooms and still do exploring during the day. Together."

When had this become a place they were going to stay? Hadn't this, just a matter of hours ago been a decrepit place to crash for one cold night? Sam had had fantasies of burning cheap hotel furniture in a giant stone fireplace for their warmth, of cocooning in blankets rescued from a dozen rooms. Something had gone off the tracks. There was something strange happening here, and he wondered if it was the animals or maybe even the lodge itself.

"Hey. How do you have electricity?" Sam asked Tess.

"Why wouldn't we?" she replied calmly.

Sam stopped now, needing his concentration to be on this line of questioning and not on where he was being led.

"Because it's a system that needs to be maintained. There's a whole grid, there were nuclear reactors that powered some, but those are almost definitely gone, but even solar power and hydroelectric needs to be maintained. There's no way it could run by itself for over eight years. No way," Sam said, becoming surer with every word out of his mouth.

"I'm a wolf Sam, in case you hadn't noticed. I've learned how to keep this hotel up and running because I care about my fellow creatures, and I want any of them that need a safe place to live or stay, to have that place. I know how to get food out and ready for my kind, I know how to keep the pool clean, and I know how to keep Craig from breaking things. What I don't know, as much as I'd love to help you, is how electricity works. I told you, I'm no scientist," Tess finished without sounding mean or insulting. These were the facts as she saw them, as she knew them, and that really was all she knew.

Even though she was incredibly civil about the whole thing, Sam's whole morning welled up, and he blew a raspberry at her and ran the other way down the hallway, immediately feeling foolish for having blown a raspberry.

"Sam," Bare called after him, but Sam had already disappeared up a stairwell and wasn't about to turn back.

Sam went from room to room, taking his confusion, his anger, and his feelings of betrayal out on the quaintly furnished hotel rooms. He started on the third floor and tore through the closet of the first room, throwing empty coat hangers across the room like broken boomerangs. Then he checked the drawers, pulling them out as far as they would go, angry that there was some mechanism stopping him from fully removing the damn things.

He calmed some after wrecking half the third floor. His arms were getting tired, and he remembered his quest for new clothes, so what he was doing was actually helpful now. He hadn't found any suitcases yet, but he figured he would eventually. And eventually happened on his first try on the second floor. It was a pink roller duffel, bursting with socks, floral prints, bras, and toward the bottom, a treasure trove of women's thong underwear. He took a great handful of them and, although he didn't really understand why, he brought them to his nose and inhaled deeply. They smelled only of must that comes from being in storage for so long, but Sam felt somehow better.

He went back out into the hallway, having repacked and restored that particular bag, and opened up the next door in the row, thinking about how he was surprised no one had come looking for him. Where was Bare? Where were those dogs? Probably back to boning. He hated those dogs right now. He opened this door and realized he should really learn to knock. The rabbit crew was here, buzzing around as if they were on speed, even in private. The wife was letting a litter of tiny, hairless baby rabbits suckle at her teats, and in a squeaky, rodent voice she yelled at Sam to get out.

"Sorry!" Sam said as he shut the door again.

Well, at least the deer were still on his side. Except he had yelled at Hannah this morning. Shit. Jean-Christopher? Sam laughed silently at the thought of Jean-Christopher ever being his friend. The snotty French little shit.

Sam opened the next door in the line and found another suitcase. This one had men's clothes in it too. He pulled out a few good looking flannels, a dress shirt or two, and at the very bottom there were jeans. Sam tried them on, and with his belt they fit. He tucked a green and brown flannel into the nicest pair and cinched the belt tight. In the closet he found a tweed jacket that was much too big for him, and he wondered at the proportions of the man who had left these clothes behind. Had his shoulders been so wide a normal jacket wouldn't have sufficed? Why were the shirts so much more normal? Maybe the man had recently lost a bunch of weight and still hadn't bought himself a new jacket. Whatever the case was, Sam took the jacket off and hung it back up.

He went into the bathroom here and tried the sink. Second floor. Doesn't work. Right. He looked at himself in the mirror and realized it had been a long time since he'd done that. He'd aged in the woods. He hardly recognized himself. He still thought of himself as the gawky high school freshman who had left all his dead classmates behind and retreated to solitude. He had a flash of a body lying on the ground and the crack of a gunshot. He closed his eyes hard and shook his head.

He opened them again, and there he was, a new man. He had filled out. The years of manual labor and an overwhelmingly protein fueled diet had given him muscles that made themselves known even underneath the slightly billowing flannel. His haircut was dumb, but he did it himself with a knife when it got in his eyes, so he wasn't expecting much from that. He was handsome now though, he saw. Somehow the years had made him handsome, and this made everything even worse because he figured if there were women alive to want him, he imagined they actually might. Even with his horrible facial hair.

Sam opened his mouth wide and made the sounds that came most naturally like that. The red veins spidering toward his pupil made themselves known as he opened his eyes wide and stared himself down. This was more like the Sam in his mind. Someone crazy, someone doing things no one had any reason to do. Sam hated this person. He had a fleeting desire to smash the glass of the mirror with the novelty soap dispenser, but he didn't want any of the animals to get glass in their paws or hooves or whatever. Sam wasn't a monster, and he could see that now.

Disheartened, he walked out of the room. He resolved to make amends with Bare and then see if he maybe just wanted to go back and hang out with him at his cabin. He'd even agree to raid a liquor store, and they could get drunk every night and forget about the world. Life could be really simple, Sam had decided.

Except Hank was walking toward him down the hall now. Sam stood there, deciding whether or not he should make eye contact or just run away again.

"Howdy," Hank said as he passed by Sam and continued on his way.

Sam didn't know what to say, so he said, "Howdy," and continued on down the hallway, as fast as possible away from the dog.

Sam went back to his room to find Tess and Bare sitting patiently, waiting for him. Sam felt guilt sneak up his throat again as he said, "Hey."

"Hey, how you doing guy?" Bare asked soothingly.

"He-" Sam stopped himself from telling Tess about Bare's drug use. What would that accomplish except to further drive him away, "Sorry about that raspberry. I don't know if I've said this, but it's been a weird couple of days for me. Not sure where my head is at."

"You made a noise at us Sam. It's not the end of the world. We were just wondering if you were doing ok, if there was anything you wanted to talk about. About you, not about the world," Tess said.

"There's not much point in talking about myself if I'm not going to bridge those topics though, huh?" Sam said.

"What do ya mean?" Bare asked with actual curiosity in his voice. The bastard.

"I mean, I knew who I was out there, and now I'm not sure. And I just want to meet a nice girl, and I see you two hitting it off, and I think I'm a bit jealous, and I don't know."

It was Bare and Tess' turns to look confused. They looked at each other as if they couldn't possibly fathom what Sam was talking about. Hitting it off? As if.

"I think I'll go for a walk this afternoon. I think some fresh air will clear my head," Sam said.

"Want me to come with?" asked Bare.

"Nah, you stay here and make friends. Maybe if they like you well enough they'll forget how much they hate me."

"Nobody hates you," said Bare.

"Ok," said Sam.

"No one hates you," said Tess, trying to stress the fact that she was serious.

Sam was already pulling his coat on.

"Alright. I'll see you two later," he said as he laced up his boots and walked out the door. He could hear Bare asking if he should go after him, and then he was too far away to hear anything.

Craig ducked down under the counter as if Sam wouldn't notice him. Playing the game, Sam walked right on by and let the sliding glass doors magically part for him. A gust of winter air slapped his face, and he remembered why people stayed indoors during weather like this. He ignored his instinct though and stepped out into the blazing-white winter world.

He tried the snowmobile, and the thing sputtered and coughed for a while, angry at being left so uncaringly out in the cold. Sam played with the choke and pulled hard on the starter cord, careful to not flood the engine. He became increasingly panicked at being in front of the Lodge. He was sure someone was going to come try to talk to him. So it came as a huge relief when the little engine finally turned over and roared into life.

Sam hopped on and tore off away from the Caribou Lodge. Hey, at least his would be the only snowmobile tracks out there. It was going to make finding this place again a breeze.

42

The town was moderately sized and looked like at one point it could have been a tourist destination. Sam pulled through a short maze of fast food and diner style restaurants and found himself in the heart of the town that according to the windows of the shops was called Folly's Landry. That was confusing to Sam, as Landry was a proper noun and a Folly was a building or something, right? Wasn't that backwards? Stupid town had a stupid name but a beautiful main street. Even after years of total disuse and disrepair it still looked good. Large knotted timber storefronts as far as the eye could see, and the cars all parked well. Sam had a clear path to fly right through this beauty and find his way in the more industrial part of town. There was a modest shopping center and some garages. Gas. Perfect.

He pulled in to one of the garages and left the sled idling. He tried the door to the garage but found it locked, so he went to try the front door, which opened right up for him. Sam stepped inside and breathed in the stale air.

"Hello?" he called.

No one responded, which was probably for the best. Through a door to his left he found the garage and in it a red tub of gas with a dirty yellow spout. Excellent. He turned around and saw the skeleton. It loomed in front of him or rather lounging casually against a black Chevy pickup. Sam's heart slammed up his throat.

It had been a few years since Sam had run in to one. Still scary. This one had the scraps of brown coveralls draped across the rib cage, and that was about all Sam could make out, as the parts that weren't bone were a gnarled mess of frozen growth and decay. Sam slid along the outer wall, his back jostling tools, creating dissonant music as they clattered into each other. Sam was back out the door and to his idling ride moments later, and his fear dissipated as he went through the simple, straightforward task of filling up the gas tank, which he accomplished with style.

'Well done, sir,' he thought to himself, 'What a great accomplishment. Skeletons are out of sight and out of mind. I'm not out of my mind though. I'm a sane man, just cruising through the end of the world.'

Sam twisted the cap, snuggling it back into the grooves, and hopped back on, swinging his leg over. On his first pull it roared right back to life. It was a good feeling being able to give something exactly what it needed. This snowmobile was easy right now and happy. He could tell by her purring she was happy. So Sam twisted the throttle and made her scream.

The hydroelectric plant was obviously on the river. Sam pulled up to the monstrosity and noted it was definitely running; as he turned his snowmobile off he could hear the whirring and grinding of machinery hard at work inside. Maybe monkeys had escaped from the zoo and learned how to run the machines. Maybe it was some clever gorilla that was able to turn her years of sign language into a working knowledge of English. And then she went about deciphering the manuals to the hydro electric plant here in Folly's Landry, Can-ah-duh, so she could effectively manage all the power to the animals who had somehow gained sentience and had all decided to use their new, amazing powers to hate Sam, apparently.

Sam tried the front door, which opened easily. Thank god for the trusting Canadians. The lobby wasn't anything extraordinary. It was a throwback to a much earlier architectural style. At one point in time it might have almost passed for modern, but now it was a mess of too bright hard wood and computers that belonged in museums well before the end of the world turned everything into an impromptu museum. Sam picked up a To-Do List that had been abandoned on the front desk next to a coffee cup emblazoned with a little picture of a motorcycle and the words 'KISS MY TAILPIPE.'

1. Call Bill Michelin about Lawn

2. Order pens- the ones that draw good

(This secretary was clearly not the educated elite. Sam pictured a man or a woman, the breasts of whom were interchangeable in this scenario, of about 400 pounds with the fashion sense of a shut-in.)

3. Cheese/meat raps for Break room

Sam had to stop.

He walked down the closest hallway listening carefully to see if the noise of machinery at work was getting louder, but he could only focus on the sound of his own footsteps.

"Hello?" he called. He jumped at the sound of his own voice.

"Hello?" came back someone else's voice.

Sam's heart about stopped.

"Hello?" Sam said again, this time tentatively.

"Who's there?"

Definitely not an echo.

"Sam," he said, as if that would mean something. There wasn't a reply this time, just the sound of metal scraping against metal, or floor, or metal against something, and goddamn it, it didn't matter, it was a terrifying horror movie sound.

Then the slow footsteps. Klop. Klop. Klop. With a lighter tapping noise mixed in. Sam was frozen. It felt like he'd been caught in the act of something sinister, but all his brain could do was focus on what sort of creature could make such strange and terrible noises. His head filled in the void for him, and suddenly a sinister skeleton vision was shaking its way up the hallway toward him, bizarre skeletal limbs making the resonating beats against the cold, antiquated linoleum.

Klop, click, klop, shuffle, click, shuffle. Then a quick, KLOP KLOP. The sound was approaching. Not fast, but just at the right speed to build up the suspense without the boredom. Sam was grooving on the suspense now almost. His depression got him excited at the prospect of an easy, horrific out. It would almost be nice to go out to a horrifying monster. It would make all the banal moments in his life seem interesting just by pure proximity.

Klop, shuffle, click, shuffle, klop. Sam was caught between wanting to run toward the sound and run backwards and away for good.

And then she rounded the corner. She was about sixty-five years old and not in the best of shape for her age, but, and this was the really important bit, she was a real live, LIVING human being. Tears escaped Sam's eyes involuntarily. He didn't think he was that guy, but there they were: hot, salty buildups in the corner of his eye that left little hot roadways down his cheeks. By the time she stood in front of him, he was weeping. Or blubbering might have been more appropriate.

She embraced him and said, "Shhhhhh."

He obeyed and looked down into her ancient eyes. They were human. They were beautiful. Or they were brown and had become muddy and yellowed with age, but they were human and that made them beautiful.

"Who-" Sam tried to start, but the whole moment was a little too much for him. He had become, in his eight years of solitude, totally convinced he was the last man on earth. He was convinced his seed would be spilled to the floor of his cabin for the rest of days, no help to the salvation of a dead species, just little tadpoles floundering out in the real world. Not that a whole lot could be forged in a seventy odd year old womb.

"I'm Carol, sweetie," said Carol, her voice hinting at emphysema or at the very least a lifetime of cold, cold smoke breaks, "Well god-damn hun, I was certainly hoping I wasn't the last of us."

"I… I'm not dreaming you?"

"Sweetie, I'm all real. Real, honest to goodness woman-kind here."

"How old are you?" Sam asked, unable to control his curiosity and the disappointment at her not being a young and beautiful woman making itself evident.

"Old enough to party," she said, completely serious.

Sam looked her up and down, noting the myriad of tattoos on her wrinkled skin: knives piercing snakes and inexplicably smiling skulls framed by flames. She had one of a guitar that was being played by a skunk with an earring, and another that looked like it might have been a castle but had become so obscured with the wrinkling and flabbing of her arms that it had taken on the aesthetic of a limp accordion. He wondered if she had more tattoos as he glanced at her dowdy figure.

"What?" he asked, distracted.

"Aren't you a cute thang," she said, her inflection making it clear it was not a question.

"I'm Sam," he said.

Carol gave him a big hug and a wet kiss on the cheek and said, "You are so cute, I could just mmmm! Walk with me!"

She used Sam's arm as a support and led him down the hallway she had come from, and Sam now watched that klop, shuffle, click, klop that had intimidated him so much a moment ago. Each klop was a step, the shuffle was a dragging of the lazier foot, and the clicks were the announcements of the silver piece of tubing she used as a cane.

"How are you still alive?" he asked, following her now. He wasn't sure if this was about humanity being gone or about her age. Either way.

"How are *you* still alive?" she countered. Good question. Neither of them probably had any business still breathing.

"What are you doing *here* then?" he asked.

"I worked here, in the days when paychecks came in. I was a secretary. I also rode bikes."

Sam thought back to the note with its misspellings and general sloppy and scrawled nature, and he couldn't help but wonder. He then pictured her scribbling it while seated atop a mountain bike. It was a strange thought.

"Like, a cyclist?"

"No," she let out a laugh that ended in a coughing fit.

"'77 Harley Davidson FLH. Ruby Red. My man."

Sam was completely lost.

"A motorcycle. And a beautiful one at that."

The coffee mug now made a lot of sense. Sam felt stupid.

"What happened to it? Him?"

"Years crept up on us both."

"Yeah."

"Come on in."

They'd reached a door. Inside was what had once been the break room. The motivational posters that had presumably occupied the walls had been taken down, their shadows left permanently as clean patches in the otherwise yellowing room. But she had dragged a bed in here. He wondered how she'd managed that, being as old as she was, but then she probably did it about eight years ago, who was to say what these last eight years had done to her.

"Water? Wine? Whiskey?"

"The three W's," Sam said, unsure of what would be appropriate. Carol laughed her laugh again, coughed once, and spit onto the ground. Sam stared at the loogie as the bubbles spread and then popped.

"So have you been in here since, I mean, since everything?"

"Sure have, Sugar. "

"May I ask why? Seems to me you could live anywhere you like, right?"

Carol moved closer to Sam, as if telling a secret.

"Keepin' the power alive. Power keeps me alive. See what I mean?"

"OK," Sam said, and then, moving on, "So where do you get food?"

Carol gave a knowing smile, a smile that preceded the glorious unveiling of a secret, and she shuffled over and opened a door to her left. Sam's eyes widened as he walked toward the open door. Inside was once a supply closet for the creams and sugars that had graced this coffee-corner, but now it was wall to wall stocked with cans and boxes upon boxes of food. Sam couldn't tell if it was organized by type of food, or by color, or by a random spattering, but a shifting series of patterns popped up in his eyes as he stared.

He felt briefly like a savant code-breaker he'd seen in a movie once. The boxes of Twinkies, and stacks of cans of corn and beans and marshmallow fluff lit up like numbers and letters in a Japanese or Russian coded translation, suddenly and inexplicably making perfect sense to him. He didn't speak either language, but staring at the cans of squid packed in oil that were inexplicably lit up and present made him sure he could learn Japanese, and Russian would fall easily after that. He felt powerful looking into that room.

"Wow," he said. It had been a while since he'd seen so many colors at once. Anymore, he tried his best to stay away from supermarkets: too many people. The satisfaction to skeleton ratio was far too low to make it worth his time or mental strain.

"I've had a few projects these past years," said Carol.

"I can see that," Sam said, "Where'd you find all this stuff?"

"Stores."

"Sure."

She walked to an old wooden cabinet centered in the closet and opened the creaking doors. Liquor bottles of every size, shape, and color were shoved inside. Carol smiled, knowing how impressive the display was. Sam could assume from the dark, rich colors of their packaging and the complete lack of plastic involved that these were all good and expensive spirits.

"Wow," Sam said again.

"I didn't think I'd ever get to show this off to someone else. Back before my tumble this is what I did when I wasn't keeping the show going here. I went all around Folly and stocked up on all the goods. But you know what we need now? Celebration juice."

She moved as fast as her brittle, clubby legs would carry her to the fridge.

"Champagne," she said excitedly, "The good stuff. None of that cooler rot."

The last part was incomprehensible to Sam, and he had to duck as a cork came barreling at his head.

"Ooof! That one got away from me," she yelled gaily as the presumably expensive liquid foamed out onto the scuffed linoleum, "Grab some glasses."

"From where?"

"The cabinet. Quick!" she said. Sam grabbed two white wine glasses, but neither knew the difference, and she poured the glasses full of bitter, turned champagne foam.

"Cheers," she croaked. She cleared her throat as they made eye contact and clinked glasses. Sam half expected the glasses to shatter. It seemed like the cinematic sort of moment that would be appropriate given the surreal circumstances. Carol gave a wink that dragged her entire face into the project, and they both choked the drink down, pretending they were classy or knowledgeable enough to enjoy it.

"How'd you end up here with me?" Carol asked finally.

"Snowmobile," Sam said simply between hurried gulps of foam.

"From where though?"

"My cabin."

"Originally, sweetie. Originally."

"I'm from America. Central. North central, really. North Dakota, if you've heard of it."

"I'm from Minneapolis, Big Guns."

"Oh, like Minnesota?"

"Exactly like that. I used to ride with some folks. Got into some trouble down south and figured Canada was a good enough option for me. For a place with so few people they take great care of their roads. You don't have to constantly be on the lookout for potholes and shit, you know?"

He didn't really. He was just a boy from South Dakota. He wasn't entirely sure why he had lied and told her North Dakota. The lie tasted bad in his mouth, or maybe it was just the champagne.

"Another?" she asked, eyeing his empty wine glass. Sam nodded involuntarily, a function of hearing the hope in her voice. She slammed the rest of hers and poured them each another cup, this time with a bit less foam.

They drank the whole bottle and another in the course of Carol retelling her life. Sam marveled at how small an amount of time it took for a person to entirely recant their existence. She had been born to a single mother in the "slums" of Minneapolis. Sam didn't believe there were actually slums that far north, but he didn't interrupt. Her friends all used to call it *Murder*apolis, but she'd never actually known anyone who had gotten killed.

After high school she had worked part time in a garage where the boys had all chased after her like a "scrabbler to the dragon," and it was there she'd met Harrison Something or Other. She'd always just called him Harry. And to 19 year old Carol (Can you imagine me like that, just lithe and young and blonde?) that name was very appropriate. Harry had ridden a '72, black with a rib cage hand painted by some famous so and so on the body.

"I'd get wet just looking at the thing," she said lustily through her cigarette-voice. Sam felt his member turn over at the possibility of someone getting wet for any reason. Moist. Sam's breathing shallowed.

"He was in the gang. Or group, or you know. The group," she said. And that was how she'd gotten involved with the North Shore Satans. To Sam they didn't sound too tough. They mostly just drove around the states, taking up road space, and sleeping in tents and trailer parks and shitty houses full of drugs, but she insisted they had meant business. It was quite a shock to her friends and family to see her go anyway. Yet she had gone. She'd toured all across America and Her myriad of dive bars.

And then there was Utah. She'd never been to Utah and probably would never be back. You couldn't even get a drink over 4 percent.

They'd been driving through Utah, and one of the other men in the caravan, Harry had long since ditched or died or it didn't matter, but one of the folks, now he definitely had a last name that was a state or something, Montana or Texas or something, well he ran down a

Mormon guy who was "like a big pile of dumb shit" walking in the middle of the goddamned road "like a fuckin' stupid fuckin' asshole."

This guy, Mr. Texas Montana, gets thrown from his bike, which skids to a stop, totally killing the paint job he'd lovingly given her, and that son of a bitch, by some miracle, ends up landing in a goddamn lake! Or pond or river or water definitely. Not the damn Salt Lake, no. But he gets up out the water and starts swearin' like he's teachin' a damn college class on the shit. 'Fuck that bitch and his fuckin' stupid fuckin' shirt and tie and sneakers all fuckin' lookin' like they're some faggot fuckin' dress shoes but they're just some goddamn dead cunt's fuckin' sneakers.' And one of them sneakers had been knocked clean off the man. His sock just hangin' on by a thread. Those are the things you notice, she assured Sam. Death got you all bogged down in detail.

So one of the chicks checked the dead guy for signs of life, but that was like a total and complete waste of time. Texas Montana had been pushing seventy-five and smoked him. So Texas Montana walks up to his bike, and he's mad and drippin' wet, and he blames the dead Mormon, so he starts beatin' the shit out of the corpse with the fuckin' exhaust pipe that got tore from his ride. Thing was all beat to hell, and here he was taking it out on that Mormon corpse.

And that's when the cop rolled by.

She assured Sam he hadn't never seen a look of such utter disgust and surprise on a man's face. The cop had driven past, probably a damn fool Mormon himself, just confused, and then the siren exploded on and the car wheeled around and the cop was there with his gun out, and Texas Montana was just screaming and beating on this corpse, and the cop was yelling at him to fucking stop beating this guy to death, of course the cop didn't know the More-man was already dead, and then just BANG! and Texas Montana became Utah.

"Because you know, dust to dust, ash to ash," she explained.

So they all hopped on the bikes and booked it, and the Cop is sitting there simultaneously kicking the exhaust pipe away from ol' dead Texas Montana's hand and firing wildly at our asses as they rode off.

"I took one in the shoulder and stayed on the bike," she said proudly as she took off her sweater. Sam watched her skin, and he felt another twitch from his pants. Something about the danger of the story hit him, and the fact that this was another human being, and one with parts that fit his own, presumably were having an effect on him. She was wearing a filthy blue tank top underneath the sweater, and she leaned in, showing Sam a purple and knotted lump on her upper shoulder.

"It missed the lung, so I was all set, but I can tell you it hurt like hell. Go ahead. Give that a feel."

Sam hadn't really considered that, but now that she brought it up, why not? His fingers rolled over the mass, and it felt like what he imagined skin cancer would feel like. She shivered at his touch and leaned into him. She was close, and he could feel her breath through his shirt. His fingers ran against her shoulder as he moved his hand away, and the rest of her flesh felt like marshmallows covered in a soft cloth. It was somehow comfortable.

"So then what happened?"

They had gotten away. The cop hadn't chased because Texas Montana was still alive maybe. Probably the whole crew of Mormons had descended; the whole lot of the polygamist bastards had come down and torn that fucker Texas apart like coyotes around a fat god-damn rabbit.

"Anyway, I was really into the H then, and we got pretty fucked up, and it didn't seem so crazy, and then someone pulled the bullet out, and we had some crazy sex if I remember right. But then we had to get out of there. We got up here to Canada, and I couldn't find my fix, but everyone was so fuckin' nice, and I got a job because they were just hiring. I couldn't pay for gas or nothin' to get out at first, and once I had come down off everything and realized everything what had gone down, the gravity of it, I just figured to stay, you know?"

"Were you ever married?" Sam asked, and Carol laughed.

"Nah. Never was married. I was into it a few times, love and all that, but never tied a knot with a man. I was married to the job, you know?"

"I thought you were a secretary."

"So?"

"Ok, yeah. So is that why you stay here?"

"I figure if I keep the city running like I have, then people passin' through might come and stay."

"Has that worked yet?"

"You're here ain't you?"

He was. He guessed he was.

"Anyway, you'd be surprised at a lot of things honey," she said cryptically.

"The animals are talking now. They use your electricity. They have a pool," Sam countered.

"Oh honey," Carol said as she came at him with her huge, billowing arms.

Sam was enveloped again, and something about this, with the scent of woman, especially an older woman, who's musk brought up so many more ingrained memories, brought out the tears again. He had figured himself cried out, that hollowness that follows tears having taken over his body before, but here he was again, that hot wetness spilling onto Carol's old blue tank top, giving it a much needed cleaning.

"Oh baby. Baby," she said as she kissed the tears from his cheeks, and then she moved down to his mouth, and Sam enjoyed his first kiss in ten years. Carol's lips were velvet except for the small spattering of mustache hairs that tickled him. But the wet and the soft drew him in, and soon the passion was growing.

Carol's tongue ventured into Sam's mouth, and after he got over the sensation of another tongue against his own, he fought back with his own, and soon they were entangled and wrestling. Sam tentatively brought his arms up against her back, hovering for a moment and then digging in, kneading at the soft flesh. Carol retaliated, pulling off Sam's snowpants clumsily and then working the tail of the giant flannel out of his billowing, belted jeans.

She didn't waste time, and soon her purple fingers were toying with the zipper on his jeans. He wondered about romance and first times and young flesh for a moment, but as that zipper came down, his manhood strained violently against its fabric prison.

"I've been waiting for you stud," she whispered huskily in his ear. And then she coughed violently, as she undid his belt.

"Wait," he said as she kissed his neck.

"What sweetie?" she asked.

"I just… I haven't…"

"Shhhhhh," she shushed.

And he did, as she took his swollen cock in her hand. Softness everywhere, and he was getting into this despite the varicose veins. She slid her shirt off, and she wasn't wearing a bra. Not at all. Her areolas were like large caps, the nipples staring blankly at the floor. But these were tits. These were some goddamn sweater pups, as people used to say before they were dead. He took one and moved its stare from the floor and into his mouth. He suckled wildly, madly. He bit it, and she smacked his thigh, hard. He was new to this, but he was learning. He moved to the other nipple, hoisted the breast up and in to his exploring mouth. The nipple had apparently lost its ability to harden, but that was fine. His tongue was an eel now, slithering and exploring some new, unknown cove in the ocean. The ocean of love, he thought, proud of himself for the poetry and for his artful tongue work.

"Baby!"

She pulled her tit out of his mouth, and he took a moment to appreciate the blue veins spidering their way to that pink (and now slightly red with friction) nipple. There were tattoos of suns above each breast and a few paw prints walking their way up the side of one of them. The steps staggered with age. The tit found its way back to the resting position it'd been living in for the past seventy-five years. His cock took a hit at that and went down slightly, and in response she fought down to her knees, which seemed a real feat for her, and took him into her mouth.

This was new.

Holy Shit.

He was close.

This was too much.

She swirled that bumpy tongue around the head of his cock, and the feeling was incredible. He could feel she was short a few teeth, but every time one of the ones left scraped against the top of his ready dick he felt poised to explode.

He scooted his small ass backwards and forced himself out of her mouth, lest he embarrass himself, and went back to kissing her on the mouth. She didn't taste like cigarettes exactly, but he imagined she would, and his brain started filling in the flavor for him. There was something spicy about her breath that wasn't altogether pleasing but also wasn't uncomfortable enough to warrant stopping. He moved his way down to her miraculously tattoo-free neck, remembering how she'd done that to him, and he had liked it. He had a worry that her intimidating amount of experience was going to crushingly outweigh his entire lifetime of inexperience, and she'd decide she was done before he was. He wanted to be able to know he'd gone ahead and done it. He wanted to know he was not a virgin. It was hard being possibly the last virgin in the world.

They stood and maneuvered awkwardly to the bed, and the excitement rushed back to him.

This was happening! Really really!

He kissed down her chest again jumping from tattoo to tattoo, which took a surprising amount of time, his mouth finally falling off her nipple as he moved his way slowly down her stomach tats. It seemed to Sam like her skin had been soaked in the bathtub of life for too long and had become uniformly wrinkled and textured. But she appeared to enjoy it, as her club-legs writhed and moved beneath Sam's chest. So he kept moving down until he was at her pants. These had no buttons, no zippers, so he pulled them down as she stuck those legs out straight like fallen trees.

And there it was.

Here he was, face to face with that thing he'd imagined for so long. It was swollen and red and textured and horrifying and wonderful, and he wanted it. Her legs were awful. She wasn't attractive to him really. At all. Her legs were translucent and muddled, the color of cigarettes that had been left out in the street for too long, shadowed with veins, and the whole ordeal was topped with the great reddish gash of her vagina. His hands felt up the puffed mound around her womanhood, as he hoisted her gut up and out of the way.

He ignored it all by closing his eyes and diving tongue first into her straight-haired muff.

The pubes seemed to come off in his mouth in droves, and through licks and slurps he had to wipe his tongue to shake them off, but her moaning kept him going because her being into it was the only real reason he was able to get into it at all. And she sounded fucking into it.

He had no idea what he was doing down there really, but he felt like an expert as he flailed his tongue wildly. He tried to shove his tongue down her hole. This would be so much easier with his dick.

And then he was up for air. She kissed him again, and he was embarrassed that she could definitely taste herself on him, but it didn't seem to bother her as much as it bothered Sam. And then they were naked, and he was rolling around on top of her, her breasts and stomach flowing down into the dirty sheets. But her opening was waiting, gleaming with his spit and maybe her own wetness. His dick seemed unnecessary; it seemed useless in comparison to this space that had maybe had more action than existed in the whole world anymore. Was Bare doing this to Tess right now? That was fucking weird. Why was he thinking about that? Yikes. But this was fucking weird too right?

But it didn't feel weird as she took hold of him and guided him down to her waiting vagina. Sam felt like he could throw up. He wanted it, he didn't want her but totally wanted her at the same time.

"You ready baby?" she whispered in her smoker-voice, turning him off.

It was too late. He was dragged through the tiny grayed forest toward the wet and cavernous forever that waited.

And then he was in. He was all in.

He was no longer a virgin.

He was no longer a virgin.

It was moist and warm and wonderful.

It was magical. He was read to go, but he managed to hold on and enjoy the moment.

He marveled at how a single moment could completely eliminate that awful V-word from the vocabulary of his future life, and at the same time effect him so little. He didn't feel different inside, but his dick did feel good he supposed. He tried to imagine what a younger woman would feel like; someone tighter, and he really doubted he would have been able to deal with that.

"Yeah baby. Thrust now. In and out, baby," she said, "There you go. That's it. That's nice, ooo."

And they were fucking. This was sex, and it was pretty nice.

He slid up and down her body, bringing most of her flesh with him, his manhood in and out of her. He was moaning now despite himself, it was just happening. The showmanship of the moment was gone, and he and Carol were one. Or that's how it felt anyway. He wanted to please her.

He felt her arm slide across her back, and then her finger probed at his ass hole. Nope. He swatted away her hand, and she relented, so he went back to work. He hoisted her legs up because he'd seen that on the Internet once, and goddamn it if it didn't somehow get better.

"Oh fuck!" he said.

"Oh, oh, awhaoooo!" she responded, in apparent ecstasy.

And then it became a marathon. That feeling of being able to come right off had faded, and he felt like he was just getting further from the finish line. He had a vision of grabbing toward trees, but then he was back in the moment. It seemed the more he pumped, the longer he stayed, the more cavernous her sex became.

He thrust and thrust, tried to change positions, but Carol wasn't responding to that, so he just let her legs drop and continued in missionary position. Carol was silent now, just taking it in, and Sam was totally focused on his own feeling, the pleasure that coursed from his cock and through his entire being. He was getting back to it, and goddamn it felt good!

"Yeah, baby, you like that?" he said lamely.

She liked it. How could she not with how much he was liking it?

He grabbed a nipple again in his mouth, trying desperately to not think about why his grandparents had had plastic on all their furniture.

He was alive. He was now truly alive! And everyone else was dead!

Zoe Hart, that foxy girl who looked so good in sweatpants he'd known in Middle School was very much dead. But Sam? Sam was alive. And fucking. He wondered if Zoe had ever fucked. Or Jasmine. *Jasmine.* There weren't many exotic girls where he was from, and Jasmine also happened to be absolutely stunning. At least for a four-teen year old. And Sam tried to imagine Carol as beautiful. The Carol in her story, young Carol on a motorcycle watching people die had been beautiful. Beautiful before Canada had gotten to her, and comfortable chairs had had their way with her, and secretarial work had added wrinkles to her body and her soul. And young Jenna McJoy, who's name alone had him close, and he was picturing these long gone supple creatures and their young selves and not this over-

"Oh shit!" he yelled, his voice bouncing down the hallway to-ward nobody, and he exploded inside of her. His body jerked violently, and he just kept going. He realized she might not like that he did that inside her, so he backed himself out of her. But he was still going, and he covered her stomach with splashes of his seed. When he had finished he dropped his sweating body onto her wrinkled breast.

"I'm sorry, I'm sorry," he repeated.

He was breathing heavily and felt his body lift up off her chest and fall back down on the bed as he murmured how wonderful that had all felt and how sorry he was. About the mess, about everything, he just felt sorry.

"I was so worried I'd never have sex. I was so afraid it would never happen. I was in the woods and surviving, and I was fucking worried, you know? What if I died a virgin? Can you imagine? I can't now."

He took a pause to catch his breath.

"Can I tell you something? About my life? It's about my parents. My parents hadn't liked each other that much. I think they'd have got-ten a divorce if the world hadn't killed them, you know? I never once walked in on them having sex. Not to be weird or anything, but I'd sometimes listen at their door just to hear if they were… you know… intimate, but they'd always just be talking or even worse not talking, you know? Just talking or sitting or whatever or watching TV. That shit. It wasn't like they were fighting in public or anything, they just had stopped liking each other, and everybody knew it. It was so sad to watch."

"I thought it was my fault at the time," Sam said, "I've figured now that they just weren't meant to be maybe. My dad was always at work, and mymMom was always trying to find work, and I don't think either of them had ever figured out what they had actually wanted to do with their lives, and then we were there and they were stuck together and that all kinda fucked them forever, you know? But yeah, I was so needy for their attention. I always wanted to watch TV with them, or talk with them, or eat ice cream with them, and they never got any private time. I don't know. It's probably my brother's fault. He was the real terror. Which they say is strange for the older sibling. Usually the younger one is the terror because of like, some weird parenting thing. I don't know, it happens more than you'd think. Anyway, I don't know what I was getting at exactly, I was just, you know, I think sex is important. It's important to a relationship and happiness. I always thought that. Carol?"

Carol was still lying there, and what Sam had taken as quiet based in ecstasy now seemed more macabre. He tentatively shook her tattooed arm. The fleshed moved, but her face just stared.

"Carol," Sam said quietly, close to tears for the umpteenth time. This was not good punctuation, "Carol."

He shook her harder, got his head together, and checked for a pulse. He waited; he waited for that surge of blood through those blue, blue veins to make itself known to his fingertip. It didn't.

Carol was dead.

'When had it happened,' he thought as he straddled her naked heft and started beating down on her chest to the tune of "Stayin' Alive" by the BeeGees like he'd been taught to in first-aid courses.

Oh, oh, oh, oh,

Stayin' Alive,

Stayin' Alive,

He brought his hands down and they slid forward, propelled by his own semen, and he punched her hard in her face.

"I'm sorry, I'm sorry," he said as he checked her face to see if it was ok. He checked for breath and found none. Ok, shit. He strained to remember if they said you should or should not do rescue breaths anymore. Oxygen to the blood couldn't hurt, right? The people left on earth knew exactly how important oxygen was. He brought his lips down to hers and tried to blow in. He watched her chest rise, and fall, and the memory of kissing her was still fresh in his head. His dick perking up slightly made him feel even worse.

"Goddamn it Carol!" he yelled at her lifeless body.

When had she gone? Had he fucked a dead woman? She was definitely talking when he put it in, right? She had started out alive right? Yes, she'd been talking, he remembered. But had she? He couldn't be totally sure now. The whole ordeal soured as he beat on this chest that had only minutes before excited him so much. He felt awful for letting it turn him on in the first place. What had he been thinking? She was ancient. She was dead. It didn't matter. That was his first time. That was her last time. This was all fucked.

He punched her chest one more time and realized that was it. He rolled off her and got dressed. She didn't move.

He sat in an old folding chair that used dirty clothing as cushions, and thought about what he should do. There was no one to report her death to. No professionals to try to come and save the day with their miracle equipment and drugs that could bring people back to life. No cops to come and handcuff him, take him in for questioning, and accuse him of murder. Murder of the elderly.

"What the hell were you thinking?" asked the imaginary cop, "You know the elderly can't take that sort of stress! You're a monster. You're going away for a long, long time."

But there was really nothing to be done. Bury her? No, the ground was too cold. What had he known about her? She liked motorcycles. Blow up a motorcycle? That was crazy. Then his eyes lit on the funhouse coloring of her snack closet.

Four minutes later he had her in the nicest clothing he could find: a denim skirt and a leather jacket. Six minutes later he'd used the sweaty, soiled sheet to drag her into the supply closet. Snack brands long since forgotten by most of humanity shone brightly around her pale corpse.

'This is what she would have wanted,' Sam thought as he looked at her peaceful face. Solemnly he picked up her walking pipe, wound up and smashed it into one of the shelves. HoHo's and Twinkies and Snickers bars rained down to the floor with a sound a lot like rain. He hit another shelf and a shower of candy bears and potato chips and jars of pickles crashed to the floor. Shelf after shelf, and Carol's body was blanketed by this junk food just like it had been in life. Sam was admiring that thought when the club smashed through the wall.

Sparks licked out, and then the corn chips were on fire. Corn burned fast and apparently searched for its own because that flame traveled quickly from treat to treat, right toward the liquor cabinet. Sam just watched, dumbfounded that so much could go wrong in such a small amount of time. Hadn't he been inside of a real live woman twenty minutes ago? It didn't seem real now. He almost wished it hadn't been real.

The liquor cabinet exploded a little then, and the flames spread through the entire room. The smell of burning marshmallows filled the air, and then it was burning marshmallows and plastic, and Sam ducked away. He pulled at Carol's leg, but she was too heavy. The flames licked at his face, and defeated he retreated into Carol's room.

He tried his damndest to pull his snowpants on, which was stressful as he watched the smoke and flames tongue their way out of the door. He'd gotten one boot on when the fire found its way out and started inching toward the piles of clothes that littered the room.

Sam wondered if sweat was flammable. If so, those piles of clothing were going up like napalm. And now his second boot refused to go on, there was something jamming it. A giant pair of panties had gotten wedged inside and were slingshoting his foot right back out. He removed the purplish monstrosity and threw it into the flames, which ate it greedily and, as a thank-you, expanded further toward him. There was his sweat theory in action. Sam could feel the flames against his face, and he thought briefly if it wouldn't be better just to walk into them. Nah. Burning to death was definitely not the best way to go.

He was on his feet, and he grabbed his coat and ran toward the door. As he ran down the hallway, he pulled the coat on, but the sleeve was on fire, and it was exactly his luck that it was lighting the hallway on fire as he ran. What was this place made of? Paper?

There was another small explosion behind him. It sounded like the fire had reached something important. He considered the irony of a hydroelectric plant catching fire as he ditched his flaming coat. The lobby hadn't yet gone up, and he had the crazed thought to go grab that horrible note as a token, as something to remember his first time by. But he realized he'd much rather forget it forever. He threw open the door and jumped out into the screaming Canadian cold.

He could feel the burn of the cold even through his flannel, and he longed briefly to be close to the fire again. But then another something, something bigger this time, exploded, and all the lights went out in the plant. He had a feeling this would have some implications, but there wasn't much he could do at this point.

The cold bit hard through his flannel, and Sam could feel his own death coming on if he didn't find a coat soon. But he couldn't stay here, so he hopped on the snowmobile and hoped he wouldn't just freeze.

47

Snowmobiling was torture. He was torn between going fast, so he could find a coat more quickly, or going slowly, so the wind wouldn't bite quite so hard through his purpling skin. He settled on a sort of middle area, but sped up when he made the mistake of looking backwards and seeing the whole power plant in flames. What the fuck had those snacks been made of? Kerosene? Gasoline? Fucking napalm? Probably just sugar. Was sugar flammable? Sam wasn't sure, but he was pretty sure he was freezing to death. Fuck it, he had been looking for clothing outfitters, but this house would do.

He pulled over and walked up to the frozen little house. It was cute in a modestly poor sort of way. He opened the door, and even with the cold, the smell of decay was there. Most homes smelled like this now: food long since rotten and people the same. The smell had ingrained itself in the walls and the furniture and the clothes. Sam was surprised he hadn't gotten used to it yet. He supposed the horrors of scent never really went away; they seemed fresh and awful every time.

And there it was of course, another decayed wreck that was once a human being entrenched in the entryway. The thing was small; not a child, but it certainly hadn't made it all the way to adulthood. It was face down on something that had festered with it for the years, and was now indistinguishable. A backpack maybe? He thought of this young thing, a girl he imagined, maybe she was pretty, carrying her book bag into the house breathing in with those virile young lungs and suddenly getting nothing. Nothing at all. And she'd probably struggled for a second and then came to rest here. As good a place as any to be dead for forever. He looked in the closet because her skeleton made going upstairs impossible for Sam. There was no way he was stepping anywhere near that skeleton hand. There was something light blue, smallish, feminine, a jean jacket, and a pretty decent leather jacket in the closet, nothing warm enough to protect him from the cold outside though.

He shut the closet and tried another door. This one led to an empty garage. He looked around just in case and spotted a flashlight on the workbench. He grabbed it, and through some miracle it still worked. The light was dim and a Halloween orange, but it was light. This would be useful now that he'd fucked up the power supply for the whole town.

The thought of Carol buried in that blaze of snacks flashed across his vision, and he felt dizzy. He wasn't going to throw up again though. Too much vomit in too few days. He was done vomiting he decided. He reached his frozen hand down his pants and readjusted his manhood. It felt sticky and weird, and purely from force of habit he lifted it to his nose and sniffed. At least it overpowered the scent of decay.

He skirted the skeleton and walked downstairs, swinging the beam of the flashlight a little too wildly to register his surroundings. His thoughts were elsewhere. He took a moment, closed his eyes, and then really looked around. The basement was full of decaying boxes and done up in 70's wood paneling.

Suddenly and terribly, a scream destroyed the silence.

"Heeeeey! Oh heeeeey! There's no carpet down here!" a voice yelled.

Sam swung the weak beam haphazardly across sinister cardboard boxes and rusted tools as claws clicked sharply against the concrete around him. He was ready to run, but he was terrified to turn his back on the thing. He imagined his back was a weak point, and he wasn't looking to expose it.

His flashlight swung, and two yellow eyes shone from a corner. Sam caught a glint of white teeth too. The thing darted away with a hiss. Sam about-faced, and the gleaming eyes and teeth of the crazed opossum were right in his face.

"Shick shick shick!" the opossum said to Sam, throwing saliva onto his face. The opossum, hanging miraculously by his tail it seemed, sliced across Sam's neck with its claws. No pain yet, but he could feel the warm wetness of his blood spring up and saturate his shirt. And then Sam disappeared.

His mind went blank, the blood forgotten, the fire forgotten, Carol thankfully forgotten, and he reached out and took the crazed animal in his crazed hands and wrapped his angry fingers around the thing's throat. The opossum sputtered and croaked and tried to speak as it cut at Sam's shirt with his sharp little claws.

"WHY? WHY? FUCKING WHY THE FUCKING FUCK!?" Sam yelled to the universe as the thing dropped down and the tail wrapped itself around Sam's throat until they were caught in a battle of familiar oxygen deprivation. The lack of air brought back bitter memories that further sent Sam south, and he ripped the thing from his neck and slammed it to the floor. And then it was all boot to face and blood and squelching noises mixed with the brittle sound of bones crumbling under force. And the low, involuntary moan Sam was releasing.

Sam was still pounding at the opossum when he came to his senses and realized the thing had been dead for a while now. Everything was dying, and it was all his fault. Carol, this opossum, the pine trees, his forest friends. They were all dead and his boots were covered in their blood. He breathed heavily over the corpse before he stooped to retrieve his blood-splashed flashlight. The light was a dark red until Sam used his shirt to clean the lens. He swept the beam around the room before he lit it on the creature, which had become nothing but a puddle of gristle and hate. Sam felt at his neck, accidently mixing his own blood with that of the opossum, and he felt a touch of panic at the sheer amount of liquid that was running down his neck. The thing must have dug in pretty deep to get this sort of a showing from Sam's hemoglobin.

He felt faint as he came down from his adrenaline rush, and he dug into a box, looking for something to soak up the blood. He stashed the flashlight between his teeth and came up holding a shirt with "I Was at Zac and Emma's Wedding, and All I Got Was This T-Shirt!" written in horrible Comic Sans across the front. With a shudder he balled it up and held it to his neck. He dug through the rest of the box, hoping to find a coat, and finding none he sat on the ground and let the desperation wash over him.

This might have been the second worst day of his life, and it had been on track to be something really great for a moment there.

"Heeeeeey!" something shouted from upstairs, "No foooood, heeeeeey! No gooooood!"

Sam closed his eyes. Of course there was another. The house was probably full of these things. Why wouldn't there be more? Maybe this one knew where he could find a damn coat.

"Howdy!" Sam called out, surprising himself by sounding strangely like Bare. The other voice hissed and there was the sound of scuttling from upstairs. Awesome, here we go. Sam wearily stood up, looked behind him, grabbed a driver out of a golf bag, and choked his hands up on the grip. He could see the stairs now; his eyes had acclimated enough for him to see through the twilight. Another opossum stood at the top and then, with a horrible scream, charged at him claws first.

Sam casually swung back with the club and smashed it into the opossum's face. That would have been one hell of a drive because the opossum lifted up off the ground and smashed against the wall. The thing fell into a box and twitched a time or two. Sam slowly walked over, kicked the box open, and brought his boot down once, hard, on the thing's skull. And look at that! A nice snowmobile jacket. He took it and tried it on. It was a bit big, but he'd take it. Ok. Check. Now to attend to his neck.

It didn't look like there was a bathroom down here, so Sam walked back up the stairs. He didn't even register stepping on the skeleton's arm as he rounded the corner up the stairs.

He found a bathroom and took the wet shirt from his neck. The opossum had gotten him pretty deep with five distinct little lines that leaked freely. He figured he should check if it had nicked his jugular or something, so he used his dirty fingers to spread the wound a little, just to check, and it didn't look to him like anything permanent was damaged. He dug under the sink and fished out a first-aid kit from beneath a pile of colorful cleaning solutions. The adhesive on the band-aids had dried up, but the gauze was clean, and the tape still had some tackiness to it.

He winced as he poured hydrogen peroxide from a brown bottle onto his steaming blood. He wiped it clean with a piece of gauze and quickly slapped a fresh one over the wound. Red appeared immediately, so he stacked on another and used generous chunks of tape to secure the mass to his throbbing neck. It wasn't comfortable, but he probably wasn't going to bleed out like this, which was probably a good thing.

He left the bathroom, and this time he stepped over the skeleton as he beelined for the door. The cold of outside, not that it was all that much warmer indoors, felt rather nice this time around, and he smiled as he walked to his ride. He was almost giddy actually, and he wondered when that had happened. He hoped it wasn't a symptom relating to massive blood loss. He put his helmet on, careful not to let the bottom of it muck up the job he'd done dressing his wound, and with fingers crossed, he pulled the starter cord and hopped on the running sled.

There was a relative peace in the small-world silence inside his helmet, and he managed to not think at all as he cruised the immaculate streets of Folly's Landry. He especially made sure to not look back at the glowing embers of what had once been the town's power source and, more importantly, that burning hole that had stolen away his virginity. He definitely was not going to look at that fucking mess.

He gave himself a moment to wonder if everyone had forgotten his outburst that morning, and he was hopeful as he pushed open the powerless sliding doors. But the hope was short lived.

With the help of the light of the moon, Sam saw Craig, still dressed in his cute little vest, his tongue a pink taffy peeking from his mouth, and the ringlets of the telephone cord cutting deeply into his hanging neck. Somehow he'd gotten the phone thrown over the antlered chandelier and had managed to hang himself dead.

"Craig?" Sam asked, as he poked the little body. Craig swung briefly before coming to a silent stop.

"Hey! Is anyone there? There's been an-"

A what? An accident? Probably not. This was only an accident in one of those crazy physics hyperboles that said that anything could happen at any moment, it just usually didn't. The only way this was an accident was if, by some huge blunder of the universe, all the atoms in the phone and in Craig suddenly popped into exactly the right spot to make it look like the little fox had hung himself from a chandelier. Sam doubted it though.

"Hello?" he called. As no one but the silence responded, he stepped around Craig's dangling body and down the hallway toward the kitchens. The dark swallowed him up and made even the quaint, rustic hallway seem ominous. Sam twisted on the small flashlight and walked slowly, swinging the beam behind him about every six seconds. Just in case. He was too frightened to call out now. The darkness seemed to imply it wouldn't be someone looking to help that came running.

Sam slowly pushed open the door to the great dining hall, trying to figure out which way would give him the most visibility and the least amount of chance he'd get mauled to death by some horrible creature. He had it most of the way open when he kicked it hard and jumped inside, flashlight pointed like a sword. His boots made an echoing thump, but nothing stirred inside the shadowed hall. He stood up on the giant table that graced the center of the room and swung the beam around. It couldn't penetrate every corner, but the bits the orange managed to illuminate were thankfully empty.

"Hey!" Sam yelled and then, in an attempt to cover his own tracks, "The power's out! What do we do?"

Nice play, but no response.

His feet made another echoing thump as he jumped from the great wooden hulk of a table. Sam walked to the door of the kitchen and, mid-stride, raised his foot up to kick it open. His foot bounced back, his knee jarred, and he fell to the floor, remembering too late that the kitchen door opened the other way. Shit that hurt! He stood and nursed his throbbing leg. It felt like something had twisted in there. He attempted a step and made it through it. He'd live. His leg would live. He regretted his brazenness, and like every time he did something rash, he vowed never again.

He limped into the kitchen, and here was the Jean-Christopher, his throat impaled on the sharp end of a knife that seemed irrationally large. Black blood radiated from him, and Sam had to step in it to get by. His feet suddenly slipped out from underneath him, and he felt himself being pulled in toward the knife. He saw his end, just impaled on that cartoon knife, but he slid forward a few inches and found his balance again. His heart was pounding, his knee hurting, and his flashlight seemed to have grown dimmer. He really hoped it wasn't dying. But as his luck had run today, he could only assume it was just about to die.

His feet left black boot prints with little droplets in between, and when Sam shone the light on them they glowed red like the eyes of a demon. The thought gave him chills.

As he slowly and carefully walked through the kitchen, he thought only of Bare. It helped to shut out the other fear. Where was

Bare? Surely he couldn't be dead, there's no way. Was he hurt though? Sam now had a destination.

He took the door back out into the hallway and moved toward Bare's room as fast as his limping leg would take him. He passed the pool and saw the dark humps of deer spines floating just above the water. He'd never gotten to apologize to Hannah…

Why the fuck did everyone around him die? Was it him? What had happened here?

There was the sound of movement behind him.

A patter of footsteps.

Sam wheeled around, aiming his light. It wasn't a deer. They were dead. Or were they? Had he counted them? Another patter of footsteps. It was bigger. Not a rabbit, certainly. Craig was dead. What if it was Craig?

Through the darkness he imagined Craig, cord still tight around his throat, exercising through the hallway, his eyes as black as Jean-Christopher's blood. Sam edged his way backward, away from these thoughts.

There was a patter of footsteps behind him.

He swung the beam around. Nothing but hallway.

He spun around, the footfalls having circled around. What the fuck was this? The steps stopped coming in bursts, and now there was a slow padding toward him. It was coming for him.

"HEY!" Sam yelled, surprising himself with his reaction born entirely out of lack of better options.

The footfalls stopped. And then an eerie, low howl brimming with lament rushed at Sam from the hallway. Sam tried to run backward, but the leg he had twisted shot with pain and brought him to the floor.

"Ow!" Sam said involuntarily. And as he sat on the ground the footfalls started up again. Slowly padding toward Sam from the corner break in the hallway in front of him. Sam tried to stand, but his leg crumpled beneath him.

He wondered briefly if the coyotes Bare had killed maybe had friends, or family, or lovers that had tracked Sam down. They'd known. It wasn't suicide here, Craig hadn't done himself in, those deer hadn't taken a plunge on their own free will: it was this band of coyotes bent on ruining Sam's life like he had helped ruin their friends' lives. He'd almost convinced himself when the coyote came around the corner.

No wait, it was a dog. Oh god. It was *the* dog.

Sam shone his light into the gay dog's eyes and two orange reflections beamed eerily back at him.

"He's dead. He's dead and you killed him," the dog said as he advanced on the fetal Sam.

"No I didn't... I didn't kill anyone," Sam said unconvincingly as he thought of Carol burning in that marshmallow fire.

"He climbed up there, and he tried to swallow it whole. It went right through his throat. His blood everywhere. His precious blood went everywhere," the dog explained to Sam. Sam could see the red sheen on his fur; his hair was matted and clumped with the stuff. It had congealed in spots that looked like wounds, and Sam seriously wondered if this was a zombie dog.

"I'm really sorry about your friend."

"Say his name."

The dog was closer now, and his teeth were starting to show.

"I didn't know his name."

He shook his head violently, as if trying to shake off the ridiculousness of Sam's statement.

"Yes you do. You knew. You were the only one who knew. And now he's dead because of you."

Sam scooted backward as the dog inched closer, the weak flashlight beam trained on his face.

"You knew," he said, "You saw. But you didn't see what I saw. Not everything. Not the important things. You can't know our love. I know why everyone is dying now. I know why, and you can't. And you won't. Not until it's too late. He died because of you. You could have done something. You could have saved him. But you didn't."

He was right in Sam's face now, his cold, wet nose almost brushing Sam's own, and the smell of iron, of blood was strong on his breath.

"I know the secret you want to know, and you'll NEVER," his voice rising now, "NEVER-"

The hairs off his face tickled Sam's cheek.

"HEAR IT YOU FUCKIN'-"

And then a shadow came alive, and out of nowhere Tess was on him. They were wrestling and biting at each other in the hallway, bashing and thumping into walls as they snarled. Sam looked around at the dark to make sure no other creatures were going to bolt in to this impromptu fray, but finding none, he figured it best if he moved away.

The dog and Tess growled and snarled as Sam pushed his way backward, the beam of light hitting every once and again and catching nothing but fluid and dangerous fur and aggression. Tess was bigger, but he was crazy, and it made the fight look even. He lunged for Tess's neck and caught a chunk, and Sam could hear the sound of tearing flesh. Tess howled in pain, and then she made it look like she wasn't even trying in the beginning.

She headbutted him, and he lost his footing for a moment, which she used to sink her teeth into his front leg, and with incredible strength she twisted her head and there was a loud CRACK of bone. Now it was his turn to howl in pain.

"He did it!" the dog howled, "It was him, he killed him, and I loved him!"

He tried to make another lunge at Tess, but faltered on his hanging paw and fell to the ground.

"Are you done?" she asked him.

He snapped at her throat from his position stuck on the ground.

Tess looked up at Sam and held his gaze before whipping her head down and tearing out the dog's throat.

The sound of his final gurgles echoed in Sam's head as he tried to comprehend what Tess' gaze had implied. And then all the questions came flooding back, and he started in without so much as a thank you for saving his life.

"What is happening? Where's Bare?" he asked.

Tess shook her head and then swallowed the gay dog's blood.

"Tess?" Sam asked, scared again.

She swallowed again, still staring at Sam.

"Uh, Tess?"

One more swallow, and then, "Eugh, dog blood. Foul."

"Thank god."

"For what? For Rudolf being dead? Fuck that."

"He was crazy."

"Everyone's crazy."

"Where's Bare."

"He's out."

"Dead?"

"No knocked out. He ran into a door and knocked himself out when he heard you screaming for help."

Sam's heart burned with happiness. His friend wasn't dead. His friend didn't hate him. His friend cared enough about him to accidently knock himself unconscious for him. All good things. All of these things were good. Everything was going to be ok.

"We have to leave now," said Tess, interrupting Sam's internal mantra.

"But what about Bare?"

"The buzz is filling my head. We have to go."

"That's really cryptic, Tess. I need some answers. Snap out of it."

"I'm out of it, Sam. I'm just telling you it isn't safe here now. It isn't safe at all. The buzz is back, and it's loud."

The buzz. What the hell was the buzz?

"We can't leave Bare."

"We won't."

"Ok."

Tess started walking away into the dark.

"Come on," she said.

Sam hurried along after her.

And there he was: that big handsome lug passed the fuck out in a dark hallway. When Sam first saw him he was sure he was dead even though Tess had said he wasn't. Bare looked more like a fat rug than the living, breathing beast Sam knew. So Sam kicked him; gently of course, it just seemed like there was so much Bare to have come around that a simple push wouldn't have sufficed.

"Hey. Get up."

"We have to go Bare," Tess was becoming increasingly repetitive, and no matter how many times Sam pushed her to tell him what the hell was happening, how Craig had managed his little phone stunt, what the hell had happened to the other nameless gay dog, Tess was silent as a church mouse. Sam hoped Cheese was ok.

Bare moaned, so Sam gave him another gentle kick. Tess looked around, frantic.

"Ughhnnn."

Another kick, just to be safe.

"Bare?" Sam said. He raised his leg for one more kick, but Bare swatted his other out from underneath him, and Sam hit the floor.

"Ow. What was that for?"

"Why the heck are ya kicking me?"

"I've been trying to wake you up."

"By kicking me?"

"Yeah, Tess says we gotta go."

"We have to leave," Tess said, more to herself than backing up what Sam had said.

"What happened?" Bare asked, "We had a couple drinks maybe and then…"

"A lot. You mean why were you passed out? You hit your head running to save me."

"Oh yah. You screamed. I heard you scream. You ok?"

"Yeah buddy. Now let's get up, ok?"

"My head hurts."

"I know."

Sam tried to lift Bare to his feet, but Bare weighed 600 pounds. Sam struggled.

"I could use some drugs."

"I know. Now let's get up."

"Drugs are up?"

"This buzz won't shut up. Oh god, we gotta go. We gotta get outta here," Tess chimed in helpfully.

"Yup, the buzz, definitely."

"I need a buzz."

"Not this, you don't hear it? It's in my head, telling me it's over," Tess said.

"Jesus Tess, calm it out. You're freaking us out here."

"I'm freaked out."

"You have too many teeth to be freaked out."

"I got more teeth than her," Bare chimed in. This hotel was now suddenly full of folks that were either dead or children. At least Sam felt busy now. He felt important.

"No you don't Bare," he said.

"Do too."

"Get up."

This time Bare listened and used the wall to prop himself up onto his feet. His clumsy claws left big tears in the wallpaper, but Sam figured people would probably be more concerned about the deer stew in the pool and the dead ornaments all around the building.

"Is everyone else dead?" Sam asked.

"Yes, now let's go," Tess said for the umpteenth time.

"Yeah," said Sam as he grabbed his pack and his axe, which he gripped tightly. He wasn't about to be without this again.

"Are there any guns here Tess? Should we bring a gun?"

"No," Sam said quickly and desperately.

"Jeeze, alright, no guns," said Bare, the severity of Sam's answer making its point, "No guns, sure. I forgot you weren't a gun guy."

"We should go," said Tess.

And they did. They pushed past Zeke and his puddle of life, past the deer swimming forever, past little, dangling Craig, and they were outside. But now how were they going to get anywhere. They wouldn't all fit on the snowmobile. And Bare might object.

"Well, I guess we should get a truck."

"I know a place," Tess said.

"Think we could get some aspirin or something along the way?" Bare asked as they started walking in the cold. No one answered. The sobering cold had made everything in the Caribou Lodge real, and that was just horrible.

They found a suburban. Sam took out the back so Bare could fit, and they were off. The whole thing was a blur, the last 24 or so hours having contained so many horrible moments that doing something as banal as car shopping didn't even register. Tess seemed like she might have been losing it a little. She mumbled about 'the buzz' but wouldn't elaborate; Sam imagined she didn't really know what she meant either, so he didn't press. Bare bemoaned how sober he'd become. His head hurt. His feet hurt. His lungs, his arms, his fur, the tops of his ears, and his gums were all sore. And the pads of his paws itched. Or so he said.

Sam just drove.

He didn't even stop when they passed the Caribou Lounge, and the suburban's tires spun over old Hank, who had taken to standing in the street again. Tess and Bare didn't noticed, the ride was bumpy, but Sam figured Hank had finally gotten what he'd always wanted. He was finally free. Sam envied him slightly.

The suburban's tires were big enough that if Sam went at a reasonable pace he was fine on the roads even with the snow. He was driving south, back to America. He knew that was where things were happening. Things always happened in America, and to be totally frank, he missed the place. He really hoped it was just the Canadian animals that were crazy, but he doubted it. Especially as a beaver waddled under the tire's treads. The red stain, black in the night, seemed a hell of a lot bigger.

58

The sound of Bare retching in the back made him slam on the brakes. Bare pitched forward into his own puddle of vomit, and Tess hit the front seat causing Sam to hit his head on the steering wheel as they slid to a stop.

"Oh god, I get it now," Bare said, "I get it. I need a drink, I need a dang drink."

"The buzz?" Tess asked shaking off the stop. Sam was making sure his neck bandages hadn't come loose with the force of the stop.

"That's the voice, the buzz," said Bare.

"What voice?" Sam asked.

"The voice in your head."

"Goddamn it, what is?"

"You're gonna think it's some crazy hippie stuff."

"Alright, so?"

"It's about the buzz, right?" Tess chimed in with her now token phrase.

"Yah, I guess it is," said Bare, "So there are things that distance us from nature. I admit I'm a bit of an addict when it comes to most substances. Before I met you I was just walkin' from spot to spot just findin' booze and licking it up, hey? And that sorta stuff totally disconnects you. Thank goodness too. If I wasn't boozin' I'd probably be dead like the rest of the animals. All that's runnin' through my head right now is kill yourself, trust me, it'll be better than the alternative, bud."

"That's a polite voice asking for your death," Sam added.

"It's my voice. That's the scary part."

"It is scary. It won't shut up," Tess said.

"Why don't I have these thoughts then? Other than the usual you know, contemplation of it as a concept."

"Because you're a human. You're dumb."

"Hey. Mean. And people are way smarter than bears."

"Just because you can build machines and stuff doesn't mean you're smarter. We've got life smarts. Nature smarts. We don't get hung up on things that don't exist and don't matter."

"Okay, okay. I get it. That puke smells awful, what did you eat?"

"I think I swallowed a lot of blood."

"Me too," said Tess.

"Electricity I think keeps the buzz away too."

Sam felt his gut drop again.

"What?" he asked.

"Well when the electricity went out everyone sort of started going crazy. The weaker animals gave in to the thoughts faster. Cheese."

No. Not Cheese!

"We heard the whole family yelling upstairs once the power went out. I got there just in time to see them just vibrating against everything, and then the TV fell. There was nothing I could do."

Sam thought about that giant, tube-filled television perched precariously on the dresser. And he pictured the whole Cheese Crew shaking violently with their fear, afraid of their own tiny minds, their tremors spreading to the dresser, and then that black screen just... His head filled in the sickly crunch even after he'd tried to shake the vision.

"Shit. Cheese, man," Sam said.

"All of them," Tess said.

"You okay, Tess?" Sam asked, "Please don't listen to the voices. They're not good voices."

"They're loud Sam. I think we should get drunk as soon as possible if you think that'll help."

"I do. I really do," said Bare earnestly.

"Well lets get you two some booze, huh? We'll all go get fucked up, and then you won't want to kill yourselves. Deal?"

The two just grunted in response, but Sam had already started up the ride, and they were back on the road.

The ValuKing. There it was in all of its giant warehouse-style shopping glory. The parking lot was full, which meant Sam was not at all excited to walk around in there. Bodies, bodies everywhere, but not a drop to drink. What the fuck did that mean? Sam was nervous.

"Let's get you kids some beer. My dad's out of town and we can party at my place."

"Your dad is dead," Tess said flatly, completely ruining Sam's clever little joke.

"Thanks Tess. Uplifting as ever."

"I have no job. Everyone I loved is dead, and I have this fucking buzzing in my ear telling me that something horrible is about to happen. So you tell me: what's the point?"

"Stop that. You're listening to the voices again. Let's get you some booze. It'll help, I promise."

And they were off to the ValuKing, King of Values. Someone hadn't hired great slogan writers down at the ValuKing apparently. The sliding door was propped open with what Sam could only assume was a body, but the snowdrift creeping inside had done a nice job covering it all up.

The essentials no one needed were at the very front; summer specials abound. The racks of flip-flops and tank tops seemed odd in contrast to the cold outside. He'd have to inquire with the management about getting the specials changed. Come on ValuKing, stay with the times.

There were bodies piled all around. Most had fully decomposed. It looked as if the animals had gotten to them. There were a few animals that had done themselves in here as well it seemed. Little paws and hooves stuck out from under giant, overturned shelves. Such a waste of perfectly good meat.

Sam grabbed a cart from the hands of a skeleton. This was his now.

"Check this move out!" Sam said as he put one foot on the bottom of the cart and pushed off with his other. The thing tipped upward with Sam's weight, and Sam fell over with the damn thing. He got up, dusting himself off. That did not help his already hurting leg. Goddamn it.

"Whoops. That's not- that wasn't it."

"Let's just get drunk, eh?" said Bare. Right. Drinks. Sam was so easily distracted. Had he always been this way?

And there he was. Back in 7th grade. The smell of youthful body odor and that meaty scent of used, pink eraser filled the air, and Sam was doodling on his notebook. He'd never been all that good at drawing. He would just do the same face over and over again, and it was sort of a bastard version of all the cartoons he'd ever seen: lazy Garfield eyes, a too-big nose that slanted at an impossible and strange angle, a couple slashes and a grate for teeth, and a big, misshapen potato to close it all in, to really encourage the idea that this could be a real human's face maybe.

The teacher had been talking. She was always doing that. People mostly just seemed to drone. Sam rarely had the patience to listen to them. The heavy use of 'um' and 'uhh' and 'hmmms' just couldn't hold his attention.

JUST LET YOUR WORDS BREATHE! He wanted to yell. A chorus of 'ums' surrounded him constantly, battering down the walls of his happiness and his contentedness with humanity as a whole. He wanted to learn, he really did. He read a lot; he was on the Internet searching for facts about everything from Scandinavian folklore to disproven conspiracy theories, anything that sparked his interest for a moment. The Internet was a much more efficient teacher than most of his teachers.

And now she was staring right at him. Time was moving. Sam wasn't sure why though. Now the whole class was looking at him.

"Well," she said. Miss Aldrin. No relation to the astronaut she liked to say. Why would she brag about something like that? How many people had been to the moon? Not many. Certainly no one Sam knew. No one from South Dakota probably even. And Medicine Lake, South Dakota? Definitely not. No freakin' way. So why did she feel the need to clarify, to almost brag about the fact that she wasn't related to an American hero. Sam didn't get it. Maybe because he was space's great second man? Did Miss Aldrin think she was too good for the second man on the moon? He wondered if she had a big, framed picture of Neil above her bed. Well, hey, at least when she'd talk about the people she wasn't related to she didn't get bogged down in the killer 'um.'

"Sam?"

Kids were laughing now. They were snickering at him. He was floundering, and he couldn't keep his mind on trying to swim up. Weren't you naturally supposed to swim up? Stop it. Stop it, he said to himself. Thought tangents took up most of his time.

"Where's the booze?" Miss Aldrin asked.

"What? Sorry?"

"Where's the alcohol?" Tess asked as Sam pushed the cart around, dropping candy and snacks into the red basin. Oh right. Where the hell had he gone?

"Let's find that, sorry," Sam said.

And they did. They found mountains of the stuff. Bare stood in front of the rows and rows of bottles, and Sam could just imagine a pillar of light illuminating him as he laid out his arms and fell to his knees. This was Bare's god. This was beauty incarnate. He was about to get fucked up.

Bare stood and started gesturing, soon grew too impatient and tried to grab bottles for himself, but his bear-hands couldn't grip them, and a small wave of bottles crashed to the floor. Sam thought of Carol and the snacks but got distracted as he saw his friend kneel in the broken glass and use his pink rubber tongue to lap up the lost bourbon and rye and gin.

"How about I grab what you want, and we put it in the basket?" Sam said. Bare looked up at him with a childish and vigorous nod.

"Great. Point at what you want buddy. You too Tess."

"I'm allergic to strawberries," she said.

"Ok."

"So no strawberries."

"Yup. That's totally fine. Most liquor doesn't contain strawberries as far as I know."

"Just checking."

"Ok."

Bare pointed at an entire row of good whiskeys.

The rest was the story of a drunken road trip. Bare and Tess sat in back, where Sam had loaded them up with snacks and big plastic buckets he'd taped to the floor to avoid the massive amounts of liquor he'd stashed in them from sloshing around too much on the upholstery.

Sam drove, and the hirsute duo half drowned themselves in a mash up of spirits. It was a nice bonding time, but Sam wished he knew where he was headed. He kept thinking back to Hank's story, and that cat; that cat that might have been able to help.

Sam knew it was an outrageous thing to be upset about, but everything in his life had been outrageous lately, why wouldn't a cat be able to tell him the secrets of the universe? Well, it was a moot point. He didn't know where this cat was or even if it was alive.

Sam sighed heavily as he continued to head vaguely south.

He'd stop from time to time, the couple in his trunk napping pretty consistently as he siphoned gas from abandoned cars, or watched as some woodland critter dive-bombed off a cliff or a bridge, or made mad dashes to smooch his tires. It was a whole lot of death for one little road trip, but that seemed appropriate considering their send off party at the Caribou Lodge. It would almost have concerned him more if the animals *hadn't* been offing themselves out here too.

Sam spent much of the drive thinking about nothing. Or at least that's what he was desperately going for. It felt a lot like those nights he always seemed to have: nights where he'd roll in bed, his mind racing too fast to calm down, silly snippets of old songs leaking in over his self-imposed mental silence. It was times like that he wished he were more spiritual; he wished he could meditate or clear his mind easily. But alas, he was only human, American human and cursed to think about the same banal things endlessly instead of sleeping soundly.

His mind swirled around between thoughts of Carol, of sex, of death, of the itching at his crotch he hoped to hell wasn't something sinister, but he definitely wasn't about to check for bumps. If he didn't see them they didn't exist. Right? And what about all the animals back there at the Caribou? Did any survive? Did any escape from the crazy? Was one of them a boozer? Was Cheese alive? Cheese could have been a boozer. No Cheese was a family man. He wasn't a drunk, and he was crushed under the weight of television.

Sam missed television. Television had taught him sex, and violence, and how to love properly. His family, he missed them too. His yard back home. Sitting out in the grass, summer time, the prickles of the blades irritating his skin, the hum of bug life droning out the thoughts of work. The river back at his cabin, gurgling away, rushing sometimes after a good thaw, that chill invigorating him as he shook his head through it like a dog or a shampoo commercial. He caught himself smiling, remembered how much life sucked, and then looked back at the two drunken animals and the frozen forever beyond them.

Sam sighed again, but nobody noticed.

"Watch out for that tree," Bare said calmly at one point.

Sam looked up to see a cracked tree swinging right for their roof. He gunned the motor and twisted the wheel, causing the suburban to go into a slide on the snowy road. He desperately turned into the skid, or was it away from the skid? He slammed on the brakes as the tree crashed behind them, and the suburban spun around a couple of times, miraculously staying on the road.

"Shit," Sam said when they had come to a complete stop. They'd turned completely around and were staring straight at the giant damn tree that had tried to crush them.

"Man, yer girlfriend sure's mad achew fer some reason," Bare said before he started licking the spilled whiskey off Tess's back. She giggled and writhed as his tongue probed around her. Sam felt one of his panic pangs. What did Bare know? Could he know about Carol? Could he know about the building? No. No way.

"Stop that please," Sam said as he refilled their liquor buckets.

"I'd like to switch to Vodka I think," Tess said at another point.

"That's a lot of work. Just finish your whiskey first," Sam said.

"But I want VODKA," she said, a child having a tantrum.

"No."

"BUT I WANT IT. I'M SOOO TIRED OF THIS WHIIIIS-KEY!"

"Don't make me pull this car over," Sam said. He smiled. He'd always wanted to say that.

"It's a suburban," Bare said.

"Shut up. I told you that."

"I knew what a suburban was."

"How?"

"Vodkaaaaa."

"I read."

"About suburbans?"

"Yup."

"Maybe we can mix them?"

"We're not mixing anything, and you've never read about suburbans. No one writes about suburbans."

"Military prolly does."

"I bet the military would gimmie vodka."

"Ok! Let's play the quiet game."

"What's that?"

"Shhh."

"What's the game?"

"It's when you're quiet."

"That's not a game."

"It is."

"Nuh uh."

"It is a game. It's a game because you can lose. If you aren't quiet: you lose."

"And if I win?"

"If you win I'll give you vodka?"

And everyone was blissfully silent.

"Did I win yet?" she asked five minutes later.

"If you give me vodka I'll tell you a secret," Tess said.

"No."

"It's a really good one."

"What's the secret Tess," Sam said flatly, fully annoyed with her at this point.

"I want vodka first."

"Tell me, and if it's good I'll give you vodka."

"You'll like it, just trust me Sammy. Meeeeow. Get it?"

"What was that?"

"A hint."

"A hint? Meow... wait, do you know where Hank's cat is?" Sam braked and brought the car to a stop and turned around, his heart pounding in his chest, excited. He had been talking about this cat the whole damn trip. He really hoped she hadn't been holding out on him.

"Maybe," Tess said with a smile.

"You need to tell me Tess. I know you're drunk, but this is crazy important."

"Voooodka."

"Ok fine," Sam said, angry. He got out and ripped her bucket from its cocoon of tape and dumped the remainder of the whiskey into the snow. He walked around back, fished out a 1.75 of Grey Goose and filled the bottom of the bucket. It looked dirty brown with the whiskey residue. He set the bucket down in front of Tess and looked at her expectantly.

"Yay Sam!" she moved to drink, but Sam moved the bucket away first.

"Nope, tell me where this cat is."

"I don't know, some place called Insternational Fowl?"

"What? That's not a word. Wait, International Falls?"

"Yeah! That's the one!"

Sam knew where that was. Sam had a destination. Sam was giddy as he gave Tess a big hug.

"I asked Hank. He also said something about it being a food place," she said before sticking her head in the bucket.

This was it! A food place in International Falls. A restaurant, grocery? Whatever, he could find it.

Something in the way Hank had talked about this cat had just felt right to Sam. He had a good, gut feeling about this cat in a way he'd never felt about cats. He just knew that this was right, and finally, after one of the worst days of his entire life, he had a glimmer of hope. Or maybe more than a glimmer of hope, he had actual, full-blown hope.

Sam got back into the driver seat, checked his map, and started out toward International Falls, and it seemed like things might actually be looking up.

As the sun went down, Sam figured he should find a place to sleep for the night. He was exhausted. He'd driven for about a thousand hours, and he'd had to listen to tweedle-drunk and tipsy-dee slur animal-nonsense the whole damn way. He really wished he'd picked a vehicle with a working CD player. The next town he found, that was it: that was home, at least for the night.

He'd been on the lookout for another Folly's Landry the whole trip. Not the animal massacre and burning power plant full of dead old lady part, but the part before the plant's demise; the part where a city had power. And people. Real human people. His eyes were wide and searching for that.

But of course he didn't find it. Lightening didn't strike twice, someone had once told him. Or it didn't strike twice in the same place? Except he'd heard about people that had been struck by lightening dozens of times. How did you live through that? It's like liquid fire raining from the damn sky. Sam didn't understand nature. Or life. Shit.

He needed to stop this tangent stuff. He was never going to get anything done, he was never going to get anywhere in figuring out what was happening if he kept thinking about how strange lightening was. Somehow his mind was no clearer than that drug-addled, egg-bake brain of Bare's.

Depressed again, Sam drove on.

63

Eventually Sam found a town; it was dirty, it was poor, but he found what was clearly the nicest house around and parked out front. It was the only one without a half dozen cars and twice that in buried, plastic lawn ornaments spewed across the snowy yards. Flamingos, finally seasonable Santas, and the obligatory homemade, chainsaw-carved animals all wore ninja masks and hats of snow on their unrottable heads and stood guard outside these folks' ancient poverty.

The snow wasn't quite as deep down here, so Sam was making much better time, and as he turned off the suburban he felt almost content. The twins were sleeping still. He'd have to start a fire and melt some snow because those two were going to wake up with one hell of a hangover. He wished he could make them a Bloody Mary, but at the same time, remembering the scene they made the whole ride, he also didn't want to do a damn thing for them. He kept washing back and forth between unrelenting nausea at the destruction he'd wrought on Tess,' and, by proxy, Bare's life, and then he'd flip right back to being annoyed as all get out by their drunkenness. It's never fun to be the only sober one at the party.

Sam decided on the altruistic, or rather the guilt-ridden route, which had a much stronger pull on him, and went inside the house to find some things to burn. The good news was he'd picked the right place. No bodies in the front entryway and not a single corpse in the living room. But there was a good-sized fireplace. Sam celebrated as he broke up an antique end table with his axe, freshly sharpened and gripped tightly.

He walked into the bodiless kitchen and threw the keys on the table, making himself at home. He pulled open all the drawers until he found a lighter and a box of matches, and before he knew it he had a fire crackling and snapping and a pot of snow ready to melt. He peeked through the moth-carved curtains out to the suburban where Bare and Tess looked to still be sleeping peacefully over their drink buckets. Good.

"Hello?" Sam called to the empty home, fire poker in hand. No response. Cool. He just had to check. It's not like it was crazy to consider the possibility of this place being infested with crazy whatevers. Maybe there was a zoo nearby. Maybe there was some homicidal warthog or an angry march of penguins or something just poised for attack behind some door.

Sam sang the parts he remembered from old rap songs as he wandered around the house. It was a nice place. The carpets were a delightfully neutral off-white, and were magically unsullied except by Sam's own snowy boots. If this were two days ago he would have taken them off in embarrassment of what the dead must be thinking of him. But today Sam couldn't give a shit about these dead. He couldn't even find them. Which was nice. These people were the rich of the town. And the rich in a poor town are the truly powerful.

Sam imagined these people lording over the others and their lawn ornament armies, a feudal system crowned with this, their pearly off-white throne. The art was minimal and flowers, and the furniture was wooden and unscuffed. The place had more the aspect of museum than of a home, and Sam couldn't imagine anyone actually living here.

He found himself in a hallway with pictures of the old tenants, which were professional and could have come factory standard if they weren't of the same nuclear unit. The father had a light beard and no wrinkles where a true smiler bore them, the mother was pale, blonde, pretty and completely unremarkable at least in photo form, and the children were worse: bland little creatures, their eyes small, like tiny adults, and their clothes starched and unlived in. Sam felt little sympathy for these dead people.

He opened the first door he came to, was confronted with a perfect bathroom, and tried the next. And here was the master bedroom, untouched, the bed still made. Bodiless. Sam walked in.

He breathed in the stale air, then ran up and threw his back onto the bed. Of course their bed would be this comfortable. He could melt into this bed. His bed up at the cabin had started out ok, but eight years of sleeping in the same position had mangled it all out of comfortability. Sam considered a nap but figured he should bring the animals inside first, lest they freeze to death. Alcohol was a known blood thinner, and that was not conducive to surviving in the cold.

As he walked back to the front door, swinging his coat on, he thought about how amazing it was going to be to drag that mattress out in front of the fire he was going to keep going all night, and have a cozy, wonderful little camp out. A good sleep on a mattress like that would have the power to make even his last 48 hours seem like nothing in the grand scheme of existing between comfortable sleeps on comfortable beds.

He stepped outside and saw the suburban door wide open. Tess was still asleep, her head nodding dangerously close to taking a swim in the bucket, but Bare was gone. Sam's head was thrown back on to that old familiar swivel. He ran up to the suburban and slammed his hands to the window, searching inside.

Bare was gone. Tracks leading up the street. Vomit there. More tracks. Sam was following now. Thank goodness for snow, the greatest companion to tracking animals a boy could have. Sam followed the tracks for longer than he'd like. How had Bare gone this far so fast? Had he run? The gait didn't suggest it. The tracks veered off and dodged a washing machine and the bed of a pickup truck to reach an adorably dilapidated home that might have been two or three trailers glued together. The door had been ripped from its hinges.

"Bare!" Sam yelled, angry with his friend for making him wander this whole way. Sam had a moment as he stepped carefully inside the home where he wondered if maybe this wasn't Bare. Maybe he'd missed something. Maybe this was another bear: a mean, angry, sober and suicidal bear who was just looking for any excuse to tear him to pieces. He thought about his old death fantasy with the bear cave gut-fiesta, and he'd put himself on edge again. He was uncannily good at doing that.

"Hey. Bare," Sam said, quieter this time. No answer, but Sam saw a furry paw laid out on the ground around a corner. And there was Bare, limbs splayed over the trash, sleeping like a damn baby. Sam kicked at him, trying to jostle him awake.

"Bare, get up."

Nothing.

"Bare. Hey Bare."

Sam was worried now. Had he fed his friend too much drink? Had Bare actually just used the booze as an excuse to kill himself on his own terms? That would be poetic but horrible. Oh shit, he'd vomited before. What if he'd done it again? What if he was Hendrixing right now and Sam didn't even know it? There was a bottle of pills on the ground next to Bare, empty and capless. Had that been there before, or had Bare, in his endless search for drugs, taken the whole bottle? How many pills would it take to kill a bear? What even were those pills?

Sam got down and did his best to push Bare on to his side like he had learned in lifeguard training freshman year. But Bare was probably 600 pounds of dead weight; it wasn't going to happen. Sam clamped his hands around Bare's jaw and pried his teeth apart. He looked down into the pink maw and saw no vomit, no pills stuck cotton to the roof of Bare's mouth.

And this of course was the moment Bare chose to jerk awake and snap his jaw shut. He lashed out with his paws and backhanded Sam onto the tiny dining room table, which snapped under Sam's weight. Sam sat in the wreckage and wrung his hands together, shocked that both were still fully intact. The force he'd shut that jaw with...

"Hey!" Sam yelled at Bare, who was muttering and flailing around, apparently confused about where, who, and what he was, "What the fuck?"

"Grruppp," Bare said.

"You hit me you asshole."

"Rfffffmmm."

Sam grabbed the axe that had been thrown from his hands and gripped it tightly.

"Hey, Bare. Yo!"

"Whhha?"

"Hey," Sam stood up and stood over Bare who had stopped thrashing.

"Sam?" Bare blinked up at him, confused.

"What the hell are you doing?"

Bare looked around, clearly having just about as much idea as Sam. Sam kept his knuckles white on the axe.

"Why did you leave the car?" Sam asked again.

"Car?"

"Suburban."

"Ugh, bourbon."

"Hey, there he is, what the fuck man? Did you take these pills?" Sam asked holding up the empty bottle.

"I nee' water. Needed water..."

"I have water ready at the house. The house we are parked right in front of. Did you take these pills?"

"Mouth so dry. Dying. This' wha death's like."

"Hey, focus! Pills?"

Bare looked cross-eyed at the bottle.

"Nah, no. Jus' needed water. So thirsty. Dyin'."

"You're not dying you drama queen, come on, I left Tess in the car. Let's get up."

"Can you gimme a han'?"

"Probably not. You're huge."

Bare pleaded with his eyes, and Sam gripped one hairy paw, felt the leather of the pads against his arm and pulled with all his might. He strained for a moment, and then Bare, deciding it was time, stretched himself up and stood. Mostly on his own.

"Thanks," Bare said.

"Don't mention it."

"Ok."

They stepped out into the cold again, Bare leaning slightly against Sam causing them to drift irreversibly to the right.

"You doing ok, buddy? Other than the thirst, I mean?"

"S'all good my man. S'all good. Tess. She's good animal, you know?"

"I know buddy."

Sam looked at his friend, drunk as hell to save his life, and he felt some hope. There was something warming about having two lives so dependent upon him. He felt like he was doing penance for Folly's here. He felt like things might be ok. Until he saw the smoke.

Black, scary smoke rising, seeping out of the pores of the nice house. Sam closed his eyes for a long blink, really, truly hoping this was just a symptom of exhaustion. He opened them again and saw the flames start to lick their way outside.

"That's too big of a fire," Bare said, his eyes glittering with the small reflections of the flames.

"Fuck."

"Was the water in there?"

"Yup."

"Dang."

The roof fell in, collapsed on itself like a soufflé at a firing range. Those perfect beams used to build up that model home were too dry for their own good apparently. The whole thing too well contained, perfect for sleeping, perfect for the flame. It looked like Sam had the makings of a serial arsonist here. The flames overtook everything now, and the heat started to lap at Bare and him, even though they were a football field away. Shit. The suburban. And Tess.

"Stay here," Sam yelled as he ran toward the flames. He shielded his face from the heat and threw the driver side door open. The heat was quickly turning the interior into an oven. He smacked at his pockets, searching for the keys. He tried his pants, his jacket, he reached inside. Where they hell—

And the image of those keys thrown carelessly on the kitchen counter as he searched for matches crystallized in his mind. Just making himself at home. Sam looked out the window at the inferno and could smell the rubber of the tires starting to melt.

No spare in the glovebox, none in the center console, under the visor? No. Maybe there was a spare in a magnet box at the back. His family had done that. Sam climbed to the other door, away from the flames, and snuck out into the heat. There were times when he'd day dreamt about being around infernos like this. Times when he'd walked his trapping route in negative 20 degree weather, the cold snow packing and thawing in the tops of his boots, soaking his ankles with water like needles. But there was precious little time he could spend out in heat like this. No matter how cold it was.

Sam used the opposite side of the suburban for cover as he groped beneath for some hidden key. Finding nothing, he reached a bit further, and the metal felt super heated even through his gloves, which came back melted. Sam retracted his stinging hand and shoved it into the melting snow. The key wasn't going to happen, but it looked like a gnarly blister was. Bare was yelling something at Sam now, but Sam couldn't make out what. Sam opened Tess' door, and tried to lift her out of the backseat. But she must have weighed two hundred pounds. She was a big girl.

"Tess! We gotta go Tess. Wake on up here."

Tess wasn't moving. It was hotter than the sun. Hotter than coffee spilled on the lap. Hotter than Kassie Freeman in high school. Focus. Focus Sam.

"TESS!" Sam yelled in her ear. Nothing. Maybe this heavy drinking thing was a poor decision. Slight buzz would probably have done it, right?

"Get the HELL UP."

Nothing.

Sam was sweating violently. The drops flowed down his forehead into his eyes, stinging like weak, wet little bees. He looked around desperate for a flower or a feather or something to tickle her nose with, or was that sneezing? All he could find was a bottle of vodka, and he dumped it all over her face. Surprised and sputtering, she woke up.

"Whu? Heaahh? Vodka?"

"Yes, vodka. Now let's go."

"Where?"

Sam pointed out the window at the blaze and at the front of the house, which looked precarious and flaming, and sure enough, it started to tip toward them. Because why the hell wouldn't it?

"MOVE!" Sam yelled, mincing no words, and this time Tess did.

Sam ran directly away from the frame that was now crashing down, and they both jumped out of the way, right as it crumpled the roof of the suburban.

Bare was running over as Sam crawled to his feet, trying to inch away from the screaming flames.

Bare was flailing and yelling something again, but Sam couldn't hear him over the roar of the inferno. Sam squinted at him, and Bare pointed at what looked like Sam. Sam looked over his shoulder and then down to see that Tess had caught on fire. It was just her fur, and just a little, and in her drunken haze, she hadn't noticed yet.

"Tess, don't move."

"Why?" she asked, moving her head of course. And that's when the flames leapt from the fur on her back, to her vodka soaked face, and she lit up like a Christmas tree. Tess was very much on fire, and all the water was inside the burning house. Great.

Tess opened her mouth and howled sending some of the flames veering away with the force of her breath. She had never sounded so much like an actual wolf until she was lit on fire. Sam, in a moment of quick thinking, shoved a handful of snow into her face, then dragged all 200 some pounds of her kicking body face first through the snow.

Somehow Sam, upon seeing a friend on fire, summoned the strength he hadn't seemed to have a minute ago and just wrecked Tess's face in the cold earth. And it worked it seemed. Except for her back, which had fire spreading rather quickly. Sam stopped dragging and jumped on top of her, hoping his body would suffocate the flame.

After a moment Tess stopped squirming, and Sam had a horrible moment where he was sure he'd just burned, dragged, and suffocated the last breath straight out of her. But then she twitched underneath him, not a death spasm twitch, but a please-get-off-of-my-body twitch, to which Sam obliged.

"Holy Moly! Are you alright?" Bare asked as he came huffing over.

They examined Tess' face. Most of the hair had been singed from one side, and the skin underneath was red and raw, but even through the acrid cloud of burnt fur stench, they knew she'd be ok. She blinked twice, her eyes thankfully still working, and nodded.

"Yeah, I guess I am. Thanks Sam. Looks like this time you saved my tail. I guess we're even, huh?"

The power plant, Craig hanging, Hank run over, that trading card he stole from his Mark Hansson in grade school, Carol burning, the house burning…

"Sure. No problem," Sam said, looking back at the fire.

A dark figure was running toward them now. 'Fuck, what now?' thought Sam. As it got closer, Sam could see it was a moose, his spindly knees bucking wildly as he jetted through the snow and crashed through the trees. Sam looked at Bare, who was still tending to Tess. He did not want to see how Bare would react to the company of a moose right now. But it didn't make any difference, as the moose veered and ran directly into the flames, never looking back. Sam shook his head. The world was really going to hell.

82

Later, truckless, packless, foodless, and drinkless, they sat in the trailer that, thanks to Bare, was also doorless, and shivered. They were all a little nervous to start a fire, especially around all this garbage, but it was dark now, and the night was when death came quickly in the north. So they blocked the front door with a dresser, and Sam gathered whatever blankets and cushions he could muster in the dark, and they huddled together for warmth.

Sam, in some insane turn of events, couldn't find any alcohol, and when he tried to light the lighter he miraculously still had, Tess howled in fear, her hungover, singed body controlling her more than her mind. So he was forced to scrounge unsuccessfully in the dark. He knew a house like this had to contain some sort of booze, he just didn't know where their particular hiding place would be. He stumbled about, banged his shin until he thought it would pop a goose-egg the size of a new leg, and gave up to join his shivering friends in a big shivering pile and wait for sleep or morning or death, whichever came first. Tess whimpered and Bare licked her wounds, hoping what little saliva he could muster might maybe soothe the pain, and they stayed like this for the long, long night.

The morning came, bright and intense. Sam was the first to wake, and he looked at his friends, finally asleep maybe in the last hour, and he winced at the sight of Tess. Her back had big red blotches where patches of beautiful gray fur used to be. Blisters had formed and popped overnight, and the whole thing was a red, pus covered mess. It didn't look third degree, but two and a half wouldn't have been a stretch if that were a thing. Her face was a little better than her back. The whole thing looked red, and the fur was shriveled and blackened, but the blotching horror-movie look of her back wasn't there. And he was thankful for that.

Sam carefully untangled himself from the sleeping duo. His leg still hurt from his fall, and he massaged it as he walked to the kitchen, trying to step on the garbage and filth that looked like it would make the least amount of noise under his boots.

The kitchen was a far cry from the one in the house he'd razed last night. This one had newspaper stacked high under the kitchen table. The paper was almost threatening to overtake the thing, and would have if a horde of shopping bags and toys and trinkets and a filthy microwave and clothes hadn't been heaped on the tabletop. How had people lived this way?

He kicked away piles of shopping bags so he could open drawers, and all he found were more plastic bags. This house must have been fifty percent plastic shopping bags. Why had they needed so many goddamned plastic bags? Were they worried they'd just sit in some dump for eternity? Did they think turning their own home into a garbage dump was a better solution? These were the sorts of mysteries that were forever to remain mysteries to Sam. The inescapable, unexplainable past Sam had watched die. The whole world was a cemetery now, its stories buried under piles of shitty plastic bags and dirty clothes.

Sam tried a drawer above the refrigerator and found a cabinet full of cereal and booze. How he had missed this last night he wasn't sure. He recognized most of it as the bottom of the barrel, grade-A gut-rot. Maybe the years it remained untouched had improved the flavor, but he couldn't imagine anything aging well in a molded plastic jug.

Sam carried it back to the duo and then went to search for a breakfast. There were plenty of cans, and Sam found a couple non-dented cans of beans and franks, and somehow, miraculously there was a can opener right on top of the mess on the counter. Finally something was going right.

He ate one can and then another. And then he ate a can of creamed corn, which had seemed like a good idea at the time. Creamed corn, it turned out, was never a good idea, and the moment the gelatinous squeeze pushed down his gullet he regretted it. That taste, that candied, strange corn flavor swirled around his mouth, refusing to relinquish its hold on his taste buds. But once the horror of the corn faded, boredom set in.

He had hoped the two would have woken up by now. He wanted to get on the road, get to International Falls. He should find Tess some aloe. That would be a good friend thing to do. That would help him feel slightly less like the worst person in the world, which for all he knew he could have been.

He walked down one of the narrow garbage chutes that passed for a hallway until he found what must have been the bathroom.

Even now, eight years after these people had died, the bathroom was still covered in a black tar of human filth and hair. Hair everywhere. Everything looked sticky and hairy all at the same time. Sam pulled back the shower curtain, and wished he hadn't. Two skeletons huddled together for warmth inside the black tub. Sam was able to just look at them for a moment; that deep unsettling feeling he had once gotten staring at these monstrosities had diminished since the opossum and really just everything.

What had these two been up to when they'd run out of air? They were huddled together, bodies entwined. Probably this, with the water running, was the only relatively clean place in the entire house. This was their sanctuary, their soap scum sanctuary in the midst of their sea of trash. They could have been fucking or fighting or just plain cleaning themselves, and doing it together to try to conserve water, try to conserve money so they could go out and buy more plastic bags. Any which way, they weren't holding any aloe, so he closed the curtain on them.

He looked at himself in the scummy mirror, and even through the haze of the dirty glass, he could see he did not look well. It had been a long few days. Big purple bags cradled his eyes, his skin was red from the sunburn he'd gotten from the fires, and his patchy facial hair and eyebrows slightly singed appearance really just set the whole look off. He tightened his hat down on his head and opened the cabinet. It wasn't pretty, but he found some aloe surprisingly. It was, like everything here, gross, but it would definitely help.

He also found a first aid kit buried at the back of the cabinet under the sink. It had surly been there for ages, forgotten entirely under the myriad of cleaning supplies, but it looked in good condition considering. Sam was glad that even in a house of such disorder, something so routine and normal still existed. It seemed like every home he walked in to he could find a first aid kit hiding in the depths of a bathroom cabinet. There was a comfort to that. It felt a little like always having a home. Which he did, it was just really far away now.

He gently peeled the tape from his neck and inspected the gashes. The five marks had become inflamed, but they didn't look infected, at least not yet. He clenched his teeth as he poured cold, cold rubbing alcohol on it and placed a new strip of gauze down as the alcohol ran down his back.

The aloe was frozen, but a fire would take care of that. At least as long as Tess didn't wake up and freak out. She whimpered slightly as he crunched his way across the room, but she didn't stir. And Bare was still out like a bearskin rug. Sam shifted the dresser and made his way outside.

The day was beautiful, and Sam breathed in the cold, crisp air. It wasn't a killer cold day, maybe 10 or 15 degrees out, which for this winter was balmy. Maybe the fire had warmed up the whole area for a bit, Sam thought despite all his knowledge of how the world worked. He trudged back inside, having forgotten to grab any fire starting materials.

He came back out a few minutes later, a bucket for melting snow full of burnable trash, and he carved out a little fire pit, a reasonable distance from the house. He used some cardboard as kindling, and soon his fire was roaring. And then the bucket was on top, and the aloe was in the water, hopefully melting, and he had nothing to do but wait. Boredom set in quickly again, and it felt like forever since he'd been bored even though he'd been almost dying of it on the road. He hardly was ever bored when he lived up at his cabin. His routine kept him busy. There was always something to do up there, some project to work on, something good to occupy his time. He had direction there. He wasn't going anywhere, but at least he wasn't going anywhere in a way that had made sense to him. He wanted to move; he felt a little like the world could end at any moment, and here he was wasting time watching snow melt.

Sam took the fifth of gin he'd found and twisted off the plastic cap, and even though it had been forever since the lips of the old residents had touched the plastic grooves of the rim, Sam wiped the thing clean on his jacket. Dirty like this place did not dissipate quickly. Sam took a swig and clenched his eyes tight, as if that were going to make the shitty gin taste any better. It didn't.

Sam remembered his father, many years ago now, probably 20 or more in the past. He remembered his father, younger then, his hat a shade of safety yellow that wouldn't be in style again ever, sitting in his white cut off T-shirt: a giant watching golf. He was drinking from a can, and at his age Sam wanted everything to be his.

"Gimmie! Gimmie some Poppy," because Sam had unfortunately called his father 'Poppy' for many years. That nickname could possibly even be attributed to their almost complete lack of a relationship for much of Sam's life and now all of his Poppy's death.

"This is beer," his Poppy had said, "You're not gonna like it."

"Yuh huh. I like beer," said Sam.

"You think so huh? Alright, have a taste, ace," his Poppy had said, his mustache twinkling with the Natural Light. Sam grasped the can, noted its texture or lack thereof, the slight moisture to it, the complete and inescapable warmness of that aluminum.

"Well, go on now. Don't be a pussy."

Sam put the can to his lips and drank some in. It was warm to the point of seeming hot, and the flavor... it tasted bad. Icky: like tub water but without the perfume of the soap. It tasted like he imagined the dishwater tasted after his Mom was done washing; it tasted like death.

"Son, one day you'll learn to love this stuff."

Sam took another hit of the gin, winced. The snow was still snow, and the plastic shell on the aloe hadn't even hardly heated up yet, let alone started melting its sweet, soothing contents.

Sam was going to make sure those two drank moderately today. Sam was a skilled survivor. He practiced moderation, he practiced responsibility, and he was going to put those skills into practice today. He thought this as he took another hit of gin. It was warming. Soothing. Maybe Tess didn't need the aloe. Maybe she just needed some gin. Some of this sweet, horrible pine-water.

Sam missed his cabin. He thought about his bed, molded all out of shape, or exactly to his shape was more accurate; he thought of his favorite chair that didn't start as a rocking chair but had a bit of a motion to it now. He missed the river, and the groves of birch and elm and maple and pine trees, and the sounds they made when they all got together. The elm and maple trees canvassed the ground, the birch threw up fences with their small, intricate bodies, and the pine trees with their splayed needles added the volume, they added the filler that really made it feel intimate, like home. He missed his lawn in the summer. He missed his lawn in the winter, sans frozen critters of course. He took another swig of gin.

It had taken him ten years to recover from his father's Natural Light stunt. He wondered about this now, having only seen his father drink that particular brand of Light Beverage that once. His father tended toward more normal brands like Miller and Coors Light: cheap drinks that you could really just slam all day and still be coherent. But Natural Light? Especially one so warm and horrible? It must have been a test. It must have been his Poppy's big parenting move: the Warm Beer Lesson. A lesson disguised as a gift, as a moment. But it had worked. Sam hadn't been one of those middle school punks, spiriting away single beers from their parents' fridge and drinking them alone in a field. He already knew it would be an absolute wasted effort.

His year of high school brought his first break in the lesson's teachings. And it was another miraculous failing. There was a pool party, an honest to goodness pool party, with girls in bikinis and chips and dips and splashing and fun, and he could only come if he brought a bottle of something. It was Sara Jo Tiki's house, and that was her rule.

Sara Jo wasn't the prettiest girl at school. She wasn't ugly by any means, it was just one of those freshman things that were done, putting girls into a hierarchy based on how much they titillated the boys nervous hormones. And Sara Jo wasn't even top 15, but her father, who had built his own wealth by inventing some computer chip that was .35 percent smaller than the previous iteration, had sold his creation to a huge company for a terrifying amount of money, and now they had a pool. Sam wondered, with all that money, why he and all the other poor kids in town had to provide the alcohol. Sam was off to the party with Marcus Cudd, probably his best friend at the time, maybe his best friend until Bare.

He and Marcus had huddled together the whole week, as they'd been given the tentative invite on a Monday after promising alcohol, and the party wasn't until Friday night. They whispered about how they were possibly going to scrounge up that magical, alcoholic ticket. Marcus' parents were recovering alcoholics, his mother a cop and his father had worked demolition for a construction crew before his drinking had led to an unfortunate jackhammer slip up that relieved a fellow worker of three toes. So Marcus' house was pretty much out of the question as a place to find alcohol, although Sam had his suspicions about a few hiding places. But Marcus didn't want to think that way, so an alternative it was.

What if they stood outside the liquor store and asked an old man to buy them a bottle? Yeah, but what if the old man was a cop? What if he said no? What if he knew Marcus' mom? Then they'd both go to jail, and their lives would be ruined, and they'd miss the party.

Well then what? Try to walk in to the liquor store and just look confident? I've done this a thousand times, oh, thank you for the compliment, I haven't been asked how old I was in many years, ho ho ho... oh, no this is adult onset acne, very sad, and we both just have incredibly young faces...

Sam considered talking to the kids who loitered in the art hall, the art kids who smoked out back every lunch period and were trying their best to keep the grunge look alive even though that was basically their parents' generation's music. They seemed like exactly the type of people who could help them, except both Sam and Marcus were too intimidated by them to ask. So that was out too. Marcus suggested Sam ask his older brother Rodney, but Sam didn't want the fact that he'd gotten booze to find its way back to his parents. Rodney could be a loose cannon like that.

In the end they decided it would be safest and easiest to just raid Sam's parents' liquor cabinet. His folks mostly drank beer. His mother was sometimes inclined toward wine, but they did have a liquor cabinet in the kitchen high above the stove away from the prying fingers of children. It was stocked with whatever bottles had been gifted to them, or they had bought on sale or a whim. There were bottles of vodka, sometimes used for Bloody Marys, there were bottles of rum for the obligatory summertime Rum 'N Coke, and probably a dozen other bottles that Sam didn't know and couldn't remember.

So when the day came, Friday, a glorious school Friday where the clock on the wall just seemed to crawl along its circle, Sam and Marcus came back to an empty home. Sam pulled a chair up to the stove, and perched himself atop the thing. He reached his hand way, way back into the unseen, untouched depths of the cabinet and pulled out what felt to be the most full bottle of the forgotten bunch. Score!

As fast as he could, as if in that one moment of holding the bottle, the bottle that spelled his victory, the bottle that was his ticket to a next-level flesh show, might be spirited away from him if it were exposed to the open air for more than a few seconds. He passed the bottle to Marcus' waiting hands and open bookbag, and they were done. They'd done it.

Sam's heart pounded violently as he carefully placed the chair back, making totally sure it went back to its exact, original position. He just knew if his mother saw the chair out of place even a millimeter she would know what mischief it had been a party to. And then they waited, Marcus' bookbag the white elephant in the room, waiting for Sam's mother to return from work so they could ask her for a ride.

Finally, after what felt like an eternity of waiting and straining to not to look anywhere near the bag, the garage door sprang to life, and they both shuffled to try and look like they had been busy.

"Hello?" his mother called to the house.

"Hey Mom! How was work? How are you today? You're looking nice," Sam blurted as he walked to greet his mother, Marcus trailing a few steps behind.

"Yeah, you look nice today, Mrs. M," Marcus said. Sam shot Marcus a dirty look. Don't call my mom good looking you perv.

"Ok, what do you want?" his mother had said, knowing she only ever got a greeting like this if there was something in it for her children.

"I was just wondering if you could maybe, pretty please, please please, please drive us to a party? Not like a party party, but a party at Sara Jo's tonight? Please? You wouldn't even have to pick us up; we'll walk to Marcus's house after and sleep there. It'd just be a little drive."

Sam's mom gave him a look as if she knew what he was up to, and that made Sam's heart jump into his throat.

"Then why did you take the bus back here if it's walking distance from Marcus' house? Ay yi yi, you kids," she said easing Sam's tension.

"Sam wanted to drop off his bookbag is all," Marcus said. Sam glared at Marcus again. Don't bring up the bookbags stupid! Marcus' eyes widened as he realized what he'd done and looked down at his own bag clasped between his hands.

"I also wanted to change. It's a pool party. Needed a towel. I'm going to go grab a towel."

"Alright. Do you need to bring anything to this party? Food or drinks or anything?"

"No," Sam replied too forcefully and too quickly, "No, her dad is super rich. They'll have everything. We just needed swim suits and stuff."

"Oh that's right, they're the ones with that mansion over in Elm Bluff, right?"

"Yeah! That's the one."

"That's one heck of a place. You ought to make nice with her Sam. She could be your meal ticket."

"Mom."

Marcus giggled, and Sam's mom winked.

"Ok, well what time do you need to be there by?"

Sam looked at Marcus. They were doing it; they were pulling this heist off!

"Seven, seven-thirty?"

"Ok, I'm going to go get some groceries, and I'll give you a ride after that. But you'll have to help me unload. Deal?"

"Deal," they said in unison.

At seven forty-five they walked through the wooden gate, flip-flops smacking and the party already roaring, and it felt like a movie. Sam's mother had dropped them off down the street, out of view of any debauchery that might have been happening, and she had told them she hoped they had a really nice time. If only she knew! They walked into the back where a beautiful, multi-tiered pool and hot tub housed beautiful, almost nude creatures. The whole thing fenced in tastefully by rows of fir trees and sweet scented lilacs and other beautiful bushes all draped in nets of white, twinkling Christmas lights. It was a tropical paradise somehow uprooted and nested into the middle of South Dakota. There were circles of girls and boys, all wearing as little as possible, placed strategically around the backyard for maximum coolness, and a table full of bottles of alcohol and single beers and some chips and cookies and other things that make a party more rounded. Empty pizza boxes littered the ground; pizza didn't last long around a team of high schoolers.

The popular music of the time added weight to their glorious entrance, and they both took on the swagger of people they'd only ever seen on TV. The world slowed as Marcus swung his backpack off, and they rolled up to the snacks table. Lisa Franklin, Sara Jo's best friend in the whole world stopped the boys with a wave of her hand: showing them her palm and then turning that palm up and beckoning them to hand it over. Marcus, an excited grin overtaking his face, unzipped his backpack as Sam nodded coolly at a group of girls, and Marcus pulled out the full bottle of vermouth. No one knew any better. They didn't know the difference between alcohols and mixers for horrible drinks. Fortified herb wine.

"Great," Lisa said, "Take a shot!"

She poured two large, large, too large shots into red solo cups.

"Enjoy guys, have fun or whatever, and like, don't piss in the pool. I'm serious. Like totally serious. And don't perv on us or anything ok? Great thanks!" she chirped and disappeared into the party.

Sam and Marcus looked at each other, raised the red cups in a cheer, and shot the vermouth down. Their faces couldn't come close to hiding their disgust. This was worse than warm Natural Light, this was like drinking a full cup of soy sauce, and as they tried to keep it down, the whole experience got great punctuation when Chaz Bertlett slamming his giant, football handling palms into Sam and Marcus' backs.

"Boys! Ya made it!"

They coughed, and Sam threw up a little but managed to swallow it back down. It wasn't any better the second time.

"Hey, uh, hey Chaz," Marcus said as Sam managed his vomit situation.

"What'd you boys bring?"

"Uh," Sam read the label, "Vir-mouth, sweet vir-mouth." Sweet?

"Ha. Ha! HA HA HA! HEY BOYS!" Chaz waved over a group of boys that pretty much all looked like him: large, muscular, stupid. They were cartoon characters, but cartoon characters every high school seemed to possess. They may have had some redeeming or interesting qualities hidden deep down, but years of sports and peer pressure had buried any of that nonsense under thick layers of testosterone.

"Check out what Spaz and Spazrina brought to the party!"

The cartoons gwaffawed; they didn't really understand the joke yet.

"Boys, do you like vermouth?"

"Not much, Chaz," a boy everyone called 'Hammer' said. Chaz looked at Hammer, hating his stupidity but still loving the moment.

"I was askin' Spazrina here," Chaz said as he punched Sam in the chest.

"Why am I Spazrina?" Sam asked, rubbing where he'd been hit.

"Let's see you drink a little more of that vermouth, fellas. You look thirsty!"

"Actually, I'm ok for now... thought I might swim for a minute, maybe say hi to some people," Sam said.

"No, I think you look thirsty. Doesn't he look thirsty boys?"

They all thought Sam and Marcus looked thirsty, so Chaz took the bottle of vermouth and poured it into their waiting red cups, letting the liquid slap inside the bottle as the cups filled to the brim.

"Drink up."

"Really, we're ok," Marcus said weakly.

"Drink it," Chaz said, his tone dropping from jovial to incredibly serious. They, with their muscles and hip swim trunks loomed over Sam and Marcus, who wavered, trapped, cups dangerously full of the horrible brown swill.

So they drank it. What other option did they have? Chaz and Hammer and the boys watched as the liquid disappeared. And they did it, and somehow, under the mean, watchful gaze of their greater peers, they managed to keep it down.

"Great job boys," Chaz said.

"Yeah!" Hammer added uselessly.

"Now enjoy the party. Losers," he said as he faded away into a sea of high fives.

And then they waited. They mingled, but they mingled like a kamikaze pilot mingles in line at an airport: they knew they were ticking time bombs. They just had to be. And then it happened. The momentum of the party itself tuned up, and they tuned up with it. Except instead of staying rational and flirty like the rest of the partygoers, Sam and Marcus turned wild. Their gangster leans turned into stumbles, their party chatter turned into slurs and sloppy winks, and when they hit the pool? That's when it turned from a little wild to complete, irredeemable mayhem.

The rest of the partygoers recoiled in embarrassment, watching in horrified awe as the two bucked and squirmed on pool toys, splashed wildly, hooted at the girls, and made complete and utter asses of themselves. Sam, at some point after he'd thoroughly lost a second invite to a Sara Jo party, tried to get up out of the pool.

But it was harder than it looked, and he slipped back, knocking his head against Marcus,' as Marcus was inexplicably waiting in line to get out of the pool at the same arbitrary point as Sam. This in absolute classic Sam style caused him to throw up all that inky vermouth into Sara Jo's beautiful pool. The black stain spread from his body, and Sam threw up again, getting the rest of the filth out of his stomach. Chunks of pretzel and ridged chip and sour cream spread floated away into the horrified screams of all the girls Sam wanted so desperately to see naked. He looked around as he pulled Marcus's face up out of the tainted water, and every peer had some level of disgust, anger, and terror etched into their grooveless features. Sam slapped Marcus awake, sending an extra torrent of blood from his already torrential nose splashing into the water.

"You fucking assholes," Sara Jo screamed at them, "My *father* is going to kill you."

"I'm going to kill 'em," Chaz added as he advanced on the pool. Luckily though, no one wanted to get into the filthy water. Even to kick their asses.

"Get out," Sara Jo yelled, and a chorus of their peers added their own slurs and hate slogans at the young boys. And they did. Sam and Marcus ran out of the pool, crashed through the bushes and trees, and fled into the woods, where naturally they got lost.

"My favorite shirt was back there," Marcus said at one point as they tried to double back, tried desperately to hear the party that must have still been raging, even in their absence.

Sam could swear he heard Chaz and the boys yelling though.

"Forget about it, ok?"

"It was my best shirt."

"We can never go back there."

"I was so drunk."

"Yeah, fucking Chaz."

"Such a fucking asshole."

"Where are we?"

"I don't know."

And after that night, lost in the woods, sleeping in the cold in nothing but their cold, damp swim trunks, Marcus and Sam drifted apart. It especially didn't help that Sam had looked up the percentage of alcohol in vermouth and found it was no stronger than that Natural Light his father had given him all those years back. The fact that they hadn't actually been drunk, or they shouldn't have actually been drunk, that their acts of foolery had really just been them, overexcited and, as Chaz had dubbed them, Spaz-like, or Spazrina-like in Sam's case, well, Sam and Marcus just couldn't face each other anymore.

But one good thing did come from their night frozen in the woods: Sam became increasingly interested in wilderness survival. He went camping most weekends, alone of course, and read survivalist literature any time he could. That failed party going experience had shaped Sam in more ways than he could count; it was responsible for his lack of friends, but it also might have been responsible for Sam being able to survive out in the woods these past years. So he was mostly undecided on how he really felt about the whole experience.

Sam took another swig of gin. He was glad he had friends inside. It warmed his heart more than the gin did.

"Aloe, aloe, aloe," he said to the bottle as he shook it. It was really getting somewhere. He was pretty sure that once Tess got up the stuff would be ready to soothe her pain. He was considering walking inside and rubbing it on while she was still out, try to soothe it so she could wake feeling nice, but the memory of Bare snapping at him was still too fresh. He liked his fingers, and he was rather inclined to keep them. He got up and peeked inside the front door. The place was still as depressing as ever, but the animals had shifted some. Sam wished he could leave them a note so he could go off and scrounge for supplies, but he didn't really want them to think he'd abandoned them or something. Or worse, he didn't want them to wander off on their own to try to find him. Was that narcissism? No, just logical thinking probably. He was their ride.

He was done waiting though.

"Psst, hey guys."

They didn't move, so he upped the decibels a bit.

"Hey, Tess, Bare, are you up? Hey are you up? Hey guys, it's morning."

He loomed over them.

"Hey guys, I've got breakfast."

Sam was sure that one would work. And maybe it still would. He went into the kitchen and got out the cans of franks and beans and a can of Spam he had found. Spam would outlast everything on this earth, he thought as he pulled off the tab on top, revealing the spongy meat-product. He walked them back and placed them under the animals' noses. Soon their nostrils twitched, then their bodies, and then both of them were sitting up, blinking at the daylight streaming through the door.

"Hi," Sam said, "Good morning."

They groaned.

"I've got some breakfast here for you," Sam said, nodding at the plates he'd prepared for them, "And when you're ready I've got some water outside and some aloe to help with your burns Tess. How do they feel? Are you ok?"

Tess gave a slight nod or headshake, and Sam couldn't tell if that was positive or not.

"Well your face looks good, I can tell you that much," he said.

"Thanks," said Tess, gritting her teeth. It looked like it hurt.

"Her face always looks like nice," Bare said, woozy from sleep.

Tess tried to smile but quit when it got difficult.

"I feel like death," said Bare.

"Well don't become death, you know? Ha, like, I am become death, destroyer of worlds, or whatever. The world's already doing pretty well on its lonesome with that, you know?"

Tess and Bare just stared at them. Tough crowd.

"Well I'll be outside when you want a drink. I've got some alcohol out here too."

Bare groaned at the thought of drinking more, but he leaned over and tucked into his plate of food. Sam smiled as he walked outside. It was nice having friends.

89

Eventually Bare and Tess got up, got fed, and drank their fill of water, although Tess made sure to stay at least ten feet away from the small fire. Sam had applied the aloe and bandaged her wounds up, and they would heal, which was good.

After they'd each forced down a little more alcohol, just to be safe, they wandered off along the road in search of new transportation. Their walk took them into the town proper, which was as squalid and unfortunate as the outskirts were, but there were trucks and cars here, and it was just a matter of time before Sam hit on the right one. Which he did in a red Chevy that happened to have a great hardtop, which would house Bare and Tess quite well once he'd found some padding. He walked down the main street and found a second hand store with two beds displayedin the window. Except it was locked.

He looked back at Bare for some guidance.

"Break it on open," he said, matter-of-factly.

Fair enough. Sam grabbed a stone and threw it at the window, but it bounced off uselessly. He tore a bench away from the ice's grasp and hurled that at the window, which now shattered cinematically. Sam used the bench to clear away the extra shards that pointed like knives from the frame and then stepped inside.

Twenty minutes later they were on their way, Tess and Bare snug in the back, and Sam alone up front. There was something eerily familiar about this situation, about this isolation that now felt awful to him. He used to thrive on isolation. What had happened to him?

He pondered this as he drove. And drove and drove.

He felt like he'd been driving forever when he saw the sign:

WELCOME TO AMERICA, it read. International Falls! They had made it.

He crossed the bridge, which meant crashing through a couple gates, weaving around a few cars, and generally causing mischief that in another day and age would have gotten him thrown in jail for a solid stretch. It felt good. It was fun, and it was nice to be able to find fun, even in all this crazy.

Northern Minnesota looked good to Sam. There was something decidedly American about it, something deeply normal, which felt nice after everything that had happened. Sam rolled down his window and waved at the imaginary greeting party as he passed by. They were jumping and cheering in his head, except he saw a squirrel jump off the bridge, presumably to splatter on the ice below. Well, it looked like the American animals were taking themselves out as well. He just had to hope that cat hadn't killed himself.

There was a grocery, a food place, Keebler's Grocery. This seemed like a reasonable spot to stop.

He walked in and called out his customary, "Hello?"

"Hello?" replied a voice. Sam backed out of the store.

"Hey Bare?" Bare was still sitting in the back of the pickup.

"Wassup?"

"Someone said hello to me in there, can you come with me?"

"Someone said hello to you?"

"Yeah, just… last time that happened it wasn't good."

"So you want me to come in with you?"

"Yes please."

"Alrighty, no problem. You think they'll have nice liquor in here?" Bare asked as he trotted over to Sam, "We're getting real tired of this crap from that house."

"You doing alright though?"

"Oh yah buddy, never been to America before. Never had a passport don't-cha-know. I do miss the Caribou Lounge though. Nice place, real nice folks there," Bare said as they stepped back inside the grocery. Sam's guilt came back full force. He really should just tell Bare. Get it over with. It'd be like a Band-Aid and then they could just get back to finding people with power, somewhere they could live and not feel the need to kill themselves.

"Hey, who's there?" Sam asked as he walked in again.

"Who are you man?" the voice asked back.

"Uh, my name's Sam, and this is my friend Bare," said Sam.

"You ain't crazies is ya?"

"No, I don't think so," said Sam.

"Good, I don't allow any crazies in here. No way."

"I hear that," said Bare.

"What the heck was that?"

Bare looked at Sam and shrugged.

"Can we come in?" asked Sam.

"Oh yeah man! Come on in. Been a while since I saw some other folks," said the voice changing its tone on a dime. Sam and Bare walked further into the grocery.

"Woah," the guy said as Bare and Sam rounded an aisle and saw him camped out in the dark, melted into a comfy office chair surrounded by blankets and wrappers. The guy was scrawny, his hair long, but Sam could see a halo of baldness forming. The guy's mouth dropped when he saw Bare, and Sam could see he had one snaggle tooth out front.

"Is that real?"

"Howdy, I'm Bare," said Bare.

"You do know there's a bear right next to you dude," the guy said to Sam as if he hadn't heard Bare.

"Bare like Barry, not like Bear, but I guess also like bear. He's cool," Sam concluded, "Oh, and I'm Sam. It's great to see another human being."

Sam went in for a handshake, but the guy was too busy staring at Bare to notice. Sam looked at his extended palm and then tentatively lowered it, pretending he had to wipe something off on his pants.

"This is trippy man."

"What is?"

"You got a bear right *there* man. Did you train it or something?"

"Bare? What, no. Hey, this is gonna be a strange question, but you haven't seen a cat around maybe?

"Like Mister Fresh?"

"Mister Fresh?"

"Yeah, we listen to the radio together."

"Radio? What?"

"Radio man. Got me a crank radio. It's dead right now, but there's some funny shows on man," the guy said as he demonstrated through gesture what a crank radio was.

"Wait, seriously?"

The guy was staring at Bare still, transfixed.

"That's fuckin' crazy man."

"Let's go back to the radio," Sam said.

"Can't man, it's dead right now. And I ain't about to crank the damn thing just so we can hear the same stupid shows, you know?"

"No, I really don't. I was living up in Canada."

"Canada…"

"Yeah Canada, and I didn't have a radio. Didn't figure… how many radio stations are there?"

"Like in the world, man?"

"Why are you living up here all alone?"

"Man… that's a story."

"What's your name again?" Bare chimed in.

The guy stared at Bare again and then looked at Sam with a look that said, can you believe this shit? Sam was losing patience with this guy, and he didn't even know his name yet.

"Your name is," Sam suggested.

"Oh, man, yeah, totally, I'm Lewis but my friends call me Buck."

"Dibs on calling him Buck," Bare said with a sideways smile at Sam.

"That bear isn't going to like maul us or anything, is he? He's freakin' me out."

"Ok Lewis-"

"Buck. Please, we're a rare breed now, we're all brothers man. Want a hit?"

Buck lifted up a big purple bong, and it put a lot of their conversation into perspective. Sam had never been good at smoking weed. He'd only tried it once, and naturally he'd thrown up. The doctors all told him he didn't have a stomach issue, that all the vomit was probably nerves, but what did doctors know?

"I would," Bear said.

Buck looked at Bare confused.

"Where'd you get weed?"

"Man, why do you think I'm up here all alone man?"

"You got lost?"

"Ha, dude, no," Buck said laughing hard, "No, check it out, International Falls is home of some of the dopest kush on the green globe my man."

How had this guy survived the apocalypse? Sam took a moment to consider the only people he'd met so far had been big time drug addicts. What if the only people to survive were himself and a bunch of dope heads? A bunch of tweaking meth addicts and coke fiends and like, whatever other drugs were out there that Sam hadn't even heard about in his days in society.

"Yeah man, there was just this like sick patch up here my buddy ran, like shit from the government, so you know it's bomb, and like after the shit went down, like when people all took the plunge, I figured I'd come up here and save the stuff. I wasn't doin' much else, just like chillin' you know?"

"Sure."

"Yeah, so I came up here, and I been keepin' the dream alive man. Mad quiet up here though."

"Where's the greenhouse?" Sam asked.

"Oh, ho ho ho, yeah, ok, like I'd just tell you where my fuckin' stash is, man. You think I was born yesterday? No way."

Sam had been working his ass off to stay fed, to stay alive for the last eight years, and this guy had clearly just been sitting here getting high and eating decade old Oreos. Sam's anger rose right up in him as he scratched at his crotch.

"You want a hit of this dudeski?"

"You won't get much out of him," a feminine voice said from the back of the dark store.

"What?"

"You want a hit?" said Buck again.

"Who's back there?"

"Back where?"

"I believe you're looking for me," the voice said, "Follow me."

"Where?"

"What?" asked Buck.

Sam walked past Buck and into the back.

"Wait! You can't just leave me here with a fuckin' bear man," Buck said as Sam walked away.

"Could I have a hit?" asked Bare.

She was an orange tabby, shaggy haired, but noble looking: like a tiny lion.

"In here child," she said to Sam as she circled against a door with a sign written in crayon on a beer insert. The sign read: Danger!!! Keep Out! Dangerus!!!

Sam opened the door and followed the cat inside.

He was pretty sure he was getting high just standing in this room. There were rows and rows of plants that had grown at least four feet tall. Their splayed leaves danced with the breeze from the open door. The smell wasn't unpleasant, but it was strange like some sort of cleaning solution, like some alternative hippy shampoo or something. Not unpleasant but not nice either. It was like a mildly pleasant fart.

"You've come a long way."

"How do you know?"

"I know much."

"I heard there was a cat in this town who was incredibly... wise. Connected to nature I guess. Is that you? Because that would be amazing."

"You are searching for answers. Answers to why you survived, why our brethren have taken to killing themselves now."

"Yes. Yes that's exactly what I'm looking for."

"There is danger, worse than ever before facing us. I have seen a man."

"Buck?"

"No. Well yes, I keep him around to feed me. My meditation leaves me no time to hunt," she said.

"So there are other people alive?"

"Many, but not for long. There is a man threatening to destroy everyone."

"Alright, who is he? Let's take care of it."

"I know not who he is, but I do know that you possess something he wants."

There were more people alive. Possibly many. His self-induced exile might not have been necessary. He wasn't alone! Hopefully these people weren't all like Buck and Carol, but at least there were people! Sam smiled. It was a big, genuine smile.

"What's your name?"

"I am a receptacle for Nature, I have no true name. But my servant out there refers to me as Mister Fresh."

"But you're a woman, or ah, a lady cat."

"This irony is not lost to me," she said as she hopped up onto a table littered with gardening supplies and food wrappers. And there was the crank radio, "Take this radio now, it will prove the things I say."

Sam did as he was told. He grasped the cheap little device in his hands. He turned the switch to 'ON,' but it was dead. Buck hadn't been lying. Sam imagined Buck didn't really have the capacity for lies. He unhooked the hand crank that slid into the plastic body of the thing and started to crank. It resisted slightly and made a sound like a roller coaster approaching a big drop off, and that's how Sam started to feel. This was it! He was about to get some answers. He was about to find people and girls and answers and hopefully girls!

Carol was a big mistake. He shouldn't have given it away like that. Not to someone like Carol. She could have been his grandma if his grandma had been a smack addict and had been like 60% tattoos. All he could remember now were the veins around her nipples and the stifling fragrance of her body odor. All her odors. And her corpse bursting into flames. That would probably never leave his head. Well he definitely wasn't going to start a fire here.

He cranked at double speed for a moment, one last push, and then flicked the thing into the 'ON' position. A light static popped into the room, serenading the plants and Sam with hope. Sam began to get nervous as he twisted the dials, searching the channels... And then through the static:

"-have it and get more, too. You know Marty?"

"I sure do Jake."

"So a reminder ya'll, the world isn't dead, it just held its breath for a moment."

"But don't hold yours. Join us in Chicago, that's right the Windee city. We have food, more attractions than you can shake a stick at-"

"That's right ladies and gentleman, and don't forget to visit everyone's favorite: The Michael Crichton Memorial Zoo!"

"Also don't forget, our glorious leader Mr. Smith, his real name folks, believe it or not, is still looking to complete his collection!"

"His collection?"

"Oh that wily, rich old wonderful man, Mr. Smith and-"

KRSSHHKK, the radio cut out for a moment. Sam desperately wound it until:

"Just a few more and maybe he'll leave the city to me!"

"Dream on big man."

"Hey a man can dream, Marty."

Under their breath:

"I just said that Jake. You repeat me like that and we sound stupid."

"Sorry, Marty."

"So come on down because we're alive and most of your friends aren't!"

"We're gonna take a quick break, but leave you with this old classic by-"

And the thing died again. Sam didn't rewind it, he had heard enough, and it was wonderful.

Chicago.

"Do you believe me now child?"

"I didn't really not believe you in the first place."

"Good. You will know the one by the crescent moon. But remember, you hold the key to his plans. Your sickness is his key."

"My sickness? Wait, what? That's too cryptic."

Mister Fresh started to cough, and she bent her head down, hacking now. She spit out something shiny and bloody. That didn't look good. Maybe she'd meant her own sickness?

"I'm not long for this world," she said, "I needed to pass the message on to you before I went though. I am glad you came child. Hold me a moment, my voice grows weak."

Sam leaned over and picked her up, a little tentative as he looked at the gross bloody glob.

"It will not be easy to stop him, but you must. If you don't the whole world will die. Nature has told me she's given up, she was not strong enough to destroy the human plague, no offense, but she doesn't want her followers to suffer. Thus the deaths.

"Wait, by Nature, do you mean like… like a god?"

"No, I mean Nature. Nature is above man's gods; nature exists and is logical and true. You humans just never learned to listen to her. And you were killing her."

"Sorry, I didn't know."

"It's not your fault you're blind. Now you must stop the man with the crescent moon, and perhaps you can change the world. Prove once again to Nature that man can do good, that he can cause something but suffering and there will be peace. You are special. You would not be able to understand me if you weren't, and that means you are capable of greatness. Now good luck, child," Mister Fresh said as she started to cough again. She made choking noises, and what looked like a lung started to push from her open mouth. Sam, freaked out and dropped her to the ground. She made one last push and got whatever that gross red sack was halfway out her mouth and then stopped moving.

Mister Fresh's eyes were open. She was dead.

Ok, he could have used a bit of clarification on all that. He didn't know what a crescent moon-man was. And his sickness? Was he sick? That wasn't good. Even if he was, how did this cat know?

Ok, this wasn't going to get him anywhere. Chicago. That's where he had to go. He backed out of the greenhouse.

Buck and Bare were lounging and eating potato chips.

With his mouth full, Buck said, "Hey, what's up man, I'm Buck. This is my friend. He's a bear."

"We've met."

Buck tried to bite at the air around where a middle finger should have been.

"Woah," he said.

"Please don't tell me you're surprised you don't have a finger. That cannot be a thing you just forget."

"Ha, weird. I don't even bite my nails anymore," he said, showing them the rest of his digits. The nails were indeed long and filthy.

"Do you mind if we take some food for our trip?"

"Sure man, whatever. Just don't take any of the good stuff. Like, don't touch the cookies. I got dibs."

"I think I'm gonna go check on Tess, hey?" Bare said.

"Sounds good. I'll be out in a minute."

"You look pretty crazy talking to that bear dude," Buck said as Bare walked away.

"Might be," said Sam. Could Buck not hear the animals?

Sam grabbed a cart and filled it right up with whatever cans struck his fancy as he pondered that. He also grabbed a box of cookies because apparently he was in a spiteful mood.

"Bye Buck," he said as he left. Buck responded with a coughing fit, which seemed appropriate. Sam felt bad about Mister Fresh. There went Buck's only friend.

"Nice guy," Bare said as Sam approached the truck.

"Tess, how you feeling?"

Tess' lips lifted around her teeth in a weak smile.

"Like new," she said, "Thanks for the aloe, that really helped."

"Hey, my pleasure. Guys, guess what!"

Bare and Tess were surprised by Sam's sudden giddiness.

"What?" they said at the same time.

"Chicago."

"What?" Again in unison.

"It's a city, and apparently there are people there! I found the cat. She's dead now, but-"

"You killed a cat?" said Tess.

"No," Sam said his guilt at the forefront again, "No, she just died. I think she was old. But she told me the reason there's the buzz is because Nature has given up. She said there's someone in Chicago we need to stop, and if we do then everything will go back to normal."

"That's great," Tess said, wincing at the burns.

"Ok, the burns still look bad. Let's see if Buck has any burn cream or anything. I'll be right back," said Sam, at his friend's pain. He walked back into the grocery.

"Hello?" said Buck.

"It's just me again."

"Who?"

"It's Sam."

"Hey man, I don't want any crazies in here."

Seriously?

"Is there a pharmacy or something in here Buck? I need to find some burn ointment."

"Hahaha, burn. Yeah man."

And there was the sound of that bong. Sam would find it himself. He grabbed more food as he went along; he figured he might as well. Buck would never notice, and International Falls probably had another grocery somewhere. And here was the pharmacy.

He grabbed some Vicatin despite his own distaste for the stuff, and he grabbed some burn cream. Also some Tums; it probably wasn't going to hurt him to keep his stomach regular. He wanted to make a good impression in Chicago, and he didn't want that to include vomiting on some poor, pretty girl who deigned to talk to him.

On that whim he grabbed a stick of deodorant, a razor, and a pair of scissors as well. And he was at the door once more.

"Bye Buck. Good luck up here."

"Later dude! Come again."

"We'll see."

"Big time."

"By the way, how'd you lose your middle finger?"

"Oh man, that? Airplane crash, man. Crazy shit."

"Have a good one, Buck," Sam said.

"Always."

Plane crash? Yeah fucking right.

And Sam was out the door and back to the truck. He doctored Tess up and then they were off: the Big Chicago Road Trip.

94

He'd made this trip once before, the Chicago drive, but that was way back in eighth grade. Many eighth grade classes, he was told, made treks over to Washington DC: a troupe of hormones wandering around America's precious history. But his school had been more than broke. They'd wasted a huge amount of their money on a swindler who had come into the town and promised to revolutionize their building by adding solar power, for a small price of course. He promised they'd make the whole fee back in less than a year with all the money they'd be saving on electricity costs. His pitch had been charming and enthusiastic. How could they say no?

And it was a dream come true. Completely worth the arts budget and the music budget and most of the extracurricular budgets for that matter. The man had put on a big show as he installed black tag board with sheets of tin foil glued to them. He'd traced out the pattern of power cells on the things, and from the ground they did look a lot like the solar cells they'd all seen on TV. So the school had secretly shelled out the money, and the man had disappeared into the depths of America to trick other Americans out of their government sanctioned educations.

They didn't even get through the first month to find out they'd been saving no money on electricity though when a small, regional aircraft containing twelve people had the tin foil on the top of the school reflect back a beam of hot light at their pilot's eyes like a giant magnifying glass. This, he yelled at whoever was listening as they went down, completely blinded him. It was a fluke, but the plane went down and crashed apart in a cornfield. There were only two survivors, and they and the families of all who had died sued the school district for their irresponsibility in having giant reflectors covering their roof.

And then, of course, the swindle and the scandal came to light, and Sam's school was out about ten years worth of budgets. Whoops. Anyway, that was how it came to be that Sam's class, even with the high co-pay on the field trips, were not able to afford DC and were forced to drive down to Chicago instead on an old bus that had once been used to house prisoners. It even had the caging separating the driver and the teachers from the students. The chaperones wondered at how no one had ever thought to use these for educational purposes before. It saved them a whole lot of headache.

So Sam knew the drive in good conditions would probably take only about 10 or 12 hours, and he absolutely couldn't wait. He was giddy as he pulled away from Buck's Weed Emporium and distanced himself further and further from where he had come to identify as home. But it mattered less to him now that he had a real destination. Chicago here he came!

They worked their way down Minnesota, and crossed into Wisconsin, taking roads that skipped Minneapolis. Minneapolis was connected in his head with his own past and with Carol's, and it held some connotations that he had no interest in confronting. About halfway down Wisconsin his drooping eyelids told him he needed to be done for the day, and he pulled up to the first nice house he could find. He opened the back of the truck bed, and Tess and Bare piled out.

"How'd you guys manage," Sam asked them.

"Pretty good. It's warmer down here," Tess said. She was looking better too. Her burns looked less angry beneath the bandages. That was good.

"Let's get inside though," Bare said, "It ain't that warm out, hey?"

Everything was a question with Bare. He wondered if that was a Canadian thing. Americans never questioned anything.

They walked into the skeleton-free entryway of the home. It was incredible how many homes were unlocked. Did no one believe in locking doors in this part of the world? Although Sam couldn't actually remember his parents locking their door either. Yet every night, in the middle of nowhere Canada, Sam had dead bolted his. He wondered what this said about him as a person. He locked the door behind them. Better safe than sorry.

Sam built a fire in the fireplace, but only under the promise to Tess that he'd put it out before they went to sleep. She *had* almost burned to death. He could give her this one, but he really wasn't looking forward to the night of freezing cold. What these beasts didn't seem to get was that Sam didn't have a nice fur coat to keep him warm. He had a swatch of chest hair, a bit of facial hair, a good bushel of pubes, and that was about it. And those hairs were basically decoration. So it was another evening of collecting as many blankets as possible and building a sleeping nest for the three of them.

After he'd gotten some water he went to the bathroom, shaved, and cut his hair. He thought he looked pretty presentable now. He'd even picked up some new clothes in one of the closets. He wanted to look good for his big day.

He walked back out to his friends, excited for them to fawn over his new look.

"Where were you the night the power went out?" Tess asked, dropping him out of his narcissism and plunging him directly into the place where all his guilt swirled and gnawed at him. Maybe that's why he threw up so much; all that guilt just tore at his stomach lining, churning those juices so much that they had no choice but to come flying back up at the smallest provocation.

"I just went for a ride. I needed to cool my head."

"Yeah. I just can't shake this feeling though, this thing where it just seems so perfect that you disappear, and then the power goes out, and everyone goes crazy. It's just weird you know?"

"Yeah," said Sam. Bare shifted, uncomfortable.

"How are those burns?" he asked Tess.

"They're about the same as they were five minutes ago," she said in reference to the time five minutes ago he had asked the same exact thing, with the same exact intonation, and with the same exact results.

"Oh, good. I'm glad they haven't gotten worse."

Bare yawned, his teeth glinting yellow in the light of the fire.

"Tess, I feel like I don't actually know that much about you. You have to have a story," Sam said, dodging. He would tell them what happened, he really would, but right now he just wasn't ready. It was too soon, and they... he wanted them to be comfortable in Chicago first. He couldn't tell them he destroyed their old home before he'd delivered on a new one. He just couldn't do that.

"Oh, it's all boring, and Bare's heard it all already," she said. Sam felt a pang of jealousy, he wasn't a fan of being left out, and he supposed he was still nervous that Tess was on track to steal all of Bare's time and attention away from him.

"Oh, I don't mind one bit," Bare said, happy that some of the tension was leaking out of the cozy room.

"Like, how'd you end up at the Caribou?" Sam asked.

"Are you actually interested?" she asked back.

"Yes," the boys said in unison.

"I love this story," Bare added as he made eyes at Tess.

"Alright, well, let's see…"

And despite her burnt face, she started her story for them. She was born a regular gray wolf pup. Her father, who was an archetypical alpha male, led her pack. He was an imposing wolf, even by wolf standards. He was monstrous, muscular, and intimidating. His hair was longer, shaggy, and regal, as if his parents had been a she-wolf and a lion. The coloring of his face made it look like his eyes were housed in white diamonds as well, adding to the regality. He was also a complete asshole, and Tess, being cleverer than many of her relatives and taking more of the empathetic cues from her social culture, hated the way her father made the pack kill for fun.

There weren't many wolf packs around when Tess had been born. The older wolves told stories of how there used to be battles over territories, how wolves had fought each other as opposed to working together to take down caribou or moose so they could eat. And then, when they were weak and tired, that was when the humans came in and took them out.

"No offense, Sam," she said.

"Oh none taken. I've never killed a wolf before," he said.

"If you'd met my pack, you'd have been dead before you could scream," Tess said. Sam just nodded. It was probably true, although Sam *was* fast to scream.

So Tess' father, to show just how far he'd broken from this cycle he'd been born in to, killed at every chance. He killed for fun and taught Tess' brothers and some of her sisters to do the same. She was always heartbroken when one of her people would howl over a kill, summoning the rest who hadn't been party to the murder, and Tess would come trotting over to see a fawn, those big doe eyes still shining even in death. Or a young coyote, what Tess perceived as her own cousins, murdered at the feet of her family. It was disgusting to her. Not that she didn't share in the eating when it happened, but it was the ones they just left there to rot, more as a message to other creatures about who was in charge; those corpses bothered her. It was senseless and dumb, and she hated her father for it.

Sam smiled as he thought about Tess full of teenaged angst. A black hoodie pulled over her gray fur, her large, pointed ears pierced in non-traditional ways, her black lips smeared with greasy, blacker lipstick. He held in his laughter though, he didn't really want to explain that thought process aloud. He didn't imagine his company would understand the humor. Or what a hoodie was.

Tess was saying how she was always surprised the rest of the animals in their territory didn't just up and leave. Why didn't they just walk away from this place of senseless and ceaseless murder? It was their home too, she supposed, and no one ever expects the worse to happen to them.

So finally, in a fit of youthful rebellion, she ran away. It was unprecedented, someone leaving the pack, but she really wanted to show her father what was what.

She left after a particularly gruesome display perpetrated by her father and three of her oldest brothers. They had come across a field swarming with prairie dogs and had cracked open the skull of every single one they could find. They had just taken down two bison earlier in the day, and the entire pack was more than full, but they still killed every single one of those prairie dogs, leaving their pink and red brains scattered across the otherwise pristine field. When they summoned the rest of the pack with a howl to show off what they had done, this genocide being a badge of pride to them, she walked away. She wanted to teach the rest of them a lesson, but mostly she wanted to be somewhere else. So she kept on walking.

That was in the middle of a beautiful Canadian spring, and she could remember the smell of the woods more than anything. The scent of flowers and moss and the smell of water somewhere, although she wasn't really all that close to the river. There was just that moisture in the air. And she loved it. She walked deer trails mostly, trotting through the trees, loving the shade when she was in it, and the feel of the sun warming her monochrome sheath when she found herself in the openness of a field. She was also pleased every time a field wasn't dressed up with the tiny brains of a hundred prairie dogs. That tended to be the way she preferred her fields. Flies and gnats buzzed lazily around her, and their buzz, the sound of the birds in the trees, and her own panting breaths were the only sounds she could hear. No prairie dog screams at all.

For the first time she could remember she felt content and worthwhile. She was doing something meaningful now in teaching her pack a lesson. She imagined they were mourning her loss already, sniffing and hunting her down, an integral part of them gone missing! And this made her trot and trot and trot because she couldn't get caught now; the thought of their anguish was just too delicious.

But soon, and it was a moment without a catalyst, it simply happened, she found herself acutely aware that she was now in unfamiliar territory. The bird calls sounded strange, more distant, more distracted. There were noises in the distance she couldn't place, they were clunky, they were mechanical she knew now, but at the time, they were frightening and alien.

"When the unknown folds in around you," Tess explained, "the world seems to get a bit darker. The clouds didn't go over the sun, the trees didn't grow higher around me, but it sure felt like that. Everything seemed worse, scarier. I'm sure if you waited, if you got to know the place it would open up and seem wonderful and sunny again, but at the time, I was lost and getting hungry."

"Sure," Sam said to convey he was listening.

So Tess had kept moving because at this point it would have been embarrassing to go back. And then she started to feel it. That pressure at the back of her skull, similar to the one they had felt back when the power went down at the Caribou, except this one was just her. This was well before all the animals started to kill themselves. She was strong, but this was stronger. This voice in her head that said, you are nothing, you are absolutely worthless without your own. You've deserted your people, and for that you should die. You should fall off a cliff, you should lay down for the rest of forever, you've made a terrible, terrible mistake. This voice spoke to her as she walked, and the further she got from her family, the more insistent the voice seemed to become. Why should she go on living? Wouldn't it teach her family a lesson if all they found was her rotting corpse? She would rather die than live the way they did? That was poetic. It was beautiful. It made sense. So why not? Why the hell not?

"Can I say something that has been bothering me?" Tess asked, breaking up her story, "I just need to get it off my chest."

"Of course," Bare said, feeling none of Sam's stress.

"When Hank was telling his story," she started, easing Sam's guilt, "You were completely rude Sam. I wanted to make my peace with that, especially now that Hank is actually dead."

"How do you know Hank is dead?" asked Sam, remembering the dog's eyes reflected in his headlights and the thuds beneath the suburban as the wheels rolled over his body.

"Because they all are. You weren't there for when it all started to fall. It was horrible. Bare and I were very lucky to have made it."

"How did you two not get the whole I-have-to-kill-myself-right-away-thing?" Sam asked, attempting to deflect this conversation away from his own misdoings.

"We were…"

"Nothing," Bare finished.

"You were what?" asked Sam.

"We were nothing," Tess repeated.

"Yah, nothin'," said Bare.

"You know that dog you killed to save my life?" asked Sam to Tess.

"His name was Rudolf and that was the hardest thing I've ever had to do. If you weren't so important to Bare I probably wouldn't have even stepped in to be completely honest. Rudolph was like family to me."

That one stung.

"Well… yeah, I had walked in on him and that other dog, the lab, I had walked in on them, you know… doing it."

"What?" asked Bare.

"Yeah, they were gay dogs," said Sam.

"I'm going to bed," said Tess angrily.

"Listen, I'm sorry, I'm not trying to be mean or anything, but I seriously walked in on them. I guess I don't know why I brought it up, but I just… I can't get it out of my head, and then that dog, I mean Rudolf saying I'd crashed his whole life down on him… it was such a horrible day."

"Yeah, I guess we all knew. None of us cared though. Not really. They just liked to be secretive. I guess they found it… whatever."

"At this point it probably doesn't matter who they've been intimate with, ya know?" said Bare.

"I just want to say, it's totally cool if you guys are hooking up," Sam said, "I don't think it's weird at all. I get it. You're both beautiful creatures. If I wasn't so keen on human females, you know, I wouldn't be against the whole interspecies thing. I mean, I'm not racist or anything. One of my best friends was black. Seriously. Jackson, his name was Jackson. Sorry, where were you?"

Tess rolled her eyes at Sam. She lapped at the vodka once more and shivered at the taste.

"I just wanted to say my piece is all," she said, "About you and Hank. I don't think you're a bad person Sam, I just think you're self-centered. It's not unconquerable, it's just something you should be aware of."

Sam looked at Bare as if to confirm this. Was he self-centered? Hadn't he… shit, hadn't he thrown Bare in the back of a freezing trailer as he snowmobiled for a day? Hadn't he thrown a tantrum and stormed out and burned down a power plant that was inexplicably keeping everyone in Folly's Landry from killing themselves? Hadn't he just tried to defend his credit with a made up black friend? Sam hadn't had many friends, and none of them had been black. He grew up in goddamn South Dakota. You were white or red or somewhere in between out there. Not that he called Native Americans 'Reds.' Shit. Why was it ok to call black people black and white people white but not red or yellow people their colors? Probably because they were weird approximations. Sam shut down that line of thinking.

"I lied about having had a black friend," Sam blurted, "Sorry, I just don't want you to think less of me."

It seemed like he was constantly explaining and justifying the things he said these days. Although maybe that had always been the case. He was great at putting his foot in his mouth. He was like a master yoga-man, flexible as hell, except in Sam's case every bend led his boot right through his front teeth. It just seemed worse now because he actually had to deal with sentient beings again. Life was so much easier when the only things he had to apologize to were trees.

"I'm a brown bear, not a black bear. Does that count?" asked Bare.

"Ok," said Tess, clearly unsure of what that meant or what to do with it, "So, I found myself in new territory."

"Yes," said Sam, glad to be moving on, "And sorry about Hank. I know it doesn't mean much, but I was still pretty freaked out about everything. My life- sorry, there I go again. I'm sorry. I'll try to be less self centered in the future. I really will."

"Ok," she said, which irked Sam. Apologies were hard. Give him a little something. But instead she just continued her story.

She had found herself in this new, dark world. It was frightening, but she wasn't about to go back. She had things to prove to her people, and that was that. But she needed food. All the walking had tired her, and those hunger pangs were becoming less of a nuisance and more of a full time thought process. But killing for herself didn't feel right at the moment either, so she was stuck in a middle ground of immobilizing indecision. So when she ran into the deer, she had a tough choice to make, but she decided to talk to the thing as opposed to ripping out her jugular and gargling the warm, delicious blood, as was her first instinct.

"Hey," she had said, "I'm Tess."

This deer was Hannah, from the Caribou as it would later turn out.

"Huh-hi..." said Hannah nervously. She wasn't used to being friendly with predators before they murdered her. Not that she was used to being murdered, but it was a bit of a cultural thing for them.

"So, I'm new around here," Tess had explained, "Do you know where I could find something to eat?"

Hannah had looked around and then down at herself, hoping this wasn't some twisted game.

"Like what?"

"I don't know. I'm just so hungry."

The tension of the moment was clearly killing Hannah, and Tess could see that.

"Hey, I don't want to eat you, ok? I have no interest in that. I just want something that isn't going to hurt other animals."

"So you're a vegetarian?" interrupted Sam.

"No," said Tess, "I was just trying to make Hannah feel more comfortable at the time."

"Oh."

"Go on," said Bare, interested.

"Do you want meat?" Hannah had asked. Tess had nodded weakly. She knew she wouldn't be able to survive on just twigs and berries. She just wasn't built like that.

"This way," Hannah had said before dashing off, and Tess was right behind her. They ran through this new forest, and with Hannah leading, the newness of it didn't feel so oppressive. She felt actually free now, and she let her tongue flap out of the side of her mouth in her excitement. Those strange sounds were steadily growing louder now, the ones that were, of course, the mechanics of the human society grinding to a halt.

And then they were in the city. Tess had never been in a city before, not that Folly's Landry was much of one. Tess had only ever seen a human once before that day. It had been a hiker. She had smelled something strange in her woods and had gone to investigate. Luckily she had been alone, otherwise her pack would have probably killed the man.

She had watched him from a distance, intrigued by the way he walked, upright on two legs like a bird, swinging his front paws to his side in a strange way that looked like he was constantly about to topple over. She had made a noise then, and he had turned to look at her, Tess being only about fifty feet from the man, and the moment he saw her she could smell his fear. It was pungent, like he had suddenly covered himself in his own urine. She backed away not from the man but from that smell.

But here in this city, which was like no forest she had ever seen, were people. Dozens of them, the scent of their fear still relatively fresh in the air, but they were all dead.

"They're dead, I don't know if that's a problem for you," Hannah had said, staring at the corpses. Tess didn't know if it would be either, but she was hungry and tired of seeing death go to waste. So she ate.

She walked to the first corpse and tore into the still unrotten flesh. It looked like her pack had come through here, it looked like the field of prairie dog, except instead of brains everywhere it was shopping bags and backpacks and portable phones.

Hannah had watched her devour a full corpse. For an animal that mostly ate berries and things it was an unnerving show to watch. There was something majestic in watching a true predator work on her prey though, so it must have been hard to look away. Sam nodded at this, considering himself secretly to be a true predator.

After she'd eaten, she and Hannah had talked, and Hannah had told her how when the air went out for a few minutes, something that most of the animals saw coming and were able to prepare for, it seemed the humans were not as forward thinking and had all just died, or at least most of them had. That had been the day before.

"So where'd you go after you ate all the people?"

"The hotel. It was close by, there were lights that stayed on all the time, which fascinated me at the time, and Cheese's family was already living there."

"Did you eat some of the people that had been in there?" Sam asked, a bit freaked out that Tess had had human meat, and Sam had never had wolf meat. Or was it a jealousy thing?

"Yes, but you're doing that thing where you ask the wrong questions again."

"Sorry."

"So how'd you get to be in charge of da place then?" asked Bare.

"Well, I just figured I wanted to help animals more than hurt them. I wanted a place animals could go and feel safe. So we created a haven, and the whole being in charge thing just fell into place from there. I still was a predator, and I think a lot of them looked up to me. I'd like to believe it wasn't all through fear anyway."

"It wasn't," Bare assured, "they loved ya."

Tess looked at Bare. She really liked him. Sam could tell. That was the way he used to stare at the pictures of women in the few books he had that showed them.

"I can go sleep in the other room," Sam said, mostly joking.

"Ok," said Tess, completely serious.

"Oh, uh, ok, yeah, sure," stuttered Sam. Bare looked close to stuttering too as he checked Tess for any facial tic that might reverse the decision, but it wasn't there.

"Hey, uh, goodnight there buddy," Bare said, and then below his breath he whispered, "Thanks."

"No problem," Sam said at a regular volume as he dragged a heap of blankets off into another bedroom. He found a lovely little bed in a place that clearly had been a small girl's room. Even in the dark the pink everything seemed to glow. It was like the room was plastered with jellyfish. Sam pulled the covers around himself, cocooning up all in pink of course. Then, just to be sure, he shoved a pink pillow around his head, shutting out all sound, and went to sleep.

And he was driving again. Chicago was close. Good god was it close. He couldn't stop thinking about all the people he was going to meet. And he wasn't kidding himself either, he was nervous. What if they were all like Buck? What if they were all crazy? He just hoped there was at least one pretty girl he could talk to. Just one. That's all he needed. Just one pretty, nice, normal lady to call his own. The road kept getting bigger and bigger as he approached the border of Chicago. It was all a little different than he remembered: everything seemed more like home and a little like his cabin. The trees all were familiar, and the whole place had this nostalgic feel.

He reached a section of road that went through a river. It started as a bridge, but then the bridge disappeared into the water. He could see rocks poking out of the water, so he knew it was shallow, so he just kept driving. He was close.

He watched as the water started to swallow the car. As he drove further the water just got deeper, yet somehow he was still moving forward. It seemed like he was out of his head now, and he watched as the truck skirted through water halfway up the door. He was sure water would have been seeping in by now, but it didn't seem like it was. That was lucky. This truck was solidly constructed. The shore seemed to stretch further away. It was especially stressful as he went fully underwater.

All he could see was brown water, blue water. Water now. Bare and Tess were going to be so mad at him. He was sure they were fine back there though. And then, from the darkenss of the water, something came swimming toward his truck. Either that, or he was driving toward the thing. Or both. And it was a beautiful girl. She looked about his age, she actually looked a lot like Jasmine from high school. Which was odd. He didn't know what Jasmine was doing swimming in this river. Maybe she had survived too. He was excited to talk to her, tell her about Chicago, except, as he got closer, she started to look more and more like Carol. How had Carol made it down to Chicago? She must have fixed up her bike. Sam figured he should still go and talk to her. That was the polite thing to do. So he opened the door, and the water rushed in.

Except the water had turned to flames, and he turned, scared, and there were Bare and Tess, their tongues giant and extending from their mouths, intertwining and knotting together. The flames started to eat away at their flesh as Carol whispered to them. Their faces, even with knotted tongues, turned stoic, angry even as they turned on Sam, and there were those dead skeleton eyes again, all staring out of the sockets of Bare, Tess, Carol, Jasmine, there was his mother, there was Rodney. There was Rodney's body, the hole in his head was a crescent-moon leaking blood, and that familiar feel as the water enveloped him again, and everything was so familiar. And then it was Rodney's blood that closed in around him. The gun swirled away from his hands as he sunk deeper and deeper again, sinking into the flames-

Sam woke up, drenched in sweat. His cocoon had overheated him, and he was severely dehydrated. Why did he keep having these horrible dreams? Something important had happened in the dream. Something he'd forgotten? Or something that was supposed to happen? He couldn't remember now, and the crazy thirst he'd built up was overpowered all other thought. All he wanted in the world was some water.

He crawled from his cocoon, toweled off his sweat-soaked body, and was instantly freezing. But mostly thirsty. He walked into the living room and heard soft noises. He couldn't see, thank goodness, but he got the gist of what was happening.

He weighed his choices now. He could either: A.) Interrupt his best friend's lucky night and satiate his thirst, or B.) He could go back to his little girl room and wrap himself up in fewer blankets this time, and try his best to sleep the thirst off. He tried to think of other possibilities, ways he could get around them, ways he could find water that wouldn't disturb them. He had a quick fantasy about arms that could stretch as far as he wanted them to. But it all pretty much boiled down to those two options, and considering everything, he felt obligated to go for option B. He did note though, as he crawled back into the tiny bed, that next time he was going to bring a water bottle to bed.

He fell asleep again this time, strangely content despite the desert in his mouth. He had finally walked in on a happy couple.

114.5

This was morning right? Yes, this little room was far too strange to be in one of Sam's dreams. The walls were plastered with pictures of shirtless boys on horses. There were pink swirls with the names of the horses and then the boys underneath. Or at least he assumed that's how the names were associated. He could only guess at which was the horse's name though and which was the boy's. Thunder could be a name of a boy if his parents were horrible enough. There was a phone sitting on a pink end table that was even shaped like a horse. Who was the kid with a room like this calling?

And then his thirst hit him like a ton of sand. The hours of tossing and turning, dreaming of deserts, dreaming of drinking water endlessly and drowning forever yet never being satiated came rushing back to him a lot like a dam bursting. Except instead of water rushing from the dam's open wound, it was exactly the opposite. He ran through the house and got to the water bucket, which was mercifully full. He brought it to his mouth and swallowed it down in greedy gulps. Except it wasn't the water bucket. It was Tess' water bucket. Or vodka rather. And a lot of it. Why had he used the same type of bucket for both? He spit out what he hadn't already swallowed, and that familiar desire to throw up came right back to him.

Bare and Tess woke to Sam dry heaving on the carpet. He wasn't going to throw up. He just wasn't. The one time it would have been useful, and he couldn't do it.

"Woah, you feeling ok there big guy?" Bare said through a daze as he lapped lazily at the real water bucket. Sam nodded, desperate for some reason to make them believe he was fine, just fine.

"Are you sick?" asked Tess. Sam shook his head no. No, he was not. Ugh, why hadn't he gotten better vodka? Wasn't good vodka supposed to be tasteless?

"Oh god," Sam managed.

"What's wrong with ya?" Bare asked.

"Vodka."

"Vodka?" asked Tess as she looked at the bucket.

"Thought it was water," Sam said, his composure finally back, "This is probably not good. I just drank a lot of vodka."

"How much is a lot?" asked Tess.

"Oh you know, like the whole bucket."

"Ya gonna be alright?" asked Bare.

"Probably," Sam said, the taste coming back to him sourly, "But I definitely need that water now."

He crawled to the water and nearly drowned himself in it. The bucket was empty by the time he was done. Now his tummy hurt. He frowned as he looked down at his body which was just not cooperating today.

"How'd ya sleep then?" asked Bare.

"Ok," said Sam, ignoring his horrible dreams and the horrible thirst he'd had. He headed toward the kitchen for something to soak up that vodka with, "And you?"

"Oh yeah-"

"Great," Tess finished.

Oh great, they were getting cute now.

They had breakfast like this, Sam terrified for the moment when that vodka was going to kick in, and Bare and Tess being incredibly cutesy. Sam was ready to get to Chicago. He wanted to save the world so he could win over a lady of his own. So when Sam stood up and that vodka finally rushed to his noggin, he was disappointed, but more than anything he was drunk. His vision split into two, and the whole world felt more like a boat than it needed to.

"Woah there cowboy," said Bare, as Sam swayed, "Breakfast hit ya that hard?"

"Vodka?" asked Tess knowingly.

"No," Sam lied, "Just stood up too fast."

And, explanation enough, Bare and Tess drank enough to keep themselves from jumping out the back of the truck, and then they piled in. Sam gripped the steering wheel like it was about to fall off, except he felt like he might fall off first. This road was spinning too much for it's own good, Sam decided as he pulled away from the little pink room with all the boys who loved horses enough to show them their chests.

There was a little window between the cabin and the back that he could slide open and talk to Bare and Tess through. He hadn't known it was a window that could open until they were almost ready to stop for the day yesterday. Sam used to be so clever when it came to spotting things. His life was changing a lot.

'Ah shit,' Sam thought as he teetered back and forth on the open road. They were lucky these roads weren't often traveled, there weren't too many cars abandoned in the middle of them, and most of the cars that had been on the roads at the time of that old apocalypse were decaying in the trees now. Which made driving drunk easier.

Sam went through periods where he thought he had a perfect handle on the situation, but then he would close his eyes, open them again, and they'd be a hundred yards down the road, and he would be driving in the opposite lane. Whoops.

"How you doing big guy?" Bare called up through the window after a particularly jarring swerve.

"Oh, you know," said Sam.

"We're almost there, right?" asked Tess.

"Oh yeah, super close," Sam replied. He wasn't actually sure if that was a lie or not, but he just kept on moving down the road.

A raccoon jumped under his treads, and he didn't even flinch; they'd been doing it the whole trip. Sam looked back at the red splotch that disappeared as he moved forward. Soon they weren't going to do this. Soon he wasn't going to have to deal with this shit.

"What was that?" asked Tess.

"Nothin'."

"Just a bump?"

"Yess'm,"

He wasn't entirely sure how long he'd even been driving, but he was surprised the vodka hadn't worn off by now. He was just so focused on not being drunk that he had completely ignored the road. It was like when he thought about his tongue or his nose and then they seemed gigantic to him, when the moment before he became aware they were total nonissues. It seemed like his tongue was suddenly too big for his mouth and his nose was weighing down his face. So he looked up at the road, at the surroundings for the first time maybe since he'd started driving.

"Hey," Sam asked, trying to make sure this wasn't some form of crazy, drunk, or dream.

"What's the good word my buddy?" Bare said, craning his face toward the little window.

"Do you see that?"

"See what?" asked Bare.

"The buildings up there?" asked Tess.

"Yeah," said Sam.

"Sure," Bare said, "Hey, is dat Chicago?"

He said Chicago funny. Like the 'I' was an 'E.'

"You say Chi-cah-go funny," said Sam, still drunk.

"How are you supposed to say it then?"

"She-cah-goh," Tess sounded out.

"Chee-caeg-oh," Bare tried.

"No, Shih-cahgo," Sam said.

"Alright, make fun of the way I speak whydon'tcha. Next yer gonna say I say drah-ma funny. Or pass-tuh."

"Wait what?"

"Pass-tuh."

"What's Pass-tuh?" asked Tess.

"Wait, *pasta*?" Sam asked.

"Oh ok, whatever. Tomato, tomato."

"Isn't it Tomato, toh-mah-toh?" asked Tess.

"I give up, I give it up!" Bare yelled. They had fun.

Sam looked back at his friends and laughed with them as he crashed into the gate in the great fence.

The airbag slammed into his face, and he just about blacked out. His eyes rolled in the back of his head. Time was moving a little strangely, but Sam was pulled from the car and thrown to the ground. He looked up at a guard, maybe in his mid-forties, one hand held a gun, and the other was small and shriveled, the fingers pointing in strange, impossible directions. Sam could read the man's nametag. Leo.

Leo hit a button on his radio with one of his off kilter digits.

"Hey Frank?"

"What's happenin' Leo?" Frank replied through the walkie.

"I just had a truck crash into my checkpoint."

"Can you put that away? I don't deal well with guns."

"Get up and put your hands up on the side of the truck. Spread your fucking legs," Leo sounded nervous, his little hand twisting in the air.

"Wait, what?"

Leo waved the gun, so Sam did as he was told.

"What's happening?" Tess asked from the back.

"What was that?" Leo asked.

Sam couldn't respond.

"Open the back please," Leo ordered as the sound of a siren grew closer. Sam did as he was told and Bare and Tess, huddled together, stared out at the two like a couple of stowaways. The mattress and blankets had luckily shielded them from the impact, but they were dripping with vodka.

"Howdy," Bare said to the gun.

Leo touched at the radio again with that gnarled hand.

"Jeeps. Now!" he yelled into the mike.

And they waited like that, Leo sweating as he moved his gun nervously between his three complying and stationary perps. This is what he had trained for. This was his moment in the sun. Leo's lip curled into half a smile as the jeeps screamed up around the truck and a dozen large guns were pointed at Sam and friends.

This is not how Sam had seen this going.

"This was a huge mistake, huh?" Sam asked as his facemasked policewoman zip tied his wrists together.

"Probably," she said as she sunk a needle into Sam's neck and then plunged the contents into his veins.

Blackout.

122

Chicago was looking a lot like a jail cell right now. Presumably because that's where they'd shoved Sam, and that's where he came to: staring at a huge red door with no handle. He was on a cot, and it wasn't comfortable. Not even a little comfortable. There was a toilet on the far wall, and blinding florecent lights washed out every corner of the concrete box. But there was power and electricity here, so the buzz would be at bay. At least Bare and Tess wouldn't be suicidal.

Where were his friends?

"BARE!" he screamed, his voice strange and huge and depressing in the tiny space. There was no answer. He strained his ears for sounds of any kind and came back empty.

"TESS?!" he tried. Again he strained, and again it was for naught.

"HEY IS ANYBODY OUT THERE? DO I GET A LAWYER OR SOMETHING STILL? IF DRIVING DRUNK IS THE ISSUE, I'M SORRY, BUT I ONLY DRANK THE VODKA BY ACCIDENT! ASK MY FRIENDS, THEY'LL BACK ME UP. I MEAN, THEY WERE SLEEPING AT THE TIME, BUT THEY SAW ME AFTER. THEY KNOW. DO YOU HAVE MY FRIENDS SOMEWHERE? THEY'LL VOUCH!" he paused, just to see if there would be a reply. No luck. So he lay down on his shitty cot to wait it out. Being a man so used to solitude, he was an expert at waiting, and the silence didn't bother him. Other than the fact that he needed to get out of here and find the crescent moon-man and save the world. Little things.

"Welcome to Chicago," he said to himself as he closed his eyes again and rubbed the spot on his neck where they'd plunged that needle in.

Eventually he fell asleep and had dreams of the Chicago he had hoped for. Women of every variety walked and posed and melted into dresses, it was somehow magically warm, and everyone was waving and smiling with the classic Midwestern displays of friendliness. It was lovely and magical and perfect. In his dream it was as if everyone hadn't died those years ago, and it was as if there wasn't something happening out there that could throw the species under the bus again.

Chicago was a haven from that. The rest of the world could end, but his dream Chicago was lovingly wrapped in a bubble that gave everything the sunny glow of airbrushing in old skin mags: that deep and wonderful fuzzy blush emanating from between the legs of the earth, the bosom of the universe.

He was sitting on a lawn, Chicago the backdrop, and a lake stretching out in front of him. He had a feeling of contentedness. There was a beautiful woman next to him; he could tell she was gorgeous even though he couldn't see her face. Everything was nice and calm until that familiar terror seized him again. Where was this coming from? He looked down and the gun was in his hands. The pistol clutched there seemed to weigh a hundred pounds. And she was gone. Where was she? Sam looked out into the water, except now it was turning red. The red waves lapped at his feet, but that gun weighed him down. He couldn't move. He couldn't breathe as the water covered his head. And then there was just red and red, and he slowly became aware he was staring up at that bright light in his little prison cell, and the red was just the fluorescent trying its damndest to crack through his eyelids.

Typical.

He opened his eyes, shaking the dream off, and hoped that someone hadn't come for him while he was sleeping. He hoped they hadn't come in and said to him, "Hey, you can go. Our bad. Enjoy," and then saw him sleeping and figured they'd just let him catch up on his rest.

But that probably hadn't happened. They probably would have woken him up for that one.

What had they shot into his neck? He hoped it wasn't damaging. He hoped he wasn't allergic. Nah, he couldn't be allergic, he'd be dead by now. Unless he *was* dead, and this was hell. Or heaven. He hoped heaven would have been nicer than this though.

He didn't really believe in heaven or hell. His parents had both been non-practicing Methodists or something. He wasn't sure what the differences between all the different types were: Lutherans, Methodists, Congregationalists, Protestant, or whatever. If there even was a difference. Regardless, his parents had brought him to church only once or twice by themselves, and that was because there was some social event happening that they'd somehow gotten guilted in to attending. Otherwise it was Christmas services with Grandma and

Grandpa, but even those had fallen off after Grandpa had his stroke, and Grandma gave up smoking. She was just horrible when she wasn't smoking. She became unbearably cranky without her smokes.

Sam always considered himself an atheist, or an agnostic if he was talking to a pretty girl who was in to the whole religion thing. He had always hoped some lovely Christian girl would meet him and try to take him on as a project. Save his soul or whatever, and that would give him ample opportunities to sneak a little smooching and petting and wherever the Luck and the Lord would take him. This, of course, never happened, but it had been one of Sam's more plausible little fantasies through school.

The older boys always said it was the Christian girls who were the tigers in bed. Something about years and years of repression boiling down to sexual deviancy. It was probably never worded like that, but that's how the idea had come to rest for Sam so many years later.

He shifted to his side on the cot, finding it still uncomfortable, he sat on the floor and used the toiletless wall as a backrest. That was better for now.

Maybe this wasn't heaven or hell, but what if it was some sort of afterlife thing. What if this was his consciousness at the moment of death? Could it be possible that he'd just been choking with the rest of humanity right now? Or on a pretzel or something? Could it be that instead of life flashing before your eyes meaning a show of what had already happened, what if it meant the rest of the life you would have lived flashed before your eyes. And by flashed it meant you had to sit through the whole damn thing, even the boring, crazy parts like sitting alone in a jail cell in post-apocalyptic Chicago?

Sam had a moment as he tried to let that sink in, as he tried to let his brain make this scenario seem plausible, make it. If it were real could he just up and die at any moment? Could he choose the moment of his own true death? He had a split second where he was about to wish for death, just as a test against the idea, but then his fear got the better of him, and he did nothing.

His life probably wasn't some death-spasm fantasy, but why risk it? What if his fantasy was close to getting him laid by a pretty girl? It'd be a shame to die before that.

He scratched at his crotch and then tried to clear his mind. He tried, for the umpteenth time in his life to perform a sort of meditation.

'Think of nothing, think of nothing, think of nothing. Wait, but by thinking 'think of nothing,' you're actually thinking something. Shut up, now we're thinking of too much.' And so on until he gave up. He just wasn't built for thoughtlessness. His mind moved too quickly. Or at least was overly active. It wasn't clear to him whether or not that was a good thing.

The hours passed like that. Or maybe it was just a few minutes. Spaces like this were designed to rob you of knowledge of time. It was classic eye-for-an-eye tactics in prison. Someone robs a bank, they get robbed of their time. And then if they get thrown in solitary, which is where Sam almost certainly was unless Chicago had the most inhumane jails in the country, they stole away from their guest even the most basic understanding of how time flowed. It was like being locked in a Wal-Mart where everything was out of reach.

The only way he could tell a long time had passed was that he had shit in the toilet and now was feeling the desire to shit again, also he was ravenously hungry. So when Sam heard the door finally click open, he had no exact estimate on how long he'd been actually locked up.

"Up," said the guard framed in the red doorway.

"Hey," Sam said, scowling, "What the hell man?"

"What's your business in Chicago, son?"

"I'm here because I have something a man with a crescent moon wants," Sam said as he scratched at his itching scrotum. The guard took notice of this, and he looked disturbingly interested.

"What was that?"

Sam scratched again. His crotch had been particularly itchy today.

"What was that itch? Is it accompanied by a rash? Swelling of the lymph nodes, sleep sweats?"

Sam subtly felt at his lymph nodes, which were indeed swollen, but that could just be because one of these fuckers had pumped him full of something or other. He was sure his lymph nodes weren't psyched on random sleep inducing chemicals being pumped into his red, red blood.

"No, just an itch," Sam said, having not checked his scrotum since Carol. He really didn't want to make a thing of it.

"Take off your pants," the guard said.

"What?"

"Pants. Off."

"I'm not taking my pants off. No way."

"You *will* take off your pants, and I *will* inspect your genitals," the guard said, fingering the clip of the gun holstered at his side. Sam looked around as if there were anyone in this tiny room who might help him out of this awkward situation.

"You're not even going to buy me dinner first?" This was something he'd heard in a movie once. The guard didn't find it clever.

"Now," he said as he took a step toward Sam. There was real intent to harm on his face, so Sam quickly tucked his thumbs into the waistline and pulled them down.

The guard took a knee in front of Sam and pulled a pair of plastic gloves from his utility belt. He snapped them on and took hold of Sam's cock and raised it violently, peering at Sam's scrotum like a hungry jeweler assessing a fresh divorcee's hate-filled diamond.

"Ow, careful!" Sam protested.

"Interesting," the guard said to himself, making Sam even more nervous.

"What's interesting? Nothing's interesting."

The guard did some poking and prodding of the testes and then gave the penis a once over. Once he was satiated he released his chokehold on Sam's member and let the thing flop back into resting position.

"Is this like a hazing thing? Is this the initiation here? Because I think it's cruel."

"Pull your pants up and follow me," the guard said, removing the gloves by pinching the bottoms and pulling them into each other and then securely disposing of them inside a red biohazard bag. Sam hiked his pants back up.

"You're going to see Mr. Smith," the guard said. This would have been cryptic too had Sam not heard the name on the radio.

"I hear he has a collection of some sort, how's that going?" Sam said, trying to make it seem like he belonged there, even as they stepped into the dingy elevator that was completely foreign.

The guard just smiled at him knowingly and nodded. Sam had never seen such a sinister nod.

Sam was led through the whole prison, which was mostly empty. Here and there he heard people howling in the distance, but the guard never took him by these people. Some of them sounded like women. He wondered what the women had done to warrant being locked up. He wondered if any of the people in here had actually done anything at all, or maybe they were all like Sam and confused greatly as to why people were threatening them with guns. And then they were out on the street, and it was already night. He'd been in that room for a while. By his estimation it had to have been at least six hours.

"How long was I in there for?"

"A day or so?"

"A *day*?"

"Or so."

The guard led him through the street, which was freezing without a coat, and into a beautiful glass building nearby. He could see other buildings around with lights blazing inside, but this one was by far the tallest around, and the lobby was well lit and well manicured. A beautiful woman sat behind a table, reading a book. Sam fell in love instantly.

"Good evening sir," she said to the guard, her tone suggesting this was required by the job.

"Hi there Jenna baby," he said, trying his hardest to put sex into his voice. She didn't even look up again, and the guard shoved Sam hard when he slowed to gawk.

"Eyes forward prisoner."

This man had seen movies too. Sam wondered if before the apocalypse this man had been a cop. He doubted it. He had a mustache, sure, but it sat on the top of his lip like a mockery. You needed a certain confidence to wear a mustache, and this guard did not have it, Sam thought.

Sam gave one more look at Jenna, her red sweater dress housing those delicious secrets, and he was shoved into another elevator. Sam was reeling from how many people he'd already met. What was this now? Three? Five in the last week. That was five more than he'd suspected were even left in the world. So discounting the whole drugging and imprisonment and molestation things and the whole world ending bit, this had been a neat trip so far.

The guard pushed a key into the elevator panel, the top of which was molded into the shape of an ornate skull, and pressed the button for penthouse. The lights cut out the moment the button was pushed and a red blanket of light descended in its place. Sam thought there might have been some technical difficulty, but the elevator started up, and the guard was unphased. There was elevator music, and Sam tried to think of the last time he actually had listened to music. This might have been the first time in eight years. It was decidedly baroque though, which Sam had trouble remembering whether or not that had been the standard for elevator tunes.

"What's the music?" Sam asked. The guard looked down at him, his eyes glowing black in the red light. He didn't speak he just cocked an eyebrow and then went back to watching the little lights flashing by that were indicators of the floors they were passing.

Floor by floor dinged by as the elevator music serenaded the two. It felt a little like a haunted house. Closer, closer, closer. Where was he headed? What sort of ghouls awaited them? What monster lurked behind the sliding door?

Ding. And here they were. The doorbell chimed out again, and it sounded like it was coming from some large organ. It probably was considering everything. Except the door opened, and they walked into a completely normal, modern, and sleek room. There were small fountains built into a walkway from the elevator, rivers that flowed into themselves and led to the main room, which was black all around and totally encased in glass. There was a closet, containing mostly black items, all shrouded in glass; there was a shower and a toilet, all glass. Sam marveled at the toilet being crafted of glass. It seemed unsafe, but it looked like it worked. This was not a palace of privacy it seemed. This was the home of someone who had nothing to hide. Except for the huge steel wall at one end. That was rather suspect.

"Mr. Smith?" said the guard.

"Forward," said Mr. Smith, presumably.

And they walked toward the black couch that was thankfully leather, not glass.

"Have a sit," said Mr. Smith.

"Don't touch him," said the guard.

"Thank you Otis. You can go stand somewhere else."

"Ok sir. Yes sir."

And Otis the guard walked away, leaving Sam to meander around to the front of the couch. Mr. Smith wasn't even old. Sam was disappointed, he had imagined Smith as an old man, decrepit and creepy, but he was maybe in his mid-thirties, and he wasn't necessarily unhandsome either. He had light hair, not blonde, but close, and his eyes were like ice: blue and piercing and mean. Smith had a scar next to his mouth, a little crescent moon. It was him. He was the one. He was the one Sam had to stop. But how?

"What is your name?" he asked as he stood. Sam could see he had maybe once been an athletic man, but he was almost emaciated now.

"Sam," said Sam.

"Hmm, Sam. Sam, what brings you to my city?"

"Chicago?"

Mr. Smith looked at him with disinterest.

"Have you seen my penthouse?" Mr. Smith said.

"I have. Or I did as I walked in."

"Did you notice anything, Sam. Is your full name Samuel?"

"No. My parent's just named me Sam actually."

"Pity."

"Did you notice anything about my penthouse Sam? Anything interesting?"

"You've got a glass toilet. Is that for watching your shits disappear? I've always wondered what happened once they'd gone past sight you know? Like do they break up? Do they float just like that?"

"That is more than enough," Mr. Smith said, stopping Sam with a finger almost touching Sam's lips. Sam looked down at the finger and noticed small bumps all down the length of it.

"Yes, my toilet is glass. My penthouse is crafted of the opaque and the transparent. It is a contrast that I am quite drawn to," he said as he slipped on a pair of black, velvety gloves and ran a finger across the glass.

"It is a product of nature to be so," he said, "Nature at once so unadmonishingly *there*, so predictable in her rising and falling, her shifts between seasons and the dullness of night and day, but then there is the black behind her glass. That oblivion sense, that unknown, that is what I am drawn toward, Sam. That is where she truly speaks to me."

Mr. Smith walked over to a black wall and whisked his hand across a hidden panel. A door opened, and a blindfolded man dressed in a white gown stepped forward.

"It is your time, son," Mr. Smith said to the man in the gown who looked much older than Mr. Smith.

"Thank you, Sir," he said back with joy and fear and lust? Was that lust in his voice?

Mr. Smith led the man over to the couch and made him kneel down in front of him. Sam looked on in horror as Mr. Smith lowered his zipper and pulled out his cock. He then took his gloved fingers, gently caressed the man's cheek, cradled his chin, and delicately guided the mouth to his manhood.

"I…I can leave…," Sam stammered.

"You will stay," Mr. Smith said as a man bobbed on his cock, "Nature is so obvious at first, but She is a subtle creature who is rife with powers. The powers of destruction, and I am not merely speaking of the awesome power of a hurricane, or a tornado, or an earthquake-"

"Or a geyser," Sam said, trying to keep his eyes away from the man in the gown and what was happening with his mouth.

"Otis," Mr. Smith said, and Otis the guard reappeared, "Make sure Sam here is paying attention."

Otis pointed to Sam, as if to make sure that Mr. Smith meant the only other person in the room who wasn't blindfolded. Sam was shocked that Otis didn't find it strange they were having a conversation as a man was giving oral to another man. How did Sam keep ending up in these ridiculous situations?

And then there was a gun to his temple. Sam's heart seized. He saw blood and hair splattering, he saw red, red life leaking out. He saw the body lying in the grass. Sam shook.

"Watch," Otis said. Sam had no choice but to obey.

"The opaque and the transparent are fundamental, they go down to the very core of our beings. Did you know that at a tiny, microscopic level all of our atoms, the transparent, for we can see them and thus see through their design, they don't touch, they simply float. We and everything around us are the subtle and effortless combination of uncountable tiny bits floating in the what?"

He gestured with one of his gloved hands toward Sam. Otis pressed the gun harder against Sam's temple. And Sam, sweating now, squeezed his eyes shut.

"Open 'em," Otis said, tapping Sam's skull with the barrel, "And answer the man."

"The opaque?" Sam said, his voice shaky.

"Precisely. The opaque is the space in the middle, the ether in which all the building blocks float. It is a wall in which secrets are kept and upon which secrets are built. Are you following me?"

Sam nodded and Otis followed with the gun.

"Splendid. Nature had her way with us, but she had had her way with me from the very beginning Sam. These people, these people of Chicago, they see me as a god. Isn't that right son?" he said to the man in the gown. The man nodded, and Mr. Smith's scabby, oh holy fuck it was scabby! His cock was covered in scabs. Sam had tried not to look closely, but now he could see the entirety of Mr. Smith's shaft was covered in scabs and blisters that were popping and leaking pus.

"You will be our savior," the man said through a mouthful of that horrible penis.

Sam had never seen something so heinous in his life. The thing was an absolute travesty. It was like the pictures they'd shown Sam in health class as warnings except worse and in person. And here was a guy ignoring all of those warnings. He was blindfolded, so maybe he hadn't noticed? Except there was no way. The man's tongue pressed up against a blister that popped under the stress, and a teardrop of yellow pus dripped down the shaft... Sam felt ill.

He would have loved to look away, but there was that gun's metallic presence against his pounding temple. His body would have loved to just puke up all his fear and revulsion right now as well, but Sam was having too vivid of a moment imagining the aftermath his brains would have on the glass if he tried a stunt like that: just a sticky red mess turning that stupid, precious transparent opaque. So he just shivered in place with the gravity of it all.

"My father, god rest his soul, was cleaning our house shortly after my mother had left us, and he made the fatal error of combining ammonia and bleach, which as you may know creates deadly chloramine vapors. The vapors had cleared once I arrived home, but my father was very much dead."

"Do you know what it's like to walk in on your father's corpse?"

Sam did. He had walked in on all sorts of corpses, including his father's.

"Yes."

"Good. So you understand. As these things happen, this affected me greatly. I became distrustful of cleanliness in general, I began to collect items that others deemed trash: hair and toenail clippings, saliva, snot, semen, feces, and I tried for a while to keep all of my bodily secretions in giant mason jars my grandmother had left us. Can you imagine me?" he said as the man was still attending to his penis, "Down on my hands and knees searching for toenail clippings? Can you imagine a young me sneaking about and putting them into filthy mason jars with my saliva and urine and semen? I remember with such vividness watching the different liquids mix together. The semen floating in milky clouds through the urine, the feces islands at the top, the toenails and bits of rolled up skin and scabs whirling about like cloudy sand at the bottom. In my head I had created a whole world just from parts of myself. I managed to keep those jars for three months before the nuns decided to throw it away."

"Nuns?"

Mr. Smith nodded.

"It was at the home run by the nuns, St. Michael's School for Boys, that I discovered my true calling; it was at St. Michael's I was raped and contracted herpes. And then later it happened again and I got HPV."

"HPV?" Sam said, curious not as to what it was, but as to how the man was still sucking after hearing this.

"Genital warts," Mr. Smith said with a nod downward at his engorged and oozing member.

"I see."

"Yes. I became what was known as a bug chaser. I traveled from city to city collecting diseases. You must remember, these were different times. Sexual discrimination wasn't an issue, but it wasn't enough to simply acquire the diseases, I had to earn them you see."

Sam nodded to show Mr. Smith and the barrel of the gun that kissed Sam's temple that he was still in fact listening and did in fact see.

"I got Hepatitis A from a very pale black man I met when an acquaintance of mine took me to a white power rally outside of Los Angeles. I got B from the daughter of a senator in Louisiana."

"Southern girls, huh?"

Mr. Smith ignored Sam.

"And I bet you're wondering where I picked up HIV."

"I was, actually," Sam said truthfully.

"He was famous."

"Who?"

"Guess."

"I have no idea."

"A singer," and then after a pause: "He was in movies some. Very *American*."

"It was a guy?"

"Come on," Otis said, "Just think about it, it's so simple."

"I have no idea."

"He sang in a band."

"Mustache," said Otis.

"A moment," said Mr. Smith as his body twisted ever so slightly.

The man in the white robe drew his mouth away, and he started to cough and convulse. Sam realized the man had been foaming at the mouth for a while now that Sam was actually considering him and not just his actions, and the man's eyes were red and rolling, the bandana having fallen from his face. He sputtered as Mr. Smith's sperm flew out over his twitching face.

By the time Mr. Smith had finished unloading, the man in the gown was dead.

"Lenny Kravitz stupid," said Otis as he thankfully withdrew the insistent and cold mouth of the gun and moved to drag the body away, a trail of rabid drool and semen sketching their path.

Sam didn't know what to say. He considered voicing that he couldn't remember Lenny Kravitz having a mustache, but then he couldn't really remember what Lenny Kravitz looked like. Also, there was no way Lenny Kravitz had AIDS. He was married. To a woman no less, and lived for a long time without dying, at least probably until the whole oxygen thing. Or maybe Sam didn't really know anything about Lenny Kravitz.

"I don't know who that is," Sam said, an attempt at simplification.

"You would if you saw a picture," Otis said, closing the door behind the body he'd just stashed.

"Do you know what that man was doing, Sam?"

"Lenny Kravitz?"

"No the man in the gown."

"He was sucking your..." Smith put his fingers to his temples, annoyed.

"He had Chlamydia, and now I do. That is one step closer to my final goal, Sam."

Sam, finally acting on his most insistent impulse, turned and bolted.

"Stop!" Otis said, but this whole Chicago scene was just too awful, and Sam's desire to get away from it overwhelmed his desire to not be shot, which was an impressive break to natural instinct.

"This will accomplish nothing," Mr. Smith said calmly.

Sam frantically pressed the elevator button even though he had realized long before that it required a key to function from here. A key he didn't have. A key Otis was twirling from an extended middle finger as he walked toward Sam, his other hand firmly cradling the pistol that only seemed to have eyes for Sam.

Sam wondered what it would feel like to get shot. Would it hurt or would it be over too quickly for pain? What if he was shot right in the heart? Would his heart try to pump the bullet through his tiny, flailing veins? He imagined it would burn. He remembered times when incredibly hot water had hit his skin and had felt somehow cold. He imagined the cold pain of a bullet to be hot despite itself though. Sam raised his hands above his head. He wasn't looking to find out yet. He just wasn't.

Otis walked up to Sam, and Sam had another insane impulse that he just figured to follow. He chopped at Otis' inner elbow with his fist and then quickly jabbed his other fist up, and Otis' flat nose flattened further and blossomed with red. Otis considered which wound, the torn elbow or the flowing nose to deal with first, and in his indecision he simply fell to the ground.

Mr. Smith rolled his eyes, and, having cleaned himself up and re-buttoned, stood and walked toward Sam as Sam looked at the gun, his fear evident.

"Go ahead, pick it up," Smith said.

Sam didn't move.

"You can't can you? I saw you with that gun against your temple. I know the look of trauma. What is your trauma Sam? How did you survive the apocalypse? Pick it up Sam."

Sam wanted to desperately; he needed to end this man, this monster with the knobby cock that brought death like some horrible super power. But he couldn't pick up that gun. Something in his head, something his mind didn't want him accessing wouldn't allow it.

"I was in the hospital when it happened. The doctors all believed I wouldn't last another day, let alone a decade. But here I am, and do you know where they are? Of course you do. You've seen your own fair share of death Sam. But I don't think you were hooked up to oxygen when it happened were you? And I'm sure you knew that's what caused it correct? The earth in all her infinite and beautiful transparency depleted our oxygen for a whole of twenty minutes. Long enough to kill most people. Most people who weren't on oxygen already, or deep in the country, or what Sam? Where were you?" Smith asked as he slowly walked toward Sam, the glass glinting all around him, his eyes never leaving Sam's, probing him for the information.

How *had* he survived? It was something he tried not to think about. His mind always raced, but it always seemed to be racing away from that. Where had he been?

"I don't think you have the courage to face the things you've done. I have the courage to face my life and the courage to face the opaque and shatter it. I am not the monster you believe me to be. I am simply a man taking the revenge on Mother Nature that she has so rightly earned. She murdered us. Do you have the courage to do the same to me Sam? Pick up the gun. Stop me."

Sam stared at the gun. Why couldn't he do this?

"PICK IT UP!" Smith roared, and when Sam still couldn't, Smith pressed a button on his watch, and a myriad of hidden doors slid open, and a dozen guards, leading with the barrels of their guns, stormed into the room.

Smith raised his hand to indicate they shouldn't shoot, and Sam raised his own hands into the air. Mr. Smith got close enough to kiss Sam, and the antiseptic stench of the man invaded his nose.

"Pity," Mr. Smith said, "You are abhorrently transparent. Such childishness. I do not believe you even know who you are. Now remove your pants."

Sam opened his mouth to speak, but the guns crunched toward him and convinced him to keep his comment to himself.

"Remove them."

Sam stared around at the barrels of the guns. Smith nodded downward, so Sam, for the second time in a half hour, undid his fly and showed his penis to a man. Smith lowered to one knee and inspected Sam closely, so close that Sam could feel his clammy breath on his member. Sam really hoped that that wasn't enough to contract something.

"Splendid. And what are your symptoms?"

"You're not going to… suck it, are you?"

"Symptoms."

"I won't have to… I won't have to do that to you will I?"

"You haven't nearly earned that privilege. I see the lesions and the rash."

Smith stood and ran his gloved fingers over Sam's lymph nodes. He nodded. Swollen.

"Sleep sweats?"

Sam just stared.

"I won't do it."

"You're the last piece of my puzzle. A small, rather common one that Mother Nature almost robbed me of earning. I thank you in advance for the service you will perform to the bettering of the world. Goodbye Sam."

The butt of a rifle struck the back of his head, and the last thing he saw was Smith's face, showing nothing but pity and that crescent moon scar that told Sam his cowardice might have just meant the end of the entire world.

140

Something near him growled. Or purred. It was hard to tell exactly. Sam opened his eyes excitedly, knowing that Tess was right there.

Except it wasn't Tess. There was no one there.

"Get up," the voice said. She said.

Sam turned, ignoring the pain in the back of his skull, attempted to cajole his body into putting a face to the melody of that voice and succeeded. She was young, maybe 17 or 18, she was Asian, and she was beautiful despite herself. It was clear she gave little care to her appearance. Her hair was wild, her dress was stained, and her face was clean of paint or makeup, yet she was the most beautiful thing Sam had ever seen.

"Did you growl at me?" Sam asked.

"Up," she said, that melodic voice ringing again. There was something so familiar about it, something that reminded him of his friends. Bare and Tess. He hoped they were ok.

"What is that?" Sam said as he stood, rubbing the back of his head.

"What is what?"

"What is this? What is happening here?"

"I'm here to do a job. I'm here to have sex with you."

Nerves racked Sam's body at that. Here was a high school aged girl telling him exactly what he'd always wanted to hear from the high school girls he had known. His body shook as he tried to think of what to say, tried to figure out what the cool thing to say would be, and tried to ignore that pounding voice that assured him this had to be a trap at the very least.

She was just looking at him.

"What?" he said.

She didn't even blink.

"Um."

"You have something Smith wants, and I'm here to get it from you. And I guess that means I need to fuck you," she said as if reading from a script. Sam's body still shook as if he were quite cold.

"So wait. What?"

"Take off your pants."

People in Chicago really wanted Sam's pants off.

"Can we slow down for a minute here?"

"Let's just get this over with so I can get the fuck out of here."

"Why are you doing this?"

"Take your clothes off."

Sam looked down at his shaking hands and couldn't imagine undoing buttons with these tremorous tools.

"What's your name?" he asked, trying to buy time. She sighed or growled again and walked over to Sam. She stood in front of him, grabbed the hem of her messy blue dress, and pulled it up over her head.

Sam watched transfixed as that blue drape traveled up her legs, revealing a small jungle that hid her sex, and then her small, flat stomach, and as her elbows flipped up the dress revealed her small but shapely breasts topped with equally small, dark nipples.

"Strip. Now," she said.

"I...I," he couldn't stop looking at her. Her hip cocked to the side, her dress trailing from her hand to the floor, her face more bored than upset.

She dropped the fabric and grabbed at Sam's shirt as he twisted his torso, giggling despite himself, trying his damndest to get away. It didn't work, and soon his head was caught in the folds of his upended shirt. The darkness was nice, but it suffocated him. And he missed the sight of her naked body, but that too was burnt directly onto his eyes. He hoped forever.

There were those moments, those sights he had pledged to himself he'd never forget. Never in a million years would he forget the sight of that first nipple, that first feminine wisp of pubic hair from the side of a bikini, that first sunset over his old mountain home. That sight of Smith's scabby dick. Ugh.

"Stop wriggling," she said. Sam obeyed and was rewarded with more of that sweet, sweet nudity. He felt like he should look away for decency's sake, and because he imagined he was probably a bit too old for her. But you could never tell with Asians, he thought, and then immediately chastised himself for having thought it. There were too few people left to spend any time stereotyping them. Hell, at this point there were probably so few people left on earth that there really weren't categories anymore. Everybody was simply and finally an individual. And what was this young, naked individual's name?

"I'm Sam," Sam said with his hand out for a handshake. She walked forward letting his hand dig in between her legs. Sam instinctually drew his hand back, shocked.

"HEY!" she yelled, now suddenly in Sam's face, her nudity hidden by this surge of anger, "Stop fucking around. Let's get this done so I can move on with my life. The sooner we... fuck, the sooner I can get the hell out of here and get on with my life."

"Why do you want to... have sex with me?" Sam asked.

"I don't want to do anything, I have to have sex with you."

"If that's a compliment I'll take it," Sam said, trying humor. It fell on dead ears.

"Do I have to beg? Because I don't beg."

"I... this is a little like, sudden, don't you think?"

"Sudden would be fine by me, as long as it's done."

Embarrassment finally drew Sam's gaze away from her body and down at his feet.

"Could you at least explain the situation to me here? I feel like I'm part of some bizarre practical joke here. Like a TV crew is going to bust in here and be all like, gotcha."

She growled again, and Sam met her eyes.

"Mr. Smith has deemed you unworthy, why? I have no idea, nor do I want to know, and-"

"I punched a guard in the nose and broke his arm," Sam said.

"When I say I don't want to know, please don't take it as an invitation to tell me. I don't give a damn about you, and I don't care to give any damns about you. All I know is I need to have sex with you and then have sex with Mr. Smith, and then we're free. And that is all I care about."

"Don't have sex with him. He's heinous. Absolutely heinous."

She growled again, presumably meaning no, she had not.

"I don't care one bit what he looks like because as soon as I finish with all this I am away from this fucking place."

"It's not about what he looks like. If anything he's fairly handsome. I mean not like handsome, handsome, but I totally would have figured him to have been some old dude. But he's probably only like thirty."

"Stop. Again: don't care. Not a bit."

She came at his belt this time, her tiny hands zeroing in, and he backed off again until he was cornered by the wall.

"His dick looks like moldy cheese. The whole thing: just cheese that's been left out in the heat for years. It was oozy and scabby, and it will kill you I promise," Sam said quickly.

"Yeah, he's gross. I got it."

"He made me watch a man give him a... to uh, to pleasure him with his mouth, I mean the other man...," this was hard to explain for Sam, as he was staring at female nudity, "The man died after... Smith's jizz killed him. I swear. You're not going to be free, he thinks he's god, and I'm sure his idea of your freedom is you dying. Do you honestly trust a man whose stipulations for your freedom are that you contract a disease from a stranger for him?"

"No, I don't."

"Please, I have to save my friends."

"That's what I'm doing now."

"Please, their names are Bare and Tess. They're a bear and a wolf, and they're my best friends."

Luck actually paused at this.

"A bear and a wolf? What do you mean? Pets?"

"No. No way. Friends. I mean, we talk about life and stuff, we hang out a lot... I don't know exactly what makes a best friend."

"You talk to them?"

"Sure, yeah, we talk all the time. Why?"

"I thought I was the only one. Hmm."

"I have an idea," he said now that he had her off the offensive, "Let's first put some clothes on you, and then together we can find some way to break out of here. I-what's your name?

"Luck."

A laugh slipped out from Sam.

"What?" Luck asked.

"Luck?"

"Yes, my name is Luck."

"Is that an Asian thing?"

Luck's open palm did not feel pleasant as it slammed Sam's cheek.

"Jesus, OW!"

"You make fun of my people, and my people make you bleed," said Luck.

"That really hurt," Sam whined as he nursed the red handprint tattoed to his face, "I've never known a girl named Luck, and considering the fact that you were about to be used as a religious sex slave sacrifice, it just, you know, it's funny."

"Well I don't think my name is very funny. It was given by someone very special to me."

"Your mom?"

Luck scowled.

"So," Sam continued, sensing he was on the verge of taking something too far, "Since you actually know where we are, do you have any idea how we might possibly sneak out of here?"

Luck looked around and shrugged.

"Are there guards outside?" Sam asked her after she made no response.

"Of course there are. Obviously there are guards outside. And anyway," she went over to the door and jiggled the handle, which didn't budge, "Locked."

"Well shit. Maybe there's a grenade or something lying around? We could blow our way out?"

Luck cocked her hip again and raised her eyebrow at him.

"Just a joke. A small joke."

She swept the room with her eyes, pushed a desk to the wall, and pulled a panel near the ceiling. Behind it was an air duct, which, with a flourish, she presented to Sam.

"Think I'll fit?" Sam asked.

"I think *I'll* fit," she said.

"So what, you're going to go ahead and what? Subdue the guards? Get the key? I can't let you do that alone, it's too dangerous."

"Shut up. You're getting in the hole too. Oh, and if I find out that you're lying to me, or that you're fucking me over in any way, shape, or form, I will murder you. I know how. I may be small, but," she looked directly up into his eyes, and Sam's nethers clenched partially with lust but mostly with fear, "I know exactly where to hit you to do the damage you don't come back from. We clear?"

They were clear.

Twenty minutes later he had managed it. He'd had to remove his shirt, partially due to Luck's goading, and partially because the material made him just a touch too bulky to squeeze his body in. Luck had gone in first, and, being substantially smaller than he, had already wriggled up to the point where the ducts expanded.

Sam, arms stretched out in front, feet stretched behind, tried to claw and wiggle his way forward, but it wasn't easy going. He was trying to slither like an eel, then he imagined himself thrashing like a beached dolphin, and finally he tried rooting like a pig, but none of these really seemed to help. The pig one mostly just made him feel even larger. Eventually, after some tense moments where Sam was sure he'd be stuck forever and some mean spirited taunting from Luck, Sam had made it through to where the duct opened up.

"Be quiet, don't fall through," Luck said to Sam as he watched her ass crawl away. He was upset with himself for his complete lack of control, but he couldn't really turn his head away, and it was pretty dark in there anyway, so he wasn't seeing much. And she'd never know.

"Stop staring at my ass," she said quietly.

"Shut up, I'm not," Sam lied back.

"Ok, I figure this should take us to a bathroom somewhere, right?"

"Should it?" Sam said, thinking about every movie ever where someone fell into a fan from a duct or dropped right on to the principle's desk. When had he gotten himself stuck in a morbid high school movie?

They crawled in silence, listening intently to the nothing, hoping violently the sound of panic or gunshots didn't ring out below them. Too often the duct would bow out and make a hollow metallic sound, which would make Sam cringe and would make Luck's ass, and presumably the rest of her, stop and cringe too. But they trudged on like a bad spy movie, with Luck stopping every once and again to look down through a grate. Sam was shocked this was actually working. There was no reason for this to actually work except for the fact that it somehow was. There seemed to be a lot of that happening lately.

Eventually Luck decided they'd crawled far enough, and she stopped at a vent, which was a relief for Sam because he was now certain they'd checked the room and found them missing and their chances of actually escaping were dwindling.

"Hey, what's happening?" Sam asked, and without answering Luck maneuvered her body around and kicked out a grate.

It clattered loudly to the floor and Sam cringed again, waiting for those steamy bullets to start ricocheting around like crazy.

When Sam finally opened his eyes, Luck was out of the vent.

"Hey, let's go," she said. So he did.

Thankfully there was no tapering involved with the vent here, and Sam was able to wriggle out into the dim room without any major complications, discounting the painful five foot drop to the ground.

"We should find some clothes," Sam said, dusting himself off and looking at her thin dress. They were in a lab of some variety. Or at least there were lab tables and Bunson burners and test tubes around. Everything was white and glass, and there were two lab coats hanging conveniently on a rack. Sam grabbed them and tried to wrap one around Luck. She snatched the billowing cloth from him, and with barred teeth she stared him down and put it on herself.

"You're the tiniest scientist I've ever seen!" Sam said gaily as he put a coat on himself, "Do you think we'll fool anyone?"

"Are you asking if you think other people will think we're scientists here?"

"Yeah," said Sam as he scratched at himself.

"Not at all. Search for some sort of weapon," she commanded.

Together, or rather on opposite sides of the room, they dug through the cabinets and cupboards of the room, but they were full of beakers and chemicals in tubes and vices and other things that didn't make easy weapons.

"Can you believe there are no bazookas in here?" Sam asked as a joke.

"Yes. Why would they keep that in a lab?" Luck asked, missing the point, "Anyway, there's nothing here. We're just going to have to risk it."

Sam stared at her for a moment. The lab coat just covered her small cleavage. She looked like a tiny porn star, ready for some lightly contrived scene set for no probable reason in a laboratory. Sam was excited by the strangest things anymore.

"Let's do it," he said as Luck was already opening the door, "Wait."

"What?" she said, turning on him.

"Do we have a place to go once we get out of here?"

"I know a place."

"Ok, excellent, can I come?"

Luck stared at him, her face conveying the pity she had for his stupidity. She nodded just slightly.

"Ok, well let's go," he said.

"Let's."

And they were out the door. She turned and put a finger up to her lips with a furrowing of her brow, letting him know to keep quiet. He already knew though. She really thought a lot of him it seemed.

The hallway was empty, but lit, which made him nervous. Anyone walking down this hall would see them from a mile off.

As they headed down the hall, careful to hug the walls because apparently they felt safer along them, Sam occupied himself with worrying about whether or not they had discovered he was missing yet. There's no way they'd assume he would have lasted this long. It had been what? Almost forty-five minutes now? Possibly an hour? Sam wasn't some Tantric god. And he was sure they'd figure that out too. They had to have burst in. Maybe they'd realized he and Luck had escaped through the vents and then tried to follow, but then they got trapped in the vents themselves because they were fat guards. Except that was ridiculous. The guards were certainly not that stupid. It would be nice if they were though.

They turned down a hall and saw two people walking in the opposite direction, backs thankfully to them. Luck pushed Sam backwards, and they hugged the wall at the corner. She peeked around, waited for them to be out of sight, and then she and Sam hurried in the opposite direction.

"Do you know where we're going?" Sam whispered.

"Shhhh," said Luck.

They twisted and turned down a few hallways, and Sam's mind wandered again. He wondered where Bare was; he hoped he was all right. Where could they be? Had they locked them up in cells? Would Bare have even fit in that tiny cell they'd put him in? He hoped wherever they were, they were together. He really missed them. He missed them more than he missed his dead family, and he'd known Bare and Tess for under a week. That was insane to him. How did he miss them more than his family?

He couldn't even remember what his parents looked like. As they jogged down another set of stairs, Sam tried to picture his mom's face, but he literally could not do it. How had he not taken any pictures of his family? He knew why, of course. Deep down he did, he just wasn't ready to-

Luck stopped suddenly, and Sam bumped into her back.

"Ooof," he said automatically, and Luck turned and stared at him with fiery eyes as his outburst echoed down the hallway to the two guards who were stomping around, clearly searching for something. That something very clearly being he and Luck. Shit.

"Hey!" one of the guards shouted down the hall, "Hey you!"

"Run," Luck said. And they did. They ran as fast as they could, Sam now in the lead. He tried a door marked 'stairs,' but it was locked.

"Stop!" the guards yelled from the end of the hallway, their guns aimed, their boots making large, dull sounds as they barreled forward.

"Go, go, go, go, go," Luck repeated.

They raced through industrial style hallways now, and they could hear new boots storming in from different directions. This could be bad. No shots had been fired yet though, so Sam assumed they were looking to take them alive. And then as if reading his thoughts, someone yelled down the hallway:

"We *will* shoot you!"

Sam tried a new door now that they'd broken the sight line with any guards, and this one opened to an extra dingy and dark hallway. Sam motioned for Luck to follow him in, and they moved as fast as they could in the twilight of the hall. There was a light coming from somewhere further down, and they moved toward it. Sam moved as quickly as possible, hands out in front of him like a blind man groping for sight. Of course it was his shin that caught something.

"Oh, ho ho ho, ow," he breathed.

"What?" Luck said.

"Watch out, there's something here."

Sam groped at it and couldn't place what it was, but it was clearly mechanical and abandoned so they went around it and moved toward

that sweet light. Soon they could see enough again, and they picked up the pace. The hallway ended in an empty garage, which was freezing cold, and filthy, but the door at the dark end of the hallway had just burst open, and from the sound of it a fair few guards were running toward them.

They were just getting outside when they heard the first of the guards yell in pain as they ran in to whatever was lurking in the hallway. Sam hoped that would buy them some time.

Luckily it was still night and rather late, so there weren't many people out and about, and the streets were relatively dark. It was absolutely freezing though, and Sam now understood why they called Chicago the 'Windy City.' The wind tore through the lab coats which Sam and Luck both clung to their shaking bodies.

"This way I think," Luck said, trying to keep her teeth from chattering.

"You think?" But she had already run off. Sam followed as fast as he could away from this building and the guards with their guns.

Sam had forgotten how big and impressive cities could be. He found it hard to believe that creatures capable of constructing something like this, of a civic project on this scale, could be almost completely wiped out by something as simple as a vengeful planet. It was a little mind boggling to him.

"We should get inside soon, or we're going to get frostbite," Sam said.

"I know where I'm going."

He hoped she did. Sam visualized purple frostbitten toes and sickly gangrene deaths, although, at the rate Chicago was working, a bullet seemed more likely than a slow and painful death anyway. The cold was so distracting that Sam found it harder to enjoy the magnitude and magnificence of the city around him, which he knew would be a shame later. He doubted he'd get much time to explore unfortunately.

Sam was positive Smith's forces were barring down on them as they ran. He pictured those jeeps that tore up when he'd driven in, and he couldn't imagine they weren't out in full force right now. Was he that important though? Why *was* he so important to them? Could Smith really not live without whatever was... whatever was happening with Sam's crotch right now. He hoped Mister Fresh had been right. He also hoped to hell whatever his 'sickness' was curable. He really didn't want to be broken for life. What an absolute shame that would be he thought as he watched Luck run.

Luck turned them down another street and suddenly they were by the water, which was completely unexpected. Chicago was such a strange city in that way; you could literally walk from your office, or home, or prison cell as it was for Sam, and be right at the beach. Not too shabby for being smack dab in the middle of the country. The beach didn't look particularly appealing right now though. Snow was bunched up into great frozen drifts, and Sam could only see white until the night ate up his sightline.

"Where are we going?" Sam said, "We're too out in the open. This wind is brutal."

"We're close."

"How close."

"Close."

And it turned out they were. Maybe only five minutes later they'd found the submarine. It was moored and roped intimately with a dock, clearly not meant to be moved. The ice had eaten most of it, but it was a tourist attraction at a time, so there was an enclosure built out on the dock around it. Luck grabbed a piece of ice and jammed it into the wall, popping out a piece of the siding. Hiding behind was a key which she jammed into the lock, and then pushed inside to the blissful shelter.

Being out of the wind was one of the greatest feelings of Sam's life. Although he had no feeling in his body. He couldn't honestly remember a time he had been so cold in all of his life. His entire body shook violently in the paper-thin lab coat, and he looked over at Luck, noting her nipples were hardened to the point of knives, threatening to pierce through the fabric. It was pretty hot actually, but he had no idea how she was so nonchalant about the brutal, sickening cold.

"I'm so ca-ca-cold," Sam said, his teeth chattering. Luck shivered as she rapped on the entrance twice fast, once slow, and then three more quick raps. And they waited, shivering violently. Sam looked around for a blanket, or a coat, but only saw the trappings of a tourism office. There was a ticket counter along one wall, a rack housing fliers near the door, and a few posters of submarines with little blurbs explaining historical significance and fun facts and the like. He wanted to set it all on fire just to feel the warmth. Maybe he really was an arsonist.

He peeked out the window and saw no guards running down the dock after them. They may have actually escaped. They were lucky there wasn't fresh snow on the ground; they would have been screwed with even a powdering to preserve their bare toe prints.

"What is this?" Sam asked.

But before Luck could give him a dirty look, the door to the submarine cracked open with the sound of metal straining against echoing metal. Luck took a step back and the door swung open, spilling some light into the darkened tour office.

"Luck?" said an Australian male's voice from the shining light.

"Brick!" Luck said, showing the first enthusiasm Sam had seen in her yet as she jumped into the arms of the towering, muscular black man who emerged from the entrance. Sam was immediately intimidated.

"We all thought you was gone for there when ya didn't come back," Brick said, his accent thick and cartoonish, 'back' sounding more like 'bake.'

"I got caught up for a minute. It wasn't a big deal."

"Not a big deal? They tried to kill you through a sick, sexual ritual," Sam piped up, trying to seem big and protective too. Brick turned on him, his eyes exploring Sam's face and clearly not liking what they found. Brick was clean cut, he looked like a Marine, or whatever Australia's equivalent was, if they even had one. Tough, scary, he looked like a man who could protect the person he wanted to protect. Except that couldn't be true because Luck had been captured.

"And who are you then, mate?" he asked.

"I'm Sam," Sam said.

"He was a prisoner with me. I helped him escape."

"I mean, I helped too… I told you they were planning on killing you. That's definitely something."

"They told me if I had sex with him I would have been brought to Smith. But I freaked. I just… I'm sorry," Luck said to Brick.

"I didn't want ya out there in the first place. You never have to be sorry," he said.

"Could we maybe go inside?" Sam asked, "I think I might be freezing to death."

Brick looked at the shivering Luck, who nodded her approval, and then with a beckoning wave he disappeared back down into the hull.

"Welcome home," he said to the tight, echoing space. The submarine looked like it was in working order, or at least the lights were on and it wasn't as cold as the ice it was surrounded by, so Sam assumed things weren't totally fucked. He could feel his body warming already. It was a relief, but the warmth reminded him of his missing friends, and his inability to kill Smith. He had fucked up. He had really fucked up.

172

"I fucking keel them," said Pavel the Russian in comically broken English.

"I *will* kill them," Hartley a beautiful woman who reminded Sam of some of his mother's old friends if his mother's friends had been a bit younger and way more intense.

"How often must you correct him before the futility sets in, love?" asked Reece, the Englishman who appeared to be in a relationship, or at least wanted to be in a relationship, with Hartley. This group's dynamic was already becoming clear, and Sam had only known them for a short time. He liked that though. They all seemed interesting. Brick was the leader, and Pavel, who based on the curve of his spine, the general shittiness of his beard, and the greasiness of his hair, Sam assumed was a scientist of some sort. Or at least some type of nerd-job. Reece was almost too tall for a submarine, and, as he had already brought it up three times, he was the chef on board. Along with other duties. But he was the chef, and Hartley was… honestly Sam had no idea what she did. But she looked pretty good doing it. And then there was Misty. She was the quiet one. Sam had only heard her speak once, and it was when she'd greeted him. Which was something, he supposed.

They were in the dining room slash multipurpose room now, where they'd retired after Sam and Luck spent some time warming up with warm sponge baths and desperate checks for frostbite.

"I'm all for killing all of these fuckers, but-" started Luck.

"Language," Harley said.

"You are not my mother, Hartley. You're not, and I can say fuckers or fuck any time I fucking please, got it?"

"Luck, please," said Reece, his accent making the two words sound somehow incredibly intimate. Luck's rage seeped out as she folded her arms into a pout. She acted so different here. She was totally prepared to have sex with a stranger not two hours ago, and here she was acting like a girl her own age. It was so strange what different scenarios and different people brought out in a person.

"Vell, ve have to do something, da?" said Pavel.

"Why can't you just leave?" asked Sam, "Can't you just sail this submarine out of here again?"

The room was silent for a moment, and Sam was scared that he'd offended them in some way, but then Brick let out an echoing "HA" and then followed that up was a steady stream of more "Ha ha ha ha HA's." And of course that caught on with the rest of the group, and pretty soon Sam felt that blood rise into his cheeks and his balls shrink up into his stomach to hide from this unexplained embarrassment.

"You think we got our submarine into Lake Michigan?" Brick asked after they'd all caught their breath again, "Nah, nah, no mate, nah. That'd be bloody impossible. Do ya reckon the canals are open without these buggers manning them? Not to mention the whole bloody lot of mines out there! Ha, no skip, this old wreck has been here for some time. We just moved in when we needed a place to crash here in Chicago."

"Oh, ok," Sam said, looking around. How the hell was he supposed to know all that? He probably should have guessed though with all the fliers up top, "But I mean, why can't you just leave? Couldn't you just find a truck or something and go?"

"They've got all the exits sealed, or busted, or blocked," said Hartley.

"They say it's for the people's protection, that it's used to keep out the unwanted, the crazies, the… the whatever. But you can't just leave."

"I mean, couldn't you walk out? This seems crazy to stay here."

"We can't leave," said Misty, tripling the amount of words he'd heard her say. She had a pretty voice. It was like a shy wind chime.

"Why?" asked Sam, looking at Misty, who had now resumed looking at her feet tucked in under the rungs of the metal chair.

"Why can't you just leave?" Sam asked the rest of the group.

"Smith needs to be stopped, OK? We can't just go. If we leave it's not going to matter. If we leave we'll all be dead," Luck said.

"I know he needs to be stopped. He's got to die or the world will end. That's why I'm here, I was wondering why *you* specifically can't leave."

"He is monster," Pavel added helpfully.

"Right, so you knew about his virus plan? And you're on our team, right?"

"Well yeah. Wait, what's he doing with viruses?"

"He's planning on infecting the entire world with his viruses," Luck said.

"That explains a lot," Sam said thinking of that penis, "But you were going to have sex with him knowing all that?"

"Of course I knew. Everyone knows. That's his thing. That's his entire deal. How would I not know?"

"Then why did you act surprised when I told you before?"

"I wasn't surprised, I was just reassessing my plan."

"You made the right decision," Brick finished, "We never agreed to that plan, I would never have agreed to you, you of all people, going on a suicide mission like that."

"How was having sex with him going to help anything though," Sam asked still lost.

"It was the only way to get close to him," Hartley said, "His people are everywhere, and they're well trained. He's promised them he's going to create a better world through this. He's promised them that he knows the secret to beating Mother Nature, to stopping what happened before from happening again. Stupid sheep."

"And these people want that. People don't feel safe anymore," Reece said, sliding his arm around Hartley.

"Alright, enough with the history lesson," Brick said, "Bugger's gotta go and that's that. End'a story."

"So what are we gonna do?"

"We?" asked Luck.

"I mean yeah, I want to help you guys," said Sam.

"I don't think there is a 'we.' I helped you escape, you're escaped, and now you leave us alone."

"He knows our hideout location though," Hartley said, and Sam got that sinking feeling in his stomach that came with assessing a situation wrong. He had thought these people were friends, but he could already see the knife coming for him. These people had a secret to hide. They didn't need him. Look at Pavel. He was Russian, he was greasy, there's no way he wasn't mostly crazy. He would kill on a lark. Russians were like that, right? And Brick looked like he could break a cinder block in half with his teeth. Seriously the man's teeth were huge. Every time he spoke, Sam wondered how horrible teething must have been for him, squeezing those huge suckers through virgin gums. Sam could bet that a trauma like that would be worthy enough cause for a little mental unbalance, a little hatred of the world, a little ability to kill off Sam and dump his body in the cold bath of Lake Michigan without losing much sleep. Shit.

"I have an idea," Sam said, heading them off before they descended on him like a pack of hyenas on some wounded wildebeest. He didn't even know if hyenas and wildebeest lived in the same area, but he did know that this ragtag group of foreigners were about to rip him to pieces. Or at least that's what his mind was telling him.

"You say that Smith has this city on lockdown, that his guards are always around, always watching, always... you know, fucking vigilant," he continued, trying to sell a point he hadn't quite thought up. What could they do? How could they get to him? They didn't have that special key to his elevator; they didn't... could they blow up the building? Drop a bomb on him? What could they do?

"What we need is a distraction. We need something to occupy the guards while we go and take care of Smith, right? Wouldn't that help?"

"Probably, but-"

"And I know the layout of the building. I've been inside his penthouse, I know how it works, and I've seen the hiding places for the guards. I think we could plan this like this. I think it's really possible."

Brick sat down finally, and Sam filled himself with the stale-air, sweat perfume of the submarine as his nostrils nervously flared. Brick was mulling it over, and to an outsider it might have looked rather casual, just some grubby adults huddled in a Cold War submarine, trying to figure out who or what would be the least amount of awkward to look at, but to Sam this was an inquisition. Brick was a judge in some backwoods legal system where their laws and rules were based around their fear of the sun. Sam, as he had for the last week or so, felt his life on the precipice of jeopardy, and as his breathing calmed him, he found he had become somewhat more at peace with the whole concept. Maybe he was just becoming practiced.

"Alright mate, yeah. I think that sounds ruddy brilliant. It'll be good to have a fresh set of eyes in on this whole mess, right all?"

"Da, yes, I am much tired of thought," said Pavel. Sam could really see that getting annoying after a certain amount of time. English syntax was dumb, but it wasn't that hard.

Sam looked at Luck, and the bags under her eyes made her look twenty years older. She probably hadn't slept in a long time. Reece saw this too.

"Darling, we must get you to bed. You look absolutely ragged. No offense of course love," he said. Luck looked up at him, and Sam saw that flitter of attraction, or interest, or something that rarely got turned Sam's way, dance its way across Luck's tired eyes. Shit, Sam thought. Well... maybe she could be a project. Sam felt dirty for thinking of a person like that, and was now just confused what to think in general. Bare would know what to say to her.

The thought of Bare gave him the insane urge to run back out into the cold and try to find him, but that was crazy. It was late, the winds were unnaturally strong, he was dead tired and had no idea where to start. And maybe these guys would have some idea. His best bet would be to ingratiate himself here. These guys were trying to overthrow this system, and his friends were hidden somewhere in that system. Helping these guys *was* helping Bare and Tess. And also Sam was pretty sure he'd die if he didn't get some actual rest soon, some rest in a place where florescent lights weren't stabbing at his eyelids the whole time.

"Let's get you to your bed little lady," Reece said to Luck, and Sam saw Hartley's large, brown doe eyes squint at Reece's attention to someone that wasn't her.

"Pavel, could you make up a bed for our guest then?" Brick instructed as opposed to asked despite the inflection he actually used. Pavel nodded and stood and beckoned Sam to follow.

"Hey, goodnight everybody. It was a pleasure to meet you all. I'm really excited to find some fellow people who... It's just good to meet you. And thank you for taking me in. I truly appreciate it. And if there's anything I can do for you just let me know."

"We go," Pavel said as he led Sam down a corridor. Luck stared at him, her beautiful eyes shimmering with the low lighting of the submarine, looking right into him as he left, and Sam's heart, ever on the move, leapt into his throat. Now he wasn't sure how easy sleep was going to come.

"Bathroom is down hall," Pavel explained after he'd set Sam up a cot with a gnarled fleece blanket that felt more like steel wool than something one would exploit for warmth. There was also a dubious chunk of something that Sam was supposed to believe was or had been a pillow. At least he wasn't still in that horrible building thinking about how he'd just gotten a beautiful girl killed through inserting his itchy penis into her. 'When had his life gone this far off the rails?' he thought at he scratched idly at his genitals.

"Water is in jug by bed. Is melted snow, but is good. You drink as you please."

"Hey, thank you. Thanks for this. We're going to… we're gonna do it," Sam said lamely.

Pavel took a moment, flashed a quick frown, and walked away. Sam couldn't tell if Pavel didn't fully understand what he'd said or just didn't care, but it felt good to be alone for a moment. There was something stressful about being on a submarine. He wasn't sure how these people did it. It felt like being in a bunker, or a grave, or in one of Sam's dreams. It was confining, it was short, it was the opposite of everything Sam had been used to for the past forever. He wondered, as he stooped and weaved between pipes and severe metal toward the bathroom, what living in a place like this would do to a person.

He smacked his head on a lower hanging bar, and as angry as he was, his thoughts drifted quickly after the small echo that reverberated from the tune his skull made when combined with the metal. Even a small sound like that echoed in a space like this. He had to imagine these people's personalities did the same. Maybe that's why Pavel and Brick seemed like such cartoon characters to Sam. Or maybe it came from the fact that Sam had never actually met anyone from outside of America before.

That wasn't true. There was a German foreign exchange student his freshman year. His name was Nacho, as his father had been born in Mexico but had moved to Germany to work in an advertising firm. Sam hadn't quite gotten how that had matched up exactly, and had always secretly wondered if Nacho had been lying, but the kid had had darker skin, and Sam wasn't about to mess with a German. He'd learned too much about their whole deal in History class.

But beyond Nacho the inexplicable German, Sam couldn't really point to anyone he knew who was actually foreign. The thought struck him as sad, as he sat on the small metal toilet seat to evacuate whatever wasn't there.

Discounting skeletons, he had never even met a Canadian, and he'd lived there for eight whole goddamn years. Well he should give these guys the benefit of the doubt. They were nice enough to let him stay here, they were good enough to take him in, and he agreed with what they were planning on doing.

Well there wasn't much else to do but trust them and let his hope carry him. At this point it was definitely his best option, and despite the eyes she made at Reece, there was Luck to think about. Her straight, black hair framing her face, her small soft lips and elegant collarbones and... and he couldn't get the thought of her naked body out of his mind. It was a sunspot image he couldn't blink away. His mind would wander for a moment and then come right back to her and the three freckles living right where her stomach and hip met. And she was mere feet away. Right now.

As he flushed away his business to who knew where, and washed his hands with the frozen water from Lake Michigan around them, the thought of Luck snoring so close assaulted his brain. He could have had sex with her. He really could have. She was so insistent, but he had to play the good guy. He hadn't known why she'd wanted him, and that's what scared him out of it. Also there were other circumstances, but right now he was just trying to rationalize his sexuality.

With Carol it hadn't mattered as much. Sam knew exactly why she liked him. She was old; she didn't have choices, and he was objectively better looking than she, at least at the point where their lives had intersected. But with Luck... Luck was beautiful. He loved how small her nose was and how surprisingly big her eyes were and the thought of her small, bright lips made his mouth water and his body tremble.

He stretched out on the small cot and covered himself with the blanket. The thought of a kiss, of her lips on his, and the feel of her small body in his arms had him straining in his shorts. He turned his head stealthily as he shimmied his pants down to about mid thigh. He stopped for a moment, listening carefully to the metallic silence of the submarine. No one was up and moving, and except for the groans and strains of the ship itself, the sub was quiet. And he was hidden away under a generous amount of piping, so he felt safe as he started in on himself.

It started routinely enough. He imagined he was here, in his shitty little cot. Except no, now it was a bed. It was a comfortable bed, and this was a comfortable room instead of the evil twin of a supply closet. And here he was, stretched out, posed and ready for anyone to walk in. And here comes Luck, sauntering over, a short dress already coming off over her head and thrown to the floor inside out and knotted. Sam didn't even have to say anything as she took him in her hand and smiled up at him, her teeth beaming through the dark, her breasts somehow illuminated and shining, her entire body alive and soft and perfect. In his fantasy she moved down quickly and took Sam in her mouth, just like Carol had done, except this was infinitely better than Carol. This could have made him come at any moment.

Except he wasn't ready, and instead of the adorable mouth of the sassy young girl he'd just met, it was just his winter-rough hand clenched desperately on his own member, flying up and down on the thing now and making a bit of a racket as his hips bucked slightly, the cot squeaking and moaning in protest. As any of these sessions happened, his fantasy broke down once he'd reached the penis in vagina portion, and the already loose storyline that had existed moments before drifted into vague images and feelings and thoughts, fuel to keep his hand gripped tightly and shimmying.

"You get any of that on those sheets, and you're washing them," Luck said from next to him, "And laundry in frozen water sucks."

Sam's heart twisted inside his chest as his stomach tried to find an exit out of its prison. He fumbled with the blanket, but he was too far in, his mind was blank, in disaster recovery mode, a big error screen blinking red where his eyes should be. His body wasn't responding in the ways he'd hope it would. He managed to sit up, his hands ripping the blanket from his lap, his back to Luck as his semen flew through the air. It had been days since he'd last had a release and his youthful sperm were eager and many as they found their way to the submarine floor.

"Oh Jesus," Luck said, presumably turning away in horror. Sam was caught on that edge between feeling so good and feeling like his life was about to end. Little Death, where had he heard that before? Finally his body stopped spasming, and he knew, even in the dark, that he had made quite the mess.

"Are you happy now?"

"Not really," he finally managed to say, "Could I maybe get a minute."

"You can have as many as you like."

"Wait, I'm sorry I just-"

"Here, I came to give you this," Luck said, as Sam craned his neck around to look at her finally. She was still turned away from him as she threw the extra blanket on the cot next to him, "I'd appreciate it if you didn't use that to wipe up. It gets cold down here. I thought you could use it. So, goodnight."

"Sorry."

But she was gone. The bile tickled his throat again as the embarrassment overtook him. His life seemed to be one long string of these moments anymore. He tried to take comfort in the thought of his cabin, of solitude, but even that had lost its magic. It seemed empty now, and he seemed empty now. Had he ruined his chances with Luck just then? Did he even have a real chance in the first? How much had she seen? Had he accidently moaned her name or something? Had he?

His feet plodded on the cold steel floor, making too much noise in the silence as he went to grab toilet paper. He bunched some up angrily in his fists, taking out all his emotions on the quilted squares, and then he was back at the cot, mopping up the puddles in the dark, hoping he wasn't missing any because he really didn't want a reminder of this in the morning. Even though Luck was certainly going to be a reminder now. He didn't know how he was going to face her tomorrow. He imagined in quarters as tight as these it was difficult to avoid someone, but maybe he'd manage.

He lay back down on the cot, which now felt colder, stiffer, as if all the energy that had recently been in his cock had flown down and starched the canvas that felt stretched across the poles with spite. He pulled the ratty green blanket up over himself and contemplated the blanket Luck had thrown to him. It was pink and well loved, small, maybe fit for a twin-sized bed at best. Sam could imagine it spread lovingly over the lower mattress of a bunk bed, or maybe even bunched up in a kennel for a dog. It made him sick to look at it, and he wanted desperately to just throw it on the ground. But instead he fought the urge, pulled the fraying fabric up to his chin, and closed his eyes as tightly as he could.

One deep breath.

Two deep breath.
Don't think. Three deep breath.
Four deep breath.

183

Eventually morning came. And eventually he had found sleep. It was not restful sleep, but the dreams that invaded it were not as clear as they usually were. He remembered snippets of conversations with Luck, images of Tess and Bare in cages wrapped in pink blankets, being suffocated by fraying, pink blankets. There was a lot of Mr. Smith and bodies leaking red, red blood, but the memories of whatever had happened during his night slipped away from him as the lights in the submarine increased from a low, morning tone to a brighter wake-the-fuck-up tone. So he did as they seemed to instruct.

He put his pants, the only clothing item he had taken off in the night, back on and tussled his dirty hair in an effort to look presentable. He doubted it had done much, but at least he'd be up next to Pavel, whose greasy facade made the rest of the world look like walkers on a runway.

How was he going to face Luck? He'd taken most of the night sweating over the options, which had boiled down to the most probable two. Option one was to go straight up to her and confront the issue head on. Option one entailed eye contact, a sure stride, and confidently saying something like, 'Hey, I'm sorry you had to see that last night, I'm pretty embarrassed about it, but I hope you don't judge me for it.' And then maybe close with a joke about being taught that masturbation was a beautiful thing. He was a little afraid to use the word 'masturbation' in front of her though, and the responsible way of going about things didn't feel right to him. And what if others were around? They almost certainly would be, and if he could help it he'd really not like that to be the first impressions they had of him too.

He leaned much more heavily toward option two, which was to completely ignore the elephant that would certainly be taking up any room they shared and hope for the best. He'd always been good at the ostrich technique, hell, his whole existence for the last eight years was one big ostrich play, except instead of his head in the sand it was his head buried in five feet of Canadian snow. As much as he'd like to take the noble route, what seemed to clearly be the smart route, he was almost certainly going to do the ignoble thing. At least he knew himself enough to know he was a coward.

In the bathroom his stream of piss shot out in three different directions, none of which made it into the small steel toilet. He bent to clean it up.

"BREAKFAST!" Reece yelled from somewhere down the sub. Moment of truth.

Sam walked in, and Brick, Pavel, and Misty were already seated. Reece set a huge platter of pancakes down before leaving through a hatch again. Hartley came in carrying two bottles of syrup, Aunt Jemimah's finest, and she set that next to the stacks.

"Have a seat, mate," Brick said, although Sam heard him say 'bate,' and his cheeks went red. Brick pretended not to notice as he speared a few cakes, flopped them down on his plate, and went to work spreading a red jam over the tops of them. Reece came back in with a plate of what looked, incredibly, like poached eggs.

"Can you not bloody wait for the rest of us? Sir?" Reece asked at Brick as the fearless leader fearlessly shoveled eggs onto his pile, eye contact all the while. Defeated, Reece sighed and took a seat, and soon Harley came back in with a pitcher of water and sat next to Reece. The whole crew, as if given some unspoken cue, grabbed at plates and cakes and eggs all at once. The table was alive with clattering, and despite his nervousness about when the bomb that was Luck would drop on him, the sounds and life that came with having breakfast with a group of real, living human beings was thrilling for Sam.

"Hey, you looking to go hungry?" Hartley said to him, pointing at the trays with a fork jiggling with egg.

"Gotta have your strength for today," Brick said mid chew. Somehow his voice was completely unaffected by the aggressive amount of pancake that swirled in his mouth. Sam wasn't really all that hungry, the nerves were doing the chewing for him right now, but he also didn't want to look rude or guilty, so he dragged a couple pancakes onto the scratched and dented metal tray that served as his plate. He took his time pouring the syrup on, biding his time, not wanting Luck to drop in while he had his mouth full. He wanted to be able to defend his honor on a dime.

Where was she? He wanted to ask the question, but he was also planning on ignoring her, so bringing her up now might raise suspicion. But maybe they already knew? Maybe they were aware?

"How'd ya'll sleep?" Misty asked, a slight Southern touch peeking out from somewhere.

"I slept like log," Pavel said.

"Like *a* log," Hartley corrected, and then, aiming those pretty, headlamp eyes at Sam, "Did you sleep well?"

Oh god, was that a wink in her voice? Did she know? Did Luck tell her? Sam had figured Luck hated her, what with Luck pretty clearly being in to Reece. Did they all know?

Sam looked around. They were all staring at him. Pavel and his greasy black eyes peaking out through his greasy black hair, judging him, Sam, for his own lewd and greasy activity. Brick looked like he knew, he was breathing down his neck, Reece was doing the same but in a smug, English way. Hartley's eyes were boring holes in Sam's face, and Misty was so ashamed by Sam's indecency that she couldn't even bring herself to look at him. Where was Luck? Who would save him from this? Fuck!

"OK!" Sam yelled, and everyone jumped back a little, save for Brick, who didn't even flinch mid chew. The man was aptly named.

"Ok, I did it. I masturbated last night, ok? I'm sorry. I apologize! It won't happen again I promise... I just... it's been awhile and... and..." Sam had read this situation wrong. That was clear. The whole table was staring at him now with a chorus of surprise, pity, and arched eyebrows. Who was this new tenant yelling about masturbation? Hartley looked like she was watching a sickly baby bird fall out of the nest.

A single clap came from behind him, causing him to jump up out of his thoughts, and that was followed by another clap, and then they slowly built up until Luck was applauding Sam and his performance.

"I saw it," she said as she sat down, "It was impressive. Pancakes look great Reece!"

"Thank you love."

And that did it. Luck had saved him. The whole crew went back to eating and chatting about their nights and their dreams, and Sam just stared at Luck, grateful and awestruck and totally thrown. This was not at all how he'd expected this morning to go. But he wasn't unhappy with it. There probably weren't many better ways this could have gone. He stared at Luck with puppy dog eyes that were not just for show. His gratitude was deep and fast and real.

She glanced at him, her mouth full of egg. She smiled a crooked smile, a bit of yolk escaping from the corner of her mouth which she caught with the back of her hand, considered it, and then licked clean. This might be what love feels like, he thought.

After breakfast Sam helped clean the dishes. It was the least he could do.

Reece showed him where the kitchen was, the impeccable kitchen, the spotless, beautiful kitchen. Sam felt like an intruder bringing the dirty dishes in to clean, so he went to work bringing them up to the standard of their surroundings. Reece dried and put away, and they worked in silence for a while. Luck might have shot the elephant in the ass, but it still hadn't died. Sam was just waiting for Reece to bring it up.

"Luck's quite the lady, isn't she?" Reece asked instead. Sam almost made a joke about his masturbation to try to combat the awkwardness, but he was delighted when it had nothing to do with his outburst.

"Yeah, yes. She seems pretty great. She seems to like you a lot," Sam said as he passed his dented tin plate over to Reece.

"She's a sweetheart," Reece said.

"Yeah. So are you and Hartley... is that?"

"Are we together?"

"Yeah."

"Sure."

"Sure, yes?"

"Yes, we've been together for a while now. She's a beautiful creature as well, yes?"

"Yes," Sam said, delighted that Luck didn't seem to have a chance.

"We basically raised Luck you know. Found her in Hong Kong. Starved half to death, basically rabid, didn't speak a word. We brought her along, taught her bloody everything she knows. It's incredibly really, the progress she's made. Absolutely astounding."

"You mean she didn't speak English?"

"No, she didn't speak. All she did was bark and growl, like a dog."

"Huh."

"How old was she?"

"Not sure. We think she's probably about seventeen now anyway, so nine or so back then would make sense."

"Sure."

Luck popped her head in, and smiled at Reece. She didn't look at Sam.

"Do *not* tell him anything about me, Reece."

"Wouldn't dream of it, love," Reece said to her, his voice gone buttery again. Sam just wanted a glance. This was stressing him out. 'Just look at me!' he wanted to yell.

"Well good. I don't need more lies spread about me," she said, and then finally she turned and winked at Sam. And then she was gone again.

"Adorable," Reece said, his eyes trailing her ass as she left. Shit.

Sam finished the dishes and felt lost again. He wasn't a fan of this whole never knowing what he should be doing thing. It had grown tiresome fast. He missed having constant projects. He couldn't relax unless he felt like he'd completed something, as if he had earned it. And in a place like this, he imagined he could never be relaxed. He was a man who needed some space. Not global apocalypse sort of space, that was literal overkill, but even when he was younger he'd liked to close the door to his room and just sort through thoughts every once and again. It was like social sleep. Sometimes he just needed a reboot, and there was no reboot space to be had down here.

He wandered down the hall after Reece had waved him away with a flick of his wrist and a nod of his head, possibly implying some sort of thanks as well. Sam passed an open hatch and caught a glimpse of Brick's blue jacket. He didn't know if he should bother him, but his brief pause caught Brick's attention.

"Yo," Brick called out to him. Sam assumed that was a beckon, so he ducked inside. There was another table in here with a tree's worth of paper strewn across it, chicken scratch handwriting sprawled across the pages. Brick clamped his hand down on Sam's shoulder and looked right into his eyes.

"We're doing a planning session in a few, you in then?"

"Yes, of course," Sam said, excited to be included. Something about Brick's size reminded him of Bare, and Sam felt another pang of guilt and homesickness. He should be out saving his friend right now. But that's what he was doing right? That's what these people were doing?

"Listen, they have my friends. They took them when we came in, and I need to save them. Any chance we could do that today?"

"Beauty, that's just the thing. Let's make it personal. I love it skip! Bring that to the table. Now go wash up or something," Brick said glancing at Sam's hands, "I'll meet you by the entrance in twenty."

Brick turned from Sam, and, taking the hint, Sam ducked back out the doorway.

Excellent, he thought as he walked down the corridor. He nodded to Pavel who was working with a wrench. Pavel gave him a nod back. Cool. Sam turned a corner and jumped back, scared for the umpteenth time, this round caused by Luck, her hand propping her up against the wall, her chocolaty, brown eyes staring right at him, waiting for him. Sam expected her to speak first, but apparently that was his job. He fumbled for words for a moment before settling on a simple:

"Hey, thanks for, you know."

"You've got a pretty big dick. Just thought you should know," she said, and then she slid past him, no more eye contact, just dropped a bomb like that and cruised on by.

"Uh, I, uh…" he said after her, but she was already around another corner. Was she messing with him? She'd already saved his ass, was that some sort of apology for walking in on him? Did she need to apologize? Should he apologize? What was her game?

Aware of it now, he scratched at his crotch. Was it big? He didn't really think it was, but shit, maybe he'd grown or something? Maybe all the big-dicked dudes of the world choked to death eight years ago on their own smugness, their own inborn confidence. Fuckers. Except… except what if he was one of those fuckers now? How had this girl gotten so far into his head? By talking about his dick of course. He sometimes hated how much of his life was dictated by his dick.

A penis was a difficult thing to walk around with, he realized. He was constantly aware of it, of its use, or disuse as was traditionally the case. He remembered in high school there was always talk about peoples' dicks. The girls, the guys, everyone talking about dicks. It was weird. Zane Tannemore's was like a pencil, thin but oddly long, Nick

Oldman's curved like a boomerang, Tommy Lake's was uncircumcised and gross. Fucking Chaz Bertlett's, that asshole fucking jock, had one that was reportedly gigantic. Which of course gave him the confidence needed to be a complete monster to the rest of the world. Well whatever. He was dead and his giant dick was long rotted away.

Girls were lucky like that too. Not the rotting bit. No one is lucky to rot, but they wore their badges on the outside, well in the open. Anyone could see if they had large breasts, which back then was the social equivalent of a big cock. A nice pair of breasts, as long as you also had some other good features, was a sure fire ticket into the popular circles. And no one really talked about a girl's vagina. Sam would overhear the occasional comment about girls like Jasmine, who were purported to be a touch slutty, having big vaginas, loose ones, like throwing a hot dog down a hallway, they'd say. But that was different, those were probably lies thrown around by the jealous and the stupid.

The more he thought about it, the more high school stories that cycled through his brain, the more he realized these people were all absolutely miserable. And maybe it had something to do with the age, something to do with the soul crushing setting that was high school, but the people he remembered were horrible, the whole experience had been horrible. What did people see in high school? How had the world decided it was a good idea to throw a bunch of hormones into such an intimate and stupid setting? It was almost enough to make Sam wonder if the apocalypse had been a positive thing in a grander sort of a way. If these were the sorts of choices that were made and deemed good, then what was the true definition of good?

But wait a minute? How did Luck know he had a big dick? What the hell was her point of reference if she was found at nine, mute and in Hong Kong, and then kept in a submarine? Sam smiled to himself. It probably didn't matter. She thought he had a big dick, and that was good. He could almost see himself being happy once Smith was dead, and he had his friends back, and once his crotch stopped this horrible goddamn itching.

Reece waited for Brick to move some of his plies of scribbled-on papers off the main table so he could set down a tray of assorted crackers.

"Thank you," Reece said as he was finally able to unload the beautifully presented assortment. His face twitched as everyone seated leaned forward and ruined the presentation in an instant. He sat down, a dour, English pout on his face as cracker crumbs rained down the front of his companions' shirts. Brick held up a finger as he attempted to swallow, and once he choked them down he said:

"Ok, so we've got a new set of eyes here today, which is a bloody good thing. You lot of ruffians were just sittin' around pushing a wheel on a treadmill. Reinforcements is what we need."

"Could we go door to door or something? Recruit people that way?" Sam asked. Luck looked at him with pity.

"Bad start. Dumb idea," Brick said.

"Too dangerous," Misty said.

"It is," Luck said, "Most of Chicago is in his pocket already, and the ones who aren't sure about him don't tend to last too long around here."

"How'd he get to be in charge? It seems insane that this many people would just put their faith in a man who's so clearly bonkers," Sam said.

"People just want to put their faith into something," Reece said, "Anything. After watching most of the world die, you don't think safety and stability have a certain charm and appeal? To be a part of something? To have hope. Mr. Smith is offering these people an escape and a promise that this sort of world we have found ourselves perched upon does not have to be the only world. We can make it our own, we can take it back. That's what he's preaching. That's why these people are following him."

"Anyway, most of the population here works for him in some capacity. He controls all the resources," Brick said, "We have to really scrounge to come up with food, and he only gives out rations to those who work for him."

Sam thought about the eggs they'd had earlier. Reece and Hartley must have been pretty damn good at scrounging.

"So basically everyone works for him," Hartley said, "They'd die if they didn't."

"Also he has a nuke," said Luck.

"He has a nuke? As in nuclear bomb?"

"Yep. That tower of his was a cold war secret missile silo. You Americans hid them all over the damn place. It would turn your hairs white if you knew how close you'd been to nukes before," Brick said. Sam thought about Smith's penthouse. You couldn't get much closer than that.

"Ok, well that's pretty serious. I've got at least two friends who will join us, who can help. Well I mean... they're- it's a little strange," Sam said.

"What?" said Hartley.

"Well, my friend Bare, he's a bear, and Tess is a wolf. She has some burns right now, but I've seen her fight, and she's incredible. And Bare is giant, so he's pretty tough."

"Animal friends?" Brick said, "How the hell is that going to help?"

"Well I'll tell them to distract the guards or something, maybe we can find other animals to help."

"And you just think they're going to listen?"

"Yeah, sure, why wouldn't they? They're my friends."

Brick's face dropped. What? He looked at Luck, upset.

"Ya didn't tell me your bloke was mad."

"He's not crazy," Luck said, "He's like me. Here watch. Cheddar, get out here."

A brown rat crawled from a hole and hopped up on to the table. Misty pulled back, and Hartley gasped.

"Hey Cheddar."

"Hey Luck, wassup?" said Cheddar.

"Hi Cheddar, I'm Sam," Sam said with a wave, and the rat waved back.

"Well I'll be damned," Reece said.

"Say something Cheddar," Luck said.

"Like what? They're not going to try to kill me again, are they?"

"No one's gonna kill you," Sam said, and Luck turned to him, her face lit up like a Christmas tree.

"You can understand him! Amazing! I was so worried I was the only one."

"Why... wait, why did you never tell us you talked to animals Luck?" Hartley asked, concerned.

"I figured you'd think I was crazy."

"Well how do we know you two aren't," Brick said, "Make the rat do something. Make it do a disco."

"Do a disco? I doubt he knows what that is," Sam said, "Hey Cheddar, could you do a dance for us?"

"Yeah I heard him. This is degrading," Cheddar said as he got up onto his hind legs and waved his hands around in the air, and then did a little hip-bucking move. This rat was probably a better dancer than Sam was.

"How'd you guys meet?" Sam asked Cheddar.

"We just started talking one night, and she's a real sweetheart, nice to talk to," Cheddar said, with a wave toward Luck.

"She is. So what are you guys hearing?" Sam thought back to Buck in the grocery and how he hadn't responded to anything Bare had said.

"Squeakings," Paivel said.

"Well, he's a nice guy," Sam said.

"I think so too," Luck said, and Sam wasn't sure if she was talking about him or the rat.

"Ok, so that's good," Brick said, "That's something we can use. Now let's get a damn plan together."

They talked and schemed for most of the day, Sam recounting his story, giving them any information that might be useful, his skills and interests and all that, and they in turn tried to piece him in to plans they already had. Reece would get up every now and then and return a while later with snacks or pitchers of water, which were devoured almost instantly, the talks continuing even through the animalistic mastication. Sam lost track of time; it had gotten to the point where his body had completely lost the ability to find a comfortable position on his chair when Luck asked what time it was.

It was apparently time for the Jake and Marty show. It was mostly crap, it was explained to Sam, but it was also the only form of news anymore, and sometimes you could glean some important information, even through the bullshit. Also everyone listened to it, so it was good to be on the same level.

They turned on an important, powerful looking radio and a wave of static hissed out as if the radio had sprung a leak. Suddenly the static stopped.

"Hey, hey, hey folks! Welcome to another episode of the Jake and Marty show! I'm your host Jake"

"No I'm your host Jake!"

"Just kidding folks, I'm Marty."

Luck rolled her eyes and slumped back in her chair. Clearly she enjoyed this show.

"Hahaha, alright folks, it's another ca-ca-ca-ca-cold one in Chee-cah-go, but the heat is on, and indoors feels mighty nice!"

Their banter went on for a while, covering such banal topics as Mr. Smith's words on how to best serve him (turns out the secret is to not make a fuss!) the weather was brought up about every other topic, more about Smith, and of course the exciting things to do in wintery Chicago. Misty took notes while everyone else looked a little glazed.

"Hey Marty, you hear the one about the chicken and the egg?"

"I'm not sure I have Jake..."

"They made a pretty great dinner!"

Someone hit a button that played a track of canned laughter, and then before the laughter had even died down, a button caused a rooster to scream COCK-A-DOODLE-DOO!

"And speaking of animals Jake, we've got a new attraction down at the Michael Crichton Memorial Zoo!"

"The MCM Zoo? My favorite spot in Chicago, Marty!"

"You don't have to tell me twice, Jake! Yes folks, your old favorites have a new friend you can go and meet. Our most recent addition is the king of the forest, a seriously ferocious looking forest critters. We've got a brand new, big ol' Grizzly Bear."

"He's ferocious and fun folks!"

And the laugh track button had another work out for some reason, but Sam wasn't laughing.

"That's my friend. That's definitely Bare," Sam said, looking at Luck for confirmation.

"This new attraction brought to you by the ONE-derful and only Mr. Smith. So head on down to-"

"The magical-"

"The majestic-"

"The Magnificent!"

"The one-"

"The only!"

"Michael Crichton Memorial Zoo!" they said in unison.

"Open Monday through Saturday, 9:00am until dusk, Jake."

And then they moved on to some more awful jokes and useless stories and more talk about the weather. But Sam was done listening.

"That's my friend. I have to save him. Them. They were talking about Bare, but my friend Tess is there too. She's the wolf. We know where they are, we've got to save them," Sam said.

"Sure they friends?" Pavel asked.

"You think there are many grizzly bears who have just arrived in Chicago?"

"No," Pavel said.

"Look, if you guys help, I guarantee they can help us take down Smith. Can you imagine the distractions they can run? It's probably exactly what we need. We release them, and the city will be all up in arms right?"

"Everyone does love that zoo," Brick said, thinking.

"How would we even get in there though?" Luck asked, "That place is almost as heavily guarded as Mr. Smith. Other than his diseases, that zoo is his pride and fucking joy."

"Language," said Hartley.

"Oh my god, seriously?" Luck said, sounding exactly like the high school girls Sam had known.

"I think it's a good idea," Cheddar said, having popped his head back in. He was taking full advantage of exploring the sub now that he wasn't afraid they were going to kill him.

"We can figure it out, right?" Sam asked, "We have to. I have to do it even if you guys won't help. I just have to."

"Nah skip, we'll help. Of course we'll help ya; not much would piss this lot off worse than takin' away their zoo I reckon."

"I'm not sure if that's such a great idea," Reece said, after having been quite quiet for a time, "I can not imagine it's not dangerous. Quite possibly too dangerous. Can we really risk our own lives for those of a couple of animals? Beasts whom we don't even know can help us?"

"I would lay down my life for them," Sam said, and he was surprised at how much he meant it. The thought smacked him across the face. He'd never felt prepared to die for someone before, but he was all in for his friends he met a week ago, "I would do literally anything for them, and I promise they would be a huge help. I've watched Tess fight."

"Tess?" asked Hartley.

"She's the wolf. With the burns. Remember? Bare kinda has a thing for her, and I think she has one back but-"

"Not the information we're after, ace," Luck said dryly.

"Sorry, yeah. Well she's fast and has teeth, and she's smart as the dickens."

"As dickens?" asked Pavel.

"You guys know what I mean," Sam said, nearing exasperation. He'd sort of expected these guys to jump on his idea and to run with it. He had half expected them to be up and getting dressed for the cold already. But their asses were still firmly glued to their uncomfortable chairs.

"Well come on guys, let's get a plan going. How are we doing this?" Sam asked. There was quiet. He hoped they were just thinking.

"Well…" Brick said.

"Ok, listen, we sneak in and just open the cages and let the animals run free and do the work for us."

"Just walk in?"

"No, I guess not. We'll sneak in, maybe subdue the guards? I don't know. We take out the guards. Maybe we distract them somehow? Wait, I have an idea. Recon! Do they know all of our faces? I can't go, they'd spot me for sure, and Luck too, but do they know you guys?"

"They know me," Brick said, "Had a run in a while back. Got taken, but I got released. But they've got eyes on me I reckon. They got Pavel too.

Pavel nodded.

"Reece? Hartley?" Sam asked.

"I'm no good," Reece said, "And neither is Hartley. We were taken in a number of months ago while scrounging for food. We almost didn't make it out of there, did we love?"

"You saved us," Hartley said, smiling up at him. He smiled back down at her, and Sam was disgusted at their lack of help and general adorableness. Brick wasn't too happy with the display either, and Sam realized Brick was lonely. He was surprised Brick had feelings.

"I mean, how do you know these guards will remember you? How do we know it will matter? There are probably a whole ton of guards in this city, and they can't all know what you guys look like," Sam said.

"True, but all it takes is one, and we're dead. We want to take them unawares, not the other way around. These people don't do forgive and forget well," Brick said.

"Come on, someone's got to go survey it. See the inside..." Sam said. And then he remembered Misty. She was quiet, but she was there. She was the one taking notes during the stupid radio show, she would be perfect for a recon mission!

"Misty! Please," Sam begged. She looked at the ground.

"Alright, we need to calm down here, boy," Brick said, leaning forward.

"Calm down? Calm down?" Sam said, his anger seeping up into his eyes, his frustration boiling over, "How can I calm down when my friends are stuck in some horrible, smelly cage, and the people who say they want to do something to change this place aren't fucking doing anything? How the fuck do you expect me to calm down?"

Sam was standing now, his temples pulsing annoyingly. Luck stared up at him.

"Alright mate, alright," Brick said as he started to stand. All the men were starting to stand. It was getting to be a big standing party. Good, it was getting them moving.

"There we go, yes," Sam said, he walked over to Misty, causing all the men's knees to snap them upright, but Sam just dropped to his knees in front of Misty, "Please, please, please, please, please, please. I'm literally begging you right now. I can tell you're smart, I bet you notice things well. You're my only hope. These are the only people I love anymore. Didn't you ever love someone? Someone you would do anything for? If you don't go, I'm going to have to go myself, and chances are real high that I will get shot and killed or captured there. And if I'm captured then Smith wins."

Misty squirmed in her seat, still only making eye contact with the floor.

"Huh?" Reece said.

"I, uh, I have something he wants," Sam said, his brain having cooled down enough to respond in a normal way. He turned back to

Misty, "Just please. It would mean the world to me, and I would do anything in return."

"Misty-" Brick said.

"Ok," said Misty, "If it means that much to you, I'll do it. I... ok."

"Thank you, oh my god, thank you that's incredible! You're incredible," Sam said as grabbed her hand and kissed it, "You are amazing, you're an angel, you're the best, you're my favorite, I love you!"

Misty blushed a deep velvet, her cheeks splotchy with the adoration Sam was showering on her.

"Ok," she said.

"Ok," said Brick, "Well let's map it out first if we're going to send anyone out."

"Thank you," Sam said again. Reece was staring at Sam as if he were trying to put a jigsaw puzzle together that should have been obvious but may have had some missing pieces. He glanced at Luck, and she was staring at Reece. Sam really hoped this wasn't the start of an odd triangle. But at least he was closer to getting Bare and Tess back. Positive steps. Big steps. His face stretched into a smile as they sat down and planned the shit out of it.

235

Sam's eyeballs threatened to freeze from the cold as they tried to watch the guard, naturally outfitted with a gun that looked like it was designed to take down airplanes, pace in front of the entrance of the Michael Crichton Memorial Zoo in the howling wind and snow. A savage blizzard had popped up overnight. There were some strange things happening in nature lately, and they just seemed to keep getting worse. Sam thought about the animals killing themselves, the unnatural shifts between heavy snowfall and intense, brutal cold. The killer winds in Chicago. It was almost as if the earth were trying to rid itself of something. Sam thought about this as he tried to itch his crotch through the thick snowpants.

Brick held a pistol loosely in his hands; he'd had it out of the holster since they 'came ashore' as he put it. Reece sat back a little ways from them, making sure no one snuck up from behind. Sam couldn't stop staring at that pistol. He hated it so much. It made him feel like he was on the verge of a breakdown, but he couldn't explain why. He couldn't stand feeling broken like this.

He realized he couldn't remember how he'd survived the apocalypse. He remembered walking into his house and seeing his parents dead and then feeling like it was his fault. And he'd gotten into the car and just drove. He remembered all the dead bodies. All of them everywhere. And he remembered the guilt. So much guilt and bile.

"Can you believe how incredibly ugly these people are?"

"How can you tell? The guards are all bundled up like bacon 'round a shrimp," said Brick.

"My god, of course you can tell. Look at their posturing, atrocious, and their clear weight problem, it's as if not a single one of these people have ever heard of diet and exercise. It boggles the mind."

"Does it really, Reece? Is yer mind boggled?"

"Yes, I do believe it is."

"Bah-hum-bugger, that's what you are: a bloody Grinch. It's not their weight we're worried about. Now just keep watch."

"I will keep watch. It's impossible to *not* capture them within the binocular lens."

Sam felt like he should intervene, but he also wasn't in a car he could pull over, so he didn't really know how he could deal with their sibling-like bickering.

"Would you two shut the hell up, please?" Luck asked, not nearly quietly enough.

"Would you keep your voice down darling? You'll blow our cover straight to hell," Reece said.

"I'll blow you straight to hell," she muttered under her breath. What did that mean? Was that sexual or violent? It was fine. He wasn't threatened. She thought he had a big penis. That meant something right? Unless she'd been joking. Stop, he told himself. This was not a road he needed to travel down right now. He needed to be sharp in case something happened. He needed to focus. So he peered through the lens of the binoculars Brick had lent him and squinted through the whiteout.

The guard loitering at the entrance was a touch pudgy, but it could have been the puffy black jacket he had wrapped around his body. Sam was willing to give this asshole at least that benefit of the doubt.

"Should we be worried about her at all," Sam asked.

"About Misty?"

"Yeah, about Misty."

"Nah, mate, no. She'll be fine. She's a survivor that one. You wouldn't be able to tell, but she is."

"Hey fellas?" Luck said, and they all turned to her. But she wasn't looking at them, she was staring down the hill.

"Yeah?" Brick asked, and she nodded toward the zoo.

And here came pudgy guard, marching right toward them, checking to see that his gun was loaded. Shit.

"Guns at the ready!" Brick whispered loudly. And everyone else loaded and de-safetied their guns while Sam closed his eyes tight.

"Keep your asses down. This shit is about to get real," said Luck.

The bullets hit the snow bank and quietly hissed their way to the frozen earth. Luckily none of them hit the gang crouched behind. Yet anyway, thought Sam as he pressed himself as flat as possible into the snow. He considered briefly, insanely, of making a snow angel, but the timing didn't really seem appropriate, and he thought Luck might disapprove. She had her hand raised above the bank, and Sam watched her tiny finger squeeze off shot after shot, each escaping bullet almost propelling her poor tiny hand all the way back to her side. But she fought through it and emptied her clip into, what Sam hoped, was the body of that pudgy guard. That would be nice. Except there were almost certainly more right behind him.

And then they were gone around him. Brick was gone, Luck, even Reece who had been hanging back some. Sam watched the white flakes howl and fly above him; the world was still breathing. Should he be moving too, expanding toward something?

This shootout was not part of the plan. They had hatched a great plan the night before. Misty would sneak into the zoo and pretend to be sketching the animals, but she would really be taking notes on where and how Bare and Tess were being held. She was also going to count the amount of guards, just so they knew what they were up against. If it were possible she'd also be in charge of unlocking some of the cages and telling the animals to wait until they heard others to bust out and start a distraction.

That last bit was hopeful thinking; most of the crew, Sam aside, didn't believe for one second that the security at this place would be anything besides heavy or that any animals would listen to people who weren't Luck or maybe Sam. So they'd wait until she came back out, they'd meet up, get the info on where they needed to head, and then go straight to Bare and Tess, and fight their way out from that point. Pavel and Hartley were walking around the zoo, hoping to find a back door or a secret entrance or something. Hopefully.

That was supposed to be phase one, and then they'd move on to phase two. Except phase one was now fucked and had been replaced by this blizzard shootout.

The blow to his chest took his breath away. So this was what getting shot in the chest felt like. This was it; this was the end. Except he opened his eyes, and it was the guard's handgun, heavy and slick with blood, that had knocked the wind out of him after Brick tossed it for him to catch.

"We're getting Misty and then we're getting the hell out of here," Brick said, offering Sam the hand that wasn't clutched on the dead guard's carbine. Sam dropped the pistol in the snow as if it were scalding hot to his gloved hands.

"What the hell are ya doing?"

"I can't."

"Can't what?"

"I can't do guns."

"Well too goddamn bad. We need ya in there."

"I can't do it."

Brick scowled.

"What happened? How'd... his gun was so big," Sam said.

"I come to rescue," Pavel said, having miraculously appeared with Hartley in tow. Brick picked up the handgun and tossed it to Pavel who caught it, released the clip, checked to see it was full, and then cocked a bullet into the chamber. He looked surprisingly cool and deft for how wimpy he appeared.

"Luck, I didn't want you here in the first place. You go back now and take *him* with you" Brick ordered, pointing at Sam.

"No, we've got a plan and we're sticking to it. None of you can get these animals to help, so you need us. Now let's go and get this fucking job done," Luck said as she ran toward the entrance.

"Stupid bloody girl!" Reece said under his breath, before he, and the rest of the group ran at the gates to the zoo.

A bullet flew through the window of a ticket booth, and Luck squeezed a few rounds across the glass. A few more bullets flew out, and Brick took aim and fired, turning the gunman's brains into decorations for the booth. Sam shut his eyes tightly again, but continued to run. The red spray brought the bile to the back of his throat. The crew formed together, Brick and Luck out front, Sam and Pavel in the middle, and Hartley and Reece somewhere behind.

Brick led the way through the open, dead space of the entrance plaza, as quickly as possible through the lack of cover to the entrance of the park.

Sam had heard or read or seen something on this place in his life before. The Michael Crichton Memorial Zoo was erected shortly after the famed Chicago-born author had died. It was a huge undertaking, but it was helped by the fact that Crichton, with no immediate family, had left his somewhat considerable wealth more or less up for grabs. So a large part of what the place was memorializing was Crichton's lack of close relationships: a giant tombstone full of animals bought with money he had no one to share with.

So the planners, those who the money filtered down to, decided they'd create something in the man's image: a modern-day Jurassic Park just with regular animals instead of the man-eaters of the novel and film. This homage was particularly clear as they jogged, guns ready, through the giant red doors, housed in a wood and stone frame, that opened into the great indoor zoo complex. The name, written in the classic red and yellow script, was emblazoned between two fake torches. 'Classy Chicago,' Sam thought.

Brick was firing again while Sam focused on figuring out if the sign was made of plastic or painted cement, and when he looked back down there were a couple more bodies on the ground. Sam quickly looked back up at the sign. He really wasn't going to be of much help here it seemed. He wished he could pick up a gun, but his brain simply wouldn't allow it. He didn't like not being in control.

In the entrance he spotted a fire extinguisher station next to a bold, red fire door, and perched in the top of it was a red, fire axe. Sam ran over, keeping his head down, and smashed in the glass with his elbow and reached in, gripping the axe tightly. It had a nice weight to it. This he could work with.

The place was deserted, the blizzard having thankfully cleared it of most of the tourists. Luck and Brick crouched behind a brass statue of a gorilla. Brick lay down some covering fire and Pavel saddled up and shot one of the guards in the leg and one in the arm. He kicked one gun away, and grabbed the other for himself, dropping the empty pistol from outside. Hartley and Reece took point in case more guards came down the hall, as Brick dragged the moaning men behind cover. Brick grabbed zip ties from their belts and bound them together.

"How do you open these cages?" Brick asked them, leveling the carbine at their faces.

"You don't. You can't."

"Don't fuck with us," Luck said, trying to sound intimidating. Sam pushed ahead, peeking down a hallway lined with cages. They weren't your typical, cartoon prisons here. The viewing windows were all made of three-inch thick plexi-glass: bullet proof and people proof. There had to be doors on the inside.

Brick came back jiggling keys which he threw to Luck.

"On me," he commanded, "We're splitting up. Reece, you, Hartley, and Pavel find Misty. We never shoulda sent her in here. It's too empty. They gotta know. Luck, the boy, and I are gonna go open some of these cages. These guards were kindly enough to give me the keys. Watches set?"

Everyone else looked at a watch. Sam didn't have one.

"Rendezvous in twenty. Questions?"

There weren't any.

"Alright mate," Brick said, clasping Reece on the shoulder, "I'm counting on you. Bring our girl home safe."

And they were off down the hall. Sam wasn't jealous of their job. They were out in the open. It'd be so easy to get shot like that. Sam shuddered at the thought and held his axe tightly as Luck started trying keys. Brick, back held against the wall, gave a disapproving look at Sam and his axe before he rolled out into the other hallway. He fired some shots, and a couple guards shouted in pain. Brick was a pretty good shot.

"Got it!" Luck said, as she pushed the door open. Brick and his carbine led the way into the tall and wide hallway. Dirt and grime streaked the floor, and stains were everywhere. Chains and milk crates and all sorts of debris littered the ground. Sam believed he maybe didn't much like zoos. A station with monitors and a couple chairs was abandoned. Sam checked the screens, but Bare wasn't on any of them, and he didn't know how to control the feeds.

The hallway was lined with sliding metal doors that were not locked but simply held in place with a bolt through a loop. Sam slipped the first one out and hoped to see Bare, but it was a warthog. An interesting choice for an opening exhibit, Sam thought.

"My name is Sam, and we're here to rescue you," Sam told him.

"Se-seriously?" the warthog asked.

"Yes, but we have to hurry. You have to come out here. We need your help."

"Ok, yeah, of course."

Luck had released two chimps from the other side. Now *they* were more like an opening exhibit Sam would set up. Except for the fact that he would never make a zoo. He believed in an animal's freedom too much, he decided. The conditions in here were kinda gross and bleak.

"So what, do they just speak English then?" Brick asked.

"Yeah, they sound just like people to me."

"Huh."

"I also speak a little Spanish," said one of the chimps.

"No you don't," said the other.

"Oh yeah, no I don't."

"They sound like monkeys to me," Brick said.

"The one said he could speak Spanish," Luck explained.

"But he can't," the second monkey chimed in.

"Ok, we don't have a lot of time here. I need you three to explain the deal to the rest of them we release, right? We're taking down the man who put you all in here, and we need your help. We need some distractions," Sam said to them.

"After this we're all going to go where that fucker is hidden and we're going to cut his goddamn head off," added Luck.

The animals looked surprised and looked at Sam's axe.

"It's an expression," Sam said, "But we need you to explain that to the animals we release ok? And you haven't seen a bear or a wolf have you?"

"I haven't seen anything but the inside of that cell and you humans on the other side of the glass in forever," the warthog replied.

"Ok," said Sam, "But you can help?"

"Sure, and thanks again for letting us free," said the warthog.

"We can help you open cages," said one of the chimps.

"Sì," said the other.

"Let's get moving kids," said Brick as he wrapped a chain tightly from one cell to the other across the door, hopefully barring anyone from entering on that side.

They moved down the hallway releasing a loud menagerie into the hallway. Anteaters, hippos, crocodiles, and monkeys, and another moose, and an ostrich, and a badger, and a giraffe, some coyotes, a capybara, and a whole host of other attractions emptied out and blocked the exit. Sam was glad no guards had come in yet, but he really wanted to find Bare.

They got to the end of the long hallway, and still no Bare, and no Tess.

"There must be another hallway. There must be more. I haven't found my friends yet."

Brick looked at his watch. Time was almost up.

"We have to meet back at the entrance."

"And then we find my friends?"

"We're not leaving until we've freed all these animals," Luck said, a little loudly, and the crowd of beasts cheered for her. They were beginning to feel like celebrities with a colorful, colorful fan base.

"No, we're not," Brick said.

The three worked their way back through the crowd, all of which thanked them, and questioned them. They tried their best to give short answers, and it seemed like the word on what was happening was getting around.

"Stand back," Brick said as he pulled the chain from the door and raised the carbine again.

He kicked the door open.

"Not shoot!" Pavel said. They stepped outside. They'd found Misty.

"Bloody good, you're ok," Brick said as he gave her a hug.

"Any word on my friends?" Sam asked from the back. Misty nodded.

"He's at the back. I didn't see a wolf though."

What did that mean? Where could they be keeping Tess if not in one of these cells?

"Were guards any trouble?"

"No, surprisingly not. We actually didn't see any other guards," said Hartley.

"That's odd. I would have thought this place would be sewn up like a button," said Brick.

"Peculiar, yes," said Reece, "but perhaps it is due to the inclement weather. They could be running based on the assumption that no one would be out today."

"Could be," said Brick, "Alright, well there's a large door at the end of this hallway, Misty and Pavel, you two go down and open that so the larger animals can get out, It looks to me like this whole damn place is just one big circle, and the cages all open from the backs. My guess is that these two doors lead to more corridors."

He pointed at two doors that looked just like the first one they had gone through. Luck went to one and tried the key and it opened. She peeked in and then withdrew her head.

"Yup, more fuckin' cages."

"For god sakes, you don't have to swear like that. It's unnecessary," Hartley said.

"Get off my ass about it!"

"Enough," Brick said, "Reece and Hartley, go down that side, and we'll release all the cages, and we three will take this side. Take these monkeys, they'll explain everything to the animals."

"Ok, more twenty?" Pavel asked, pointing to his watch. Brick nodded, hit two buttons on his watch and then jogged through the door. Sam and Luck followed him.

"I'm going to run ahead. I've got to see my friend," Sam said.

"I don't know," Brick started, but stopped when he saw the desperation on Sam's face, "Are you sure I can't convince ya to bring a gun?"

"No guns," he said, holding up the axe, "this will do."

"Don't die or anything," said Luck. Sam smiled at her before he turned and jogged down the hallway.

'I'm coming for you Bare,' he thought, as he peeked through the dirty picture window of door after door. Michael Crichton, you were one sick son of a bitch making a place like this. There was just no way the animals could be happy in such store bought, faux-natural environments. Sure the trees and the plants and the grass were real, but what about the air? What about the sky and the freedom? Sam had never really cared about zoos until he had a friend in one. He wondered if that made him selfish. Like celebrities who got diseases and only after it affected them did they champion the cause. Was that actually selfish? It was hard to tell.

He got to the end of the hallway and rounded a corner, and there was a guard stepping out of a door on the far side of the corridor. Sam slipped back around the corner and plastered his back against the wall, away from the guard's carbine. He had exited a door on the wrong side of the complex, a door leading to what? It wasn't a cage. Or at least not one on public display. Ok, Bare had to be in one of the cages near where that guard was standing, and the guard was definitely going to hear what Luck and Brick were doing further down the hall soon.

Think Sam, think. He peeked around, and the guard was walking toward Sam now. His hands weren't on his gun yet; he hadn't seen him. But what happened when he got to the end and saw Luck and Brick, busy and distracted down the other hallway? Sam had to do something. He considered the axe in his hands, but it would never beat the bullets. Think. Ok.

He ran out and waved an arm wildly in the air at the guard.

"Hey!" the guard yelled from down the hall as he raised his gun.

But Sam had already slid the bolt from the latch of the nearest door, and slipped inside. He slammed the axe handle into the latch, bending it so he couldn't just get locked in, and then slammed the door behind him.

"What are you doing here?" asked the massive tiger in the room with him as she sauntered toward Sam, giant haunches swaying with each step.

"Listen, we're here to help you. I'm here to free you, but I don't have a lot of time."

"You can understand me?"

"Yeah, I think it's because I was drowned for like 20 minutes eight years ago."

"And why should I believe you? Do you know what they've done to me? Do you know how they've treated me here? Why should I trust any of you?"

Sam pointed behind him where, thankfully, the animals from the middle chambers were streaming out into the giant halls.

"Because it's true, and we're the good guys," Sam said.

"Oh. Excellent. Thank you," said the tiger, relaxing her posture.

Sam took the room in: the trees, the tire hanging from a braided rope, the dismantled carcass of something. Ok, time to work.

He chopped the rope with his axe, tied a loop at one end and used it to pull a nearby tree branch near the door to the ground. He tied a slipknot on the other end, buried the axe head in the ground, and used that to hold the loop to the ground. The rope was taut, the branch straining and the trap set right in front of the door. 'This had better work,' Sam thought as he ran to the corner. He'd never set a trap that quickly before, especially not with such makeshift tools.

"Hey, get over here," Sam said to the tiger who was just staring at the animals streaming to safety, "Trust me, come on. Hurry."

The tiger bounded over, and both hunched behind a tree. The metal door slid open, and then the guard yelped as his foot caught and tripped Sam's trap. His carbine clattered to the ground. Sam peeked out to see the guard hanging upside down, blood dripping from his nose and down his face. Sam ran up to him and punched him hard in the face just to be sure. He shook the pain in his fist out and then undid the guard's belt, letting the pistol and the knife and the badass taser fall out of reach. Sam turned again to the tiger who approached slowly, as if she were stalking prey, staring intently at the hanging guard.

"We're trying to take down the people who imprisoned you all here, and we'd really appreciate your help," Sam said.

"Ok," said the tiger, "I'll be with you in just a minute."

"Alright, I have to go find my friend. There are a few other humans coming this way. They're releasing all the rest. Don't hurt them or anything."

"Yes," said the tiger, now right underneath the guard and staring up.

Sam slipped out of the room, and as he reached the first door he heard the guard's blood curdling scream. But then it was silent again, so that was good.

Sam opened that door, and then another, and another, letting the animals out, telling them to walk down the hall, and people would explain.

He got to the middle, and he found a door with a padlock on it. It was a cheapish one, like a lock from a high school locker room. This had to be it, right? This had to be. Sam took his axe, wound up, and smashed the back side into the lock. Sparks sprayed out, but it didn't give, so Sam smacked it again. And again, and again, trying to chop the metal off maybe. He checked it and pulled down on the circular face, and the lock clicked open. Oh. Sam felt a little foolish now. 'Always check to see if something is locked before you try to break in,' he thought. He'd make a real shitty burglar.

"Bare!" Sam yelled, that wavering of emotions fluttering through his chest and up into his eyes at the sight of his friend. Bare turned around, wide-eyed, ecstatic to see him.

"Sam!"

Bare bounded up, and Sam experienced the true meaning of a bear hug. Bare picked him up and held him to his warm body. Sam breathed in the scent of woods and stale alcohol that seemed to just exist on Bare's body as his ribs threatened to crack under the pressure of the hug.

"Sam. I am so sober."

"I'm sorry buddy. But you aren't suicidal or anything, right?"

"Heck no. You came to rescue me. You're a true friend you know that Sam?"

A lot of emotions rattled around in Sam, and it was hard for him to put into words what all of them meant.

"I've never missed someone like I missed you Bare."

"Alright, let's not make a whole thing of this," Bare said with a smile, clearly happy that it was thing.

"Did you find Tess?" Bare asked, excited at the prospect of seeing her too.

"You mean you don't know where she is?"

Bare's face fell. Clearly he didn't.

"It's ok buddy, we'll find her."

"She fought them Sam. She's a fighter. She really did not want them to take us. I couldn't protect her neither. They put me on some real heavy stuff Sam. I was out like a light. I woke up in here... I thought... I don't know, I've been hot and cold, and my head has hurt from missing you two."

"It sounds like withdrawal."

"Yes! That's exactly it. I was feeling withdrawal from you two."

"Well that and the drugs. How long has it been since you had any drugs?"

"Three days? Five days? A hundred years? I don't know! I can't tell time here, I was just sittin' here dyin."

"I know buddy. Hey listen, I met a girl."

"You did?!" Bare asked, excited.

"Yeah. She's beautiful, and interesting, and tough, and get ready for it: she's human!"

"Human? She sounds like just your type!"

"Yeah, but please don't make a thing of it ok? I don't want her to know I like her yet."

"Why not?"

"I don't know, it's complicated."

"Hey, I'm seeing clearly right now for the first time in a long time, and buddy it ain't complicated. You know what I see? I see that I love you man. I do. I straight up love you."

Sam felt put on the spot. He had thought about that too, but hadn't really put it into those words. What else could he say?

"Hey man, I love you too. You're the best friend I ever had. And I mean that."

"You're the best friend I ever had," Bare said back, "And you know what else I know. I love Tess. I straight up do. I love that woman. When I'm around her it's like I'm in awe, like in awe but like everything is gonna be alright, ya know?"

"Yeah," said Sam, thinking of Luck's beautiful eyes, "Yeah, I do."

Sam hugged Bare again.

"Alright, now lets get our asses out of here."

"And find Tess."

"And find Tess," Sam agreed.

299

Back in the hall, Luck and Brick were just rounding the corner, followed by a host of zoo animals, looking like a crazy version of that slow motion movie walk where everyone looks badass. Except they were all walking at regular speed and still managed to look cool as hell.

"Who is that smokeshow?" asked Bare.

"That would be Luck," Sam said smiling at them. He gave a wave and started forward.

"Guys, this is my friend Bare. Bare this is Brick, and this is Luck."

"Holy moly, you are the most beautiful lady I have ever seen in my whole life!" Bare said, "Have you seen this girl Sam?"

Sam blushed a deep scarlet and mumbled, "Come on Bare…"

"Nice to meet you, Bare? You're a bear named Bare?" asked Luck.

"Well my Ma named me Barry, ya know, she just liked the name. But yah, bear named Bare."

"That is hilarious! I love it," said Luck, showing off her token smile. Sam's heart puttied at the flashing of her teeth. They liked each other.

Brick looked in to the open door and his square jaw dropped.

Sam followed his gaze and saw the guard's lower half strung up from the tree branch, leaking profusely, and dangling intestines where an upper torso, some arms, and a head should have been. Sam wondered where they had wandered. Brick looked at Sam and then down at the red axe still in his hands, and it was clear he was reassessing the boy.

"Taken care of," said Sam, "I still need to find my friend Tess. She doesn't seem to be in a cage, but she has to be here."

"She has to be?" asked Brick.

"She's here," said Bare with finality.

"Ok, let's find her quick then, we're still on a schedule right?" said Luck.

Brick checked his watch.

"Jake and Marty are on at 1800."

"And what time is it now?"

"Are they Jake and Marty?" Bare asked, gesturing to the pair who had rounded the corner with another group of animals.

"It's 1720, and no, those buggers are Reece and Hartley," Brick explained.

"I think we should check that door back there for Tess. That'd be my best guess for where she is," said Sam before he stepped into the tiger's den and unclipped a key card from the blood and gristle soaked belt on the ground.

"This should help," he said as he took off down the hallway.

Sam got to the door and swiped the card. A little light flashed red and then green. Behind him, Brick told Reece and Hartley to bring the animals to the front and to wrap some of the more cold-blooded ones in coats or anything else they could find. It was going to be a chilly walk to the tower.

But Sam only heard a small part of this because the rest of the sound was drowned out by what he saw: green lights barely illuminated columns and rows of tiny cages, crammed to the brim with animal fur, hair, faces, paws, creatures just shoved between the bars. Sam walked in slowly, his brain working to process exactly what was happening here.

Luck made a guttural noise as she followed Sam in, the horrible scent and the dungeon quality of the room hitting her hard. Bare was next, and he reacted quickly.

"No," he said as he ran on all fours over to the first of the cages, "Tess? Tess?!"

She didn't answer, but Bare's panic snapped Sam out of his daze, and he followed suit, looking up and down the cages, hoping to find their friend. But he hoped to hell she wasn't in here.

"Spread out, please," Sam said, "We have to find Tess. She's a grey wolf; she's got some fresh burns on her face. Please hurry."

Luck walked over to Sam, his eyes still flying over cages, and put her hand on his face. She wiped away some of the tears that were inexplicably tracing Sam's cheeks. Up on tiptoes, she kissed the spot on his cheek she'd cleared of tears.

"It'll be ok, we'll find her. Everything is going to work out."

Sam nodded and then had to look away. He had to find Tess.

The animals in the cages looked sick. If their eyes were open at all they were yellow with pus. Oozing sores covered their hides, and a general chorus of shaky, wheezing breaths and low pained moans and grunts filled the room. An upper cage shook violently and everyone turned to watch a dog have a seizure, his spindly legs kicking involuntarily at the hard, steel bars. The desperation welled up in Sam as he got further and further into the room.

Fresh needles littered carts next to red biohazard bins. What were they doing here? What could the purpose of a place like this possibly be? Sam assumed they were testing something on the animals, but what? And for fuck's sake, why?

Bare made his way quickly toward the back and was whispering to a cage. Tess. Sam ran up behind his friend. Tess was looking at Bare as he told her everything was going to be all right.

"Tess!" Sam said, excited to see her, "We're going to get you out of there. Just hold on."

Sam stood and beckoned Luck over with dramatic gestures. She came running.

"Do you still have those keys?"

She handed Sam the ring, and he went to work trying each one. Tess whimpered inside the cage.

"It's ok Tess, we're here now, we've got you."

"Key's… over… there…" Tess managed to say.

Sam looked over at the far wall, which was a lab. Test tubes with gradient colors, beakers, tubing in intricate and delicate shapes, and liquids marked with stickers and hastily scrawled scripts that could only be discerned by people who already knew filled the space. Amidst this chaos was a desk calendar with an empty coffee mug, a few papers, an empty bag of chips, and a palm tree keychain with a single key attached. Sam grabbed the key and tossed it to Luck, who jammed it in the lock and opened the door. Bare lifted Tess gently out and set her on the ground.

She didn't look as bad as most of the animals in the place, thank goodness. The burns on her back looked as if they may have become infected, the swollen red was angry and dark, but she didn't have the skin lesions, and her eyes were relatively clear. Bare nuzzled her gently, his head held against hers, and it looked to Sam like she smiled.

"We find that gal of yours?" Brick asked from near the door.

"We did," Luck called back, "but she looks in pretty bad shape. It looks like they might have burned her."

"Ah, that was actually sort of me," said Sam, "It's a long story, but she looks ok."

"I think they have her drugged," said Bare.

"You…would…know…" Tess said, trying at a joke. Bare smiled down at her.

"Hey Tess, I was thinkin', and ya don't have to say nothin', but I love ya. Just sayin'."

"I love… you too… dummy," Tess said back

"Alright gang, it's already 15:30. If we don't leave now, we're not going to make it in time and all this would be for nothing."

"We've got to release the rest of these animals," said Sam, standing.

"We don't have time," Brick called back.

"We have to. Just look at them. This is sick; they're in pain."

"It's not going to matter if we don't get over to the tower for phase two. You know that."

He did. But there had to be an alternative.

Sam slid a large cart with a sheet on it over toward Tess.

"Do you think you two can get her on there for now?"

"Ya," said Bare, still stroking her fur lovingly, "Yah, of course we can, hey?"

Luck nodded, but Sam was already jogging back down toward the entrance. He sprinted past Brick.

"Yo," Brick said to Sam's back.

Sam slammed through the door to the entrance and was greeted by the sound and smell of a hundred animals. Misty, Pavel, and Hartley were trying to give directions while wrapping coats they'd found somewhere around the crocodile, the boar, and some of the other shorthaired animals. Sam couldn't see Reece through the crowd. He walked up and surveyed the animals and then pointed at an orangutan and a bearded, smaller, black and white monkey.

"You and you follow me. And hurry," he said to the two, the authority in his voice unquestionable. Sam was a man on a mission.

"Me?" asked the orangutan.

"Yes. And him."

The bearded monkey pointed a finger at his own chest, and Sam nodded and waved for them to follow him. They jogged back up the hallway to the room with the cages. Bare and Luck had loaded Tess onto the cart and wheeled her out as Sam came huffing over.

"I'll meet you guys back there in just a second," Sam said.

"Ya best hurry mate," said Brick tapping the face of his watch, "We're off in five."

"Ok," said Sam as he pushed the ape and the monkey into the stinking room. He made some prolonged eye contact with Luck as she walked past him, but he was on a mission. No time for the flirts right now. Even if she did look incredible. The thought of her naked body was gone though when he reentered that room.

"What is this place?" asked the bearded monkey.

"I'm not sure," said Sam, "But you two need to release all these animals."

"All of them?" asked the orangutan.

"There's the smell of death here," said the monkey, his nose twitching.

"That's why you're releasing them," Sam said as he handed the key to the monkey, "Get them out and try to make them comfortable. I don't know, see if you can find bedding or something? They just can't be like this. Ok? Got it?"

"Got it," said the monkey, as he raced over to the first cage and unlocked it. The orangutan helped the pained opossum out of the cage.

"Thank you guys. This means a lot to me. We'll be back. I promise."

And he meant it too.

341

They struggled through the cold, a misfit parade with no one standing around to watch their slow march.

The tower was only six or seven blocks away, but in the howling wind and stinging snow of the blizzard, it felt like a thousand. The humans led the way, gun barrels first much to Sam's continued discomfort. But they wanted to be safe. Sam had found a hammock and a blanket in one of the environments, and they had used that to secure Tess onto Bare's back in a makeshift swing. Sam couldn't just leave her behind, but she still was too groggy to do much of anything. Yet, hopefully. Hopefully that yet held promise.

They were on to phase two of the plan. Total invasion and total evisceration of Smith's credit. They were going to turn the people against Smith. That was the plan anyway.

One group would go in through the front, and one group would assault the rear. The animals had been warned that there would be guards with guns, and to be careful, but after the explanation of who Smith was and what he was doing, most of them decided the stakes were more than worth the risk. Then, while the animals were wreaking havoc in the tower, the humans and Bare and Tess would sneak their way up to where Jake and Marty broadcasted, and they would let all of Chicago in on all of Smith's horrible misdeeds. And then, while the people, hopefully guards included, were rising up against Smith, they'd break in to the penthouse and kill Smith. At least that was the plan.

Sure there were some maybes, some hopeful bits, there were some gaps that would hopefully be filled by angry followers, but given the time constraints, it was going to have to do. Smith could launch that nuke at any time.

When they were a block away they split into the two teams: Pavel, Misty, Hartley, and Luck in the group entering from the rear, and Brick with his carbine, Reece with his pistol, and Sam with Bare and the animals would take the front.

"Hey Luck," Sam said, his heart pounding hard, the bile just right at the top of his stomach. He'd been running this through his head the whole, frozen march.

"What's up?"

"I just wanted to say, just in case... you know whatever: I think I like you. You don't have to say anything, I just wanted to say I'm glad I got to meet a woman as beautiful and smart and interesting and you know, a woman like you. I just wanted to say that. And you're cool, and you're tough as hell, and you're pretty much the perfect girl. So thank you, you know, for being you. I'm sorry, I just-"

Luck punched him in the stomach. Pretty hard. And of course, Sam almost threw up.

"This is no time to get all soppy, dumbfuck. We're about to go kick some ass."

And then she kissed him full on the lips. Not just a quick kiss either. There was some tenderness there, and she even teased his shocked lips with her tongue for a brief moment before pulling away and pushing him backwards.

"Now man up, and I'll see you upstairs."

Sam couldn't speak through his goofy grin.

"Let's move loverboy," Reece said as he grabbed Sam's arm and dragged him toward the entrance. He was just jealous, Sam thought as he readjusted the shifting and ballooned member in his pocket.

The winds howled their way indoors as Sam and Reece held the doors for the animals who greedily climbed into the warmth of the large lobby. Sam wished he could see that sexy secretary Jenna's surprise as a tiger and a hippo and some coyotes and a few penguins those two chimps and a battery of zoo creatures all wearing frosty disguises came barging in to her quiet lobby with the swirling snow from outside. He laughed at the thought. He looked at Bare and nodded at his friend. He was excited now. He had his friend back, they were doing good, and he was ready to take this fucker down. 'Smith, you sick bastard, I'm coming for you,' Sam thought. It sounded cinematic. He liked it.

"Hey Smith, I'm coming for you," Sam said out loud to nobody, and the wind whisked it away.

Brick waved Sam and Reece and Bare inside, and they ran up, Brick leveling his stolen carbine at the mayhem that was the lobby. But it looked like the hippo had gotten to the surprised guard first, and now Sam knew why they called hippos one of the meanest animals on the planet. That guard would never father children now. And there went his arm out its socket. Looked like he'd never make it to the big leagues either. The guard spit out a glob of blood instead of chew and slumped up against the wall. Jenna, the spicy lobby-lady, stood screaming in her elegant, aqua dress as a boar in a coat tried to coax conversation out of her.

"Press the elevator buttons," Sam yelled to his comrades.

"Good call, let's get these critters spread out," Brick said in return, and the three of them pushed every call button and then ushered animals into the large, waiting carts.

Muted gunshots popped off somewhere deeper in the building, and Sam got another quick flash of a field in summer, small rocks jutting out, and something, something at his feet...

"Yo, hey, Sheila," Brick yelled at Jenna, "What floor do we go to find Jake and Marty's broadcast?"

"What the fuck is happening?" Jenna asked as the animals who hadn't yet made it onto elevators bound for random floors started to sing classic rock favorites, this one being Cold as Ice, by Foreigner. Sam wondered what everyone else heard.

"Jake and Marty, what floor?" Brick insisted.

"Eighteen, they're on the eighteenth floor. What is this?"

"This, darlin', is not the end of the world. Now we're gonna have to handcuff you up over here, and it's nothing personal, I've just got to do it."

"I'll do it," said Reece, holding up a bundle of black zip ties. Reece led her over to a fixture on the wall, whispering in her ear the whole time, the flirtatious bastard, thought Sam. He gingerly secured her wrists, trapping her in the now empty lobby.

"How you feeling buddy?" Sam asked Bare.

"I'm a darn sight better now that we're all back together and out of that place, hey?"

"You better believe it man. It's great to see you."

"Oh yah, and you. We probably should have had a plan coming in here though hey? And that crashing thing wasn't the best. Smacked my head pretty good."

"Yeah. Sorry about that, I really didn't think I was *that* drunk."

"Yah, how's Tess looking?" Bare asked as the last of the animals disappeared into the inner works of the building. Sam pet the part of her face that wasn't burned, and she smiled.

"That was very nice, thanks," she said in a dreamy voice.

"Still out of it. She's sounding better though."

Bare hoisted her up so she was more secure against his back.

"Alright, we've got some radio to crash brother," Sam said, "We ready?"

"They should be here soon," Brick said, "One more minute."

Two more gunshots, closer this time. Real close. Sam dragged Bare behind the front desk, and put his head down. Brick and Reece took cover behind marble lined support pillars, guns at the ready.

"Hey! Hey you can't just leave me out in the open like this!" Jenna yelled, the fear of death raising her voice an octave or so.

Another gunshot almost inside the lobby. A door burst open, and a guard stood there. Sam had a horrible moment where he was sure the rest of the crew had been killed, but the guard fell forward onto his face, and Luck, Misty, Hartley, and Pavel, pistol smoking, piled in and slammed the door behind them. Misty frantically pushed the UP button on the closest elevator.

"Everyone good?" Brick asked.

"Fuck heads shot a couple of the animals. Can you believe that shit?" said Luck.

"Are you ok?" Sam asked, running over to her, Bare close in step.

"She's got quite the mouth on her, eh?" Bare asked just to Sam. Sam just grinned as he looked her up and down.

"I'm fine, so you can stop checking me out. Perv."

Brick and Reece joined them right as the elevator doors slid open. An anteater waddled out.

"I got nervous. Sorry," he said as he wandered back out into the lobby.

"That's ok," Luck said as she got into the elevator. The rest of the gang piled in and turned toward the front. The doors slid shut, and everyone suddenly got quiet: only the sound of people nervously checking their guns.

"Could someone press 18, please?" Sam asked, hoping for a bit of levity, which fell flat, as no one had actually done that yet. Pavel leaned out and pressed 18 with the barrel of his pistol. The elevator Muzak kicked in, and Bare tapped his claws to the beat.

"This is nice," he said.

"I like this song," Tess said shakily from her hammock. The floors ticked by slowly, and the folks wearing watches kept checking them. Sam hoped the animals were doing their jobs and keeping everyone busy. He had told a few of them to try to find their way up to the top floor. Maybe disrupt things up there. Maybe even get Smith. Hopefully this bit would be simple. Hopefully.

Ding. Floor 18. The doors slid open. No one. Strange, but maybe the critters had done their part here, and everyone had just cleared off. Brick signaled Reece to cover the right while he'd cover the left, and they swung out of the elevator, guns first.

"Clear," Brick whispered, waving everyone off the elevator. He pointed fingers to indicate they were heading left. So they did.

As Sam passed by he saw a little placard that read '←Studio.' The hallway split with a bay of windows, and Brick motioned for everyone to walk below the sightline toward the door. They marched, burning up in their winter gear, doubled over and nervous toward the door to the studio. Brick motioned for the first three to swing around to the other side of the door, and when they were all in place he silently counted off 1, 2, 3!

He threw open the door and slid inside, carbine first again, firing blindly toward the ceiling.

"Everyone down!" he yelled, his accent cartoonish and imposing.

There was one man behind a control panel, in a revolving chair. His hands were as high as he could raise them, and Sam could already see the sweat greasing up the adult acne on his forehead.

"Please don't shoot!" his voice was squeaky.

Hartley walked over to him and zip tied his hands to his chair and his feet around the bottom. Pavel swung the door to the recording studio open and Jake and Marty huddled under the dark wooden desk with the microphone hanging in the middle. Jake and Marty were apparently twins, overweight, with red hair that no longer climbed above the tips of their ears. The red "ON THE AIR" sign was lit. This was broadcasting.

"Hey Jake," said Marty.

"Yeah Marty?"

"We've just been invaded by what sounds to be what's left of the United Nations."

"Shut it fatty," Brick said as he dragged Marty out from underneath the desk.

"Hey man, don't, hey! Careful I'm fragile!" Marty whined.

"Inside," Reece said holding the door, "Let's finish this job."

Hartley and Pavel went straight for Jake and dragged him out, using the zip ties on his wrists too. Pavel took off his boot and removed his filthy sock.

"I hate listen you. Your mouth is trash," Pavel tried as he shoved the browning sock into Jake's confused mug.

Luck ran straight for the microphone and dipped it elegantly.

"Ladies and Gentlemen, this is the Blue Lagoon Crew," a nickname Sam had never heard, "And we've got a few things we need to tell you about your glorious leader..."

Sam watched Luck work, entranced from the entry to the room.

"Come on buddy, I wanna set Tess down here for a sec here," and Bare bumped Sam inside, letting the door swing to a shut, cutting out the sound from outside. As Luck explained what Smith was trying to do, Sam helped Bare gingerly drop Tess in the corner, and she really was starting to look better as she turned her head with wide eyes outside.

"Tess?"

Sam turned to see the room they had just come from full to the brim with guards packing big and angry guns. And Mr. Smith himself standing there, suit crisp, arms crossed, a smug look of satisfaction on his face, a fever blister exploded on his upper lip, Reece next to him, not looking nearly as scared as he should given how many guns must have been aimed at his back.

"Uh," said Sam, and the whole 'Blue Lagoon Crew' turned to see what Sam did. Shit. The ON AIR sign went dim. They were trapped.

Brick leveled that carbine at Smith, who just smiled, his lips cracking and showing teeth, that crescent moon scar just barely flinching. Brick flipped it to semi-auto and fired one shot that ricocheted wildly and lodged itself in Jake's fat thigh. Jake gave a muffled scream into Pavel's sock, and Marty tried to worm his way over to help his brother. It would have been sweet if he didn't look like a giant, ginger slug and if the gang wasn't in so much trouble.

Smith walked over to the panel and pushed the zip tied man in the chair, sending it and the man with the acne crashing to the carpet. Smith pushed a button and leaned into a microphone.

"Who is that?" Bare asked.

"That is the bad guy," said Sam.

"Oh."

"Good evening citizens. I see you took the liberty of liberating the tenants of my zoo. That is disappointing but in the end makes little difference. They've served their purpose now, and you will, I am sure, be happy to know that you will all get to be witnesses to the final great revenge of man. It is sure to be spectacular, so be excited."

"Goddamn it!" Luck yelled, and ran to the window in front of Smith and pounded with her tiny fists, "Goddamn you you fucking piece of shit! Reece do something!"

"Language, please," Hartley said without much conviction behind her words.

Smith laughed into the microphone, and the surprisingly natural sound grated against Sam's ears.

"Oh, your friend Reece has already done something sweetheart," Smith said smiling toward Reece.

"What?" said Luck, thrown off.

"Why do you think it was so easy for you to just march in here? Why do you think it was so easy for you to march into the zoo? Look at all the guards I have. Do you truly believe there would only be a handful of men guarding that entire facility? I have hosts of paramilitary troops and ex-police. Those people you killed were simply fanatics in costume. Foolish. You are a foolish and transparent pack of mongrels. But, in case you haven't been able to process this: your friend Reece works for me. He set you up. He informed me of every step of your plan. I do enjoy the pageantry of it all though."

"You told me you wouldn't harm Hartley," Reece said, although he sounded distant and small, being a length from the microphone, "Hartley I did this for you love."

Hartley's face was stone.

"You incredible asshole," she said.

"That smell in the air is gas," Smith explained to them, "I'll see you all just in time for my own little pageant. We're going to make it fun."

Smith turned off the mike and straightened up.

"That fucking bastard," Luck said, and then, banging the window again and addressing maybe everyone, "YOU FUCKING FUCK HEAD BASTARD!"

Brick frantically searched for some way out, some crack in the defenses of the tiny, blank room. Pavel slumped into a chair, already feeling the gas, and Misty, with sudden vigor, started punching Marty in the stomach.

"NO," she roared, quadrupling the decibel levels Sam had ever heard out of her.

Bare looked at Sam with sad eyes, and Sam returned them before he went over and dragged Luck off the wall, holding her kicking and screaming little frame tight to his body.

"It'll be ok, we're still ok. It's not over. It's not," Sam whispered into her hair as he started to feel woozy from the gas.

The last thing they all saw was Smith leveling a beautiful, black handgun at Reece's head. He pulled the trigger. Reece's eyes were wide with surprise as his brains splashed across the glass wall, and, not quite aware he was dead yet, he took a few steps backwards before slumping to the floor.

Sam wasn't sure if it was the gas or the violence, but a wave of woozieness hit him. He could feel his body start to fall, but he never felt the landing.

400

They had tossed Sam in a field apparently. Or that's where he fell. Although the grass was green, which was confusing. A greenhouse maybe? The zoo? What was this place?

He stood, completely alone, all his friends gone and apparently his enemies too. The field was mostly dirt with some tall prairie grass patches swaying in the breeze. Sam looked down and saw the gun in his hands. It was a small snub-nosed revolver. Dread.

A chain link fence was off in the distance near a large rock. Sam knew there was a lake past that fence. A sheer drop from a cliff, maybe sixty feet, and then lake. Sam remembered Randy, and then he couldn't breathe, he couldn't see, he couldn't think. Except he finally could because he remembered. He remembered what he'd done.

Sam woke up, chained to the wall of Smith's glass penthouse, his heart filled to the brim with panic. He twisted his neck, searching for his brother, but he only saw the rest of his new friends chained up next to him. They were all adhered to the wall with what looked like leather, S+M bondage straps. Bare was tied up on a cart, presumably the only way they could transport his girth, and Tess was sprawled on the ground near him. She wasn't bound, and Sam hoped to hell that didn't mean what he thought it might. Everyone else was twitching slightly and muttering, except for Misty who was already groggily trying to figure out where she was.

The penthouse had changed, expanded. The steel wall was gone now and opened to a huge space that must have been the center of the building. The great space was much more industrial than Smith's penthouse, no sleek modernism but rather a cold and function driven metal. There was a metal walkway, held in place by beams connected to the floor above. The green nose of a rocket peeked up from the middle. The rocket meant to end the world. Smith stood by a great bank of control panels, tweaking dials, and pressing at glowing computer touch screens.

"Who is Randy?" Smith asked, turning toward Sam, sounding legitimately curious. Had Smith just read his mind?

"What?"

"The gas has the pleasant side effect of making people talk in their sleep. It can be incredibly informative. For example, they are having an affair," his gloved hand tick-tocked between Hartley and Brick, "And that one... well that one is Russian. I don't speak Russian, but he sounded upset."

"Where is... he?" asked Misty, trying her hardest to come up out of the haze the gas had left them in.

"Shhh," Smith said, "We are having a discussion. Shouldn't you still be asleep? Now Sam, who is this Randy? An old flame perhaps?"

Sam closed his eyes hard, but the image of Randy in the field came back to him. Sam remembered what had happened now. His mind had shut it out apparently because he simply didn't want to remember it. Now that he could, he had the thought that he probably couldn't have gone on living had he remembered it.

"None of your business."

"If you tell me a story I'll take a minute longer to push this button here," Smith said, sliding the tip of his finger in a sensual circle around a glass button that was glowing slightly green from a light source inside the consol.

"What the fuck do I care about that button," said Sam, "Let me down from here."

"You should care about this button. You should care about this button very much. This button is connected to a 50-megaton hydrogen bomb, which is, if you were unaware, an incredibly powerful explosive. The most powerful bomb ever created in fact. The bombs dropped on Hiroshima and Nagasaki combined were one thousand times less potent than this bomb. Can you imagine? Powerful enough to take all those tiny hydrogen atoms and rip them away from space, make them move at powerful, incredible speeds, and leave that wonderful, magical opaqueness of the universe vulnerable. So much empty space leaves a hole for me to fill. I have injected myself with every conceivable disease left, and when that bomb explodes my collection and I will infect the very opaqueness that keeps this world alive."

"What the fuck are you talking about. You do know you're insane right?"

"Where... is... he?" Misty tried again.

"And now that I've gotten the final piece from you," Smith continued, ignoring Sam, "It was syphilis is you were wondering, which I'm sure you were. I was able to track down every other known disease, and by some ludicrous coincidence I had never managed to acquire syphilis. I had thought it to be gone, which would have been immensely disappointing. I managed to find malaria, small pox, rabies, all of the old staples, but somehow syphilis had been out of my reach. So I thank you for that. What I don't thank you for is making me go through all this to get it. What a headache."

Sam struggled against his restraints, trying to find some trick to freeing himself while Smith paced around the room, checking on his awakening prisoners. Brick struggled weakly against his binds as he walked past.

"Where is my husband?" asked Misty as Smith passed her.

"Your husband? I haven't a clue." Smith said.

"Yes you do," Misty said quietly, "You captured him six months ago. I'm here to find him."

This was news to Sam. He looked over and noticed a wedding band around her finger. That would do it.

"I would guess he is dead if that is the case."

"He's not dead."

"He was a prisoner here? He is almost certainly dead. Human prisoners, animal's, we used them all to cultivate diseases. Now shush."

Sam thought about the room with the cages in the zoo. Jesus, Smith was sick.

"I'll kill you," Misty said.

"No, I'll kill me," Smith said, "And I'm taking the rest of the universe with me. She's not a great listener, Sam. Now that story, let's hear it. I do love a good yarn." His finger hovered above the button. Sam was quiet.

"Do I have to do something drastic?" Smith asked, drawing his beautiful, ebony handgun. He leveled it first at Hartley, and then, shaking his head, he switched to Luck. He looked at Sam, who looked sufficiently worried.

"Well?" Smith said, cocking the hammer back.

"Ok," Sam said, "Ok, fine I'll tell you about Randy."

And the others were just waking for this. Great.

It had started when Sam had found the pistol in a shoebox on the top shelf of his dad's closet. His dad had never been one to be too creative. Sam wanted to lie and say that he had been looking for something else, but he'd been looking for exactly that.

Two days before Chaz Bertlett had told everyone that Sam was gay, that he was a fuckin' queer faggot, and that Sam had tried to grab him in the showers after gym. He'd done this because Sam had talked to Jasmine the day before. That was it. They'd talked about their third period English class, and jealous, vindictive Chaz had spread a rumor that spread so fast and so violently that Sam had been called into the guidance office and talked to, the principle and, more ominous, the school's cop present. Chaz's parents wanted to press charges they said, and Sam would be suspended for the near future. They even had the gall to escort Sam out through the locker bays during a break from class so everyone could see. Every girl, every potential friend, everyone saw Sam in serious trouble, completely validating Chaz's bullshit story.

Sam saw Bare was awake now and listening as he strained at the straps that contained him. That made him sad, he'd hoped Bare would miss this. Maybe Bare wouldn't get the connotations associated with school shootings.

"Hmm, so what does this have to do with Randy?" asked Smith.

"Do you want to hear the story or not?"

"I want to hear a good story. I want these people to know who you are before I kill them. I want you all to know each other before you die together. It'll be sweet. Poetic even. I like the idea of poetry. Now continue," he said as he waved the gun once more at Luck, who still hadn't fully come to.

So Sam had been at home, his parents had grounded him as well, and all he had to do all day was sit in his room and fume. The second day he'd found the gun, and it took him two more to work up the courage to take it to school. He got all the way inside, the gun wedged behind his belt buckle, the fear eating at his stomach, the hood from his zip-up obscuring his face. It was just after lunch so his peers were all lounging by their lockers. It was busy, so no one noticed as Sam worked his way toward Chaz. He passed Sara Jo, Jasmine, Marcus, everyone; nobody stopped him. His palms were sweating, his face was sweating, his heart pounded in his chest.

Chaz deserved to die, right? Chaz was pure evil. Look at all the havoc he'd wreaked on Sam, look at how he treated everyone in his life. Sam saw Chaz and started his beeline. He was just reaching back to grab the gun from under his sweatshirt when his brother Randy stopped him, and asked him what he was doing there.

"Ahh! Randy was your brother. Now, what happened next?"

What happened next was Randy had accidently pulled up Sam's hoodie when he'd grabbed him and had seen the pistol. Shocked he backed away. Chaz was just standing at his locker, and he yawned. He looked harmless, if not a bit douchey. Sam couldn't do it. He couldn't just kill someone like that, so he started running, knocking Randy over in his windmill dash. Randy had called out Sam's name, which had gotten the attention of Chaz who gave chase, surely to try to beat the shit out of Sam.

Sam had run outside. He had run as far as he could: out past the school grounds, past the football field and the baseball diamond, out to where the country hit, out to where a broken chain link fence guarded some cliffs and a lake. He ran until his lungs burned, and his face streaked with sweat. Sam had felt trapped. He was sure Chaz was right behind him.

In Sam's mind Chaz had absolutely grabbed a baseball bat from the dugout, he was about to kill Sam for showing his face. Sam, about to be stuck against that chain link fence, about to be squeezed through the links by the force of the bat, heard the foot falls behind him, so he pulled the gun out, turned, and shot.

"It was an accident that I hit him. I was just trying to scare him. Randy just fell over. I... he just fell over. I ran over to him. You know, what the fuck was he doing following me? Chaz was following me. Not Randy. I'd walked over to Randy and saw the hole in his head, saw it seeping blood. His eyes were wide open and he just had this shocked look on his face, and I just couldn't..." Tears were streaming down Sam's cheeks.

Smith sat on the control panel, a look of content on his face as he checked his watch, but Sam had to finish now, he had to get it out. He had ceased to take in his surroundings; he was totally back in South Dakota, reliving his worst memories.

"I tried to you know, check and see if he was still alive, but he just stared up at me. I couldn't stop thinking about all the things I'd never said to him. I couldn't remember the last time I said I love you to him, I couldn't remember the last time I did something really nice for him; I could only remember the bad things. I saw people running out, and I just, you know… I didn't want to live at that point. My life was over. I was a murderer. I'd killed my own brother, one of my best friends in the world. So I ran to the fence and just slipped through a hole in it and threw the gun in the water and then jumped in myself. When I woke up I was on a little beach, a ways from the school. I must have drifted. I don't know how I lived. I shouldn't have, I had no business living, but when I woke up I didn't remember anything. I mean, I remembered who I was and all that, but the whole week leading up was totally gone."

"The mind will do that sometimes in an effort to protect itself," Hartley said, evidently listening too, "It's totally natural with traumatic experiences."

"Shit," said Luck.

"A fabulous story," said Smith, as he clapped his two gloved hands together a few times, "A real hero here, a boy who was going to shoot up the school but instead just shot his brother. Fantastic. And it looks like that took just about enough time for them to arm my atom bomb. Perfect Sam. A magnificent job."

"How were you not arrested?" asked Luck, a coldness in her voice that pierced Sam's heart.

"That's when everyone died. I'd survived the first apocalypse in the water somehow."

"At least you know your brother wouldn't have lived much longer after you shot him," Misty said.

"Yeah, if anything you saved him from the fear of the apocalypse, of suffocating to death. I understand gunshots are a fast death," Hartley said.

"That's not it though," said Sam as he looked at Bare, "Bare I'm sorry. Tess, if you can hear me, I'm sorry. That night I went away I found the power plant in Folly's Landry, and I had sex with an old woman there, she must have been 65, but I did it."

"You did what?" asked Luck.

"Carol. She died halfway through, or after, or at some point, so I tried to give her a funeral, but accidently ended up setting the power plant on fire, which then kinda burnt down and caused everyone at the Caribou to kill themselves. Or at least I think that's what happened."

"You did what?" asked Tess weakly. She was alive! Holy shit she was alive!

"I thought that dog was dead," Smith said, amused.

"I did it. I'm sorry, I kept meaning to tell you, but I just... I wanted us to find a new home before I had to explain how I accidently ruined your old one... I'm sorry."

"Sam," Bare said, hurt.

"You killed all my friends," Tess said, "You killed everyone I loved."

"I'm sorry," said Sam, "It truly was an accident. How was I supposed to know that would happen? Not that that's an excuse."

Tess stood up on shaky knees, and she hobbled over to Sam, an angry fire in her eyes.

"I'm mad at you for that, but right now we need to take out this guy," she whispered.

"Hey! No whispering," Smith said, as he leveled his handgun, "Now you were dead before, let's put you back that way."

He fired, but the gun kicked, and the bullet sliced into Sam's wrist. Icy: the pain was icy. Sam had always wondered if getting shot would be the burning pain or that icy cold one. He knew now. The bullet had cut through his skin, but it also cut through some of the leather. Sam looked at his blood, pushing red out of his skin, but also the broken strap. He was a bad guy. Or he had been. But he had an opportunity to save the world here maybe. He had an opportunity to redeem himself, for Randy, for the Caribou, for everyone. One, two, three.

Sam ripped his arm from the leather, which snapped apart fairly easily. He fumbled with the belt on the other one, his hand not working the way he'd like it to with the pain in his bleeding wrist. Smith leveled another shot, but Sam twisted away, and the panel of glass behind them started to web with cracks from the hole the bullet bore. Sam pulled the belt out of its loop and dropped to the floor.

"Get him ya little fucker!" Brick yelled.

"Fuck him up Sam!" Luck chimed in.

Sam charged at Smith who fired another shot, but only grazed Sam's thigh. Sam ran through it and tackled Smith to the ground. The handgun skirted off. Sam punched Smith in the face, and some red blood blossomed from Smith's nose.

Smith laughed as Sam punched his face. That was unexpected. Sam let up for a minute.

"What are you laughing at?" he asked as he slammed Smith's skull to the ground.

"Fuck him up Sam!" Luck screamed. Sam looked back at her. Goddamn it she was pretty.

"Sam!" Brick yelled, trying his best to gesture.

Sam turned back just in time to catch Smith with his hand poised around his watch, the one with the panic button that summoned his guards. Shit.

"You can't beat me Sam. You should know that. I'm smarter than you; I've got better resources, a host of guards, and I've got the power of retribution behind me. You can't touch me."

"Oh yeah?" Sam said as he raised his heavy winter boot. Smith pressed the button.

"Guards!" Smith called, the melody of victory in his voice, "Get this trash off of me."

Sam remembered the guards rushing in when he was first here, how fast they were, how angry their guns were. Boot still poised over Smith, he raised his hands up into the air, blood from his bullet wound wetting his sleeve. He closed his eyes, ready to hear that crack-crack-crack of machine gun fire. But none came.

"Well look who we found," said the tiger. Sam looked up, and the zoo animals were streaming in through all the open chambers in the penthouse.

"I told you that would lead somewhere good," said one of the chimps.

"I said that," said the other chimp as he climbed down off the hippo's back.

"Well holee-shit," said Brick, "What happened to all those guards?"

The tiger just licked her lips, and the hippo pushed Otis the guard inside. He was bleeding from his face, and his clothes were torn pretty badly.

"There weren't that many," said the hippo, "We had to kill two, and this one gave up."

"I'm sorry, Mr. Smith," Otis said, tears mixing in with the blood, "They all heard the radio, and the cowards deserted you. They just took off. I stayed though, Mr. Smith, I stayed for you."

Their broadcast had worked. Incredible.

"Get the gun Sam and let us down," Luck said. Sam looked at the gun. Then back at Smith. He didn't know if he could do it.

"Just think of dear Randy," Smith said, inching backwards tentatively toward the control panel, "I remember when you were first brought to me. You could have grabbed Otis' gun and shot me dead. It would have been so easy. But you didn't. You couldn't. Take the gun Sam. Do it."

Sam stared at the gun and then at his friends.

"Do it."

He couldn't. He just couldn't.

Suddenly the whole building shook, knocking everyone standing off balance. Smith pitched forward and had his hands on the gun again. Everyone froze as he pointed the gun around the room and worked back to the control panel.

"What the hell was that?" Pavel said, in almost perfect English. Everyone looked at him, stunned.

"Vat?" he asked, his accent back.

"That would be the sound of the rockets firing up," Smith said.

"But you didn't press the button!" Sam said.

"What rockets?" asked Luck.

"The rockets on my atomic missile."

"But you didn't press the damn button!" Sam said, incredulous now. Smith laughed. Sam saw the capybara was stealthily gnawing at Bare's restraints. Good.

"Do you honestly believe I would bring the only people who stood any chance of stopping my plan up to the only place where they could stop it? Do I strike you as unintelligent? Of course not. Would you like to see what this button does?"

Smith slapped his hand on the button and a door on the missile opened, and there was a cockpit inside. A digital timer counted down from 3:56. Not much time at all. Smith pressed another button, and a metal sphincter rotated its way out of the rocket's way. The smoke billowing from underneath met the snow from the blizzard still raging outside in a swirling, white haze, and the cold air from the open hatch chilled the room in an instant.

"There is no stopping this. I will have my revenge on the world. A world as cruel as this one? How do you still support it? It killed off almost all of us. It choked most of us to death. It allowed my mother to leave me, my stupid, stupid father to kill himself, my body to become riddled with disease. A world that would simply allow me to do this," Smith said, as he aimed the handgun, two hands this time, at Pavel and pulled the trigger. Pavel's throat exploded into blood. Smith must have hit an artery because the blood just rushed out.

"You son of a bitch! I'll kill you!" Brick roared.

"See?! That's madness! That man is now dead, and that is allowed! Some might even say encouraged. How can you support a place like this? How can you not want to infect the very core of it, steep its opaqueness with the very diseases it has issued to keep us fearing it, to keep us dying?" Smith said as he stepped toward the missile, "Well soon it won't matter. Soon the world will be dead. Everything will be dead. We all will be. I'm going to ride this to the end though. Right into that hole I tear in Mother Nature."

The capybara was just about through Bare's restraints. Sam had to keep Smith and that roving gun occupied.

"You're going to get in that thing?"

"Precisely. My body, my disease will infect the very core of the opaque, and it shall be me who kills Nature. Naturally I have the diseases already in there, so if you did somehow stop me, it wouldn't matter. But I want to be there when it happens. Poetic, don't you think?"

"Your definitions of 'opaque' and 'transparent' don't make any sense."

2:30 remaining. Smith glanced at the countdown.

"Of course they do. It makes perfect sense."

"No. Why do you call the invisible thing, the space in-between space, how could that possibly be the opaque and not the transparent? It's invisible. You keep calling people and things transparent, but we're clearly opaque. It's stupid."

"You are the stupid one," Smith said, mad now. They were just supposed to watch this, "You are all stupid. There was never any point. My legacy will be immortal, and you will all simply be insignificant and dead."

"Nah, I think you're probably the one who's gonna be dead," Bare said as he took those claws of his and slashed through the arm that held the gun. Smith's arm hemorrhaged blood as the pistol clattered to the ground.

"Wait!" Sam said, "We need him to tell us how to turn this thing off."

Bare put his clawed foot onto Smith's chest, keeping him in place as his torn up arm leaked freely. It looked like Smith tried to move the arm toward the gun, but it flopped weakly. Bare must have torn something important.

"You gonna talk then?" Bare asked.

Smith just looked up at Bare.

"He asked if you were going to talk," Sam translated.

"Even if I don't get to go along, that missile is still going. My revenge is assured. You have lost, all of you. You are weak, you are stupid, you are worthless pieces of-"

Bare tore open Smith's throat, and the diseased blood just streamed out. Smith's blood was definitely opaque.

"I'm sorry, I had to do it. What an *ass*hole."

Sam was pretty sure that was the first time he'd ever heard Bare swear. Shit.

"Turn that thing the fuck off!" Luck yelled, "And someone get us the fuck down from here!"

Sam sprinted over to the Luck. He undid one strap, and she slapped him across the face.

"No you idiot, stop the bomb!"

"I don't know how."

"Figure it the fuck out kid," said Brick.

"I'm sorry about all this," Sam said to Luck.

Sam ran back from the glass apartment over to the control panel and started hitting buttons.

The red clock clicked down to 59 seconds. Time was running out, and none of these buttons did a goddamn thing. What was the point of having a switch or a lever or a button if it wasn't going to do anything? Ridiculous. Nothing was working. 50 seconds left. Sam was going to have to do something drastic.

He'd done a lot of bad in his life. He had killed his brother, he had killed everyone at the Caribou, and he had hurt his friends more times than he could count. He'd even stolen those cookies from stupid, stoned Buck. If he was going to go out, he was going to go out at least trying to do good.

Luck had unstrapped her other wrist and was over at the panel, trying to hit buttons too, but nothing changed. Sam ran over to Bare and hugged him.

"Thank you for being the best friend I ever had. I love you buddy."

And then over to Tess who had collapsed again on the floor.

"Tess, I'm sorry for everything I did. I promise I didn't try to hurt you or anyone on purpose. I'm really sorry, but now I need you to get better and take care of Bare for me. Love him or whatever."

"Sam-"

But he was already over to Luck. Twenty seconds left on the clock. Nineteen. Eighteen. Seventeen.

He grabbed her like he had always fantasized grabbing a girl in high school. He dipped her and kissed her on the mouth.

"Sorry, I had to do that. I really wish I could have gotten to know you better. You seem like everything I've ever wanted in my life. Or, uh, I think you're pretty cool is all. Now get everyone out of here."

"Sam, what-"

But Sam was already running through the smoke and the snow to the bomb. He couldn't see, but the clock said 10 seconds. Nine. He climbed into the rocket and strapped himself in. The door to the thing slid shut, and there was a little window where Sam got to watch Luck frantically slam all the buttons he'd already tried. No luck. She looked up at him, desperation on her face before she waved at everyone else to get back. They started to pile into the guardrooms, away from the blast of the rockets.

"I think she really liked me too," Sam said, a smile on his face. Three. Bare knelt down next to Tess and held her in his arms. Two. That was good.

One.

518

It started as a rumble, a shaking of the cockpit, and then gravity slammed him into the chair. This was it. He fought a panel of metal off the inside and stared at the interwoven, colorful wires.

He had always been so careful in life. He'd stayed inside when the weather was bad, ate well, he always carried some form of protection, he always locked his fucking door. He lived a safe life, an easy life, and now he was flying in an atom bomb. It was funny how these things happened. Or maybe it wasn't funny. Maybe it was sad.

He hoped to hell he could get this thing to stop or to not explode. He didn't actually know what he was doing now, but he wasn't scared. He was finally doing something that made up for some of the shit he'd done in life. This is good, he thought. It felt like he'd gone a fair distance now. Gravity was pulling him down, so he assumed he was traveling away and not too far up. The missile was still going. Moment of truth. He started pulling at wires. They sparked and burnt his fingers, but he kept pulling.

Sam hoped he was doing the right thing finally. He thought of Mister Fresh and her message about Nature. About Nature having given up, about all the animals having given up. Maybe people weren't worth saving. But some were. Brick, Hartley, Misty, Tess, Bare… Luck. How could the world be all bad if people and animals like his friends existed? He started pulling wire faster.

How was this rocket still moving? What was the point of having all these wires if they weren't going to do anything? Sam thought about swimming with Bare, about drinking with him, listening to him talk. He felt special, having gotten the opportunity to meet who he met, to do the things he had done. He wished he'd had more time with them all. Especially Luck, Sam thought, as he pulled out an important looking green circuit board.

Now that he was about to die, he hoped it wasn't just a coincidence. He hoped everything wasn't just random events and things that just happened to happen. He wanted his sacrifice to mean something. He reached his arm deep up inside the hole and ripped out a huge chain of something. The rockets sputtered, and gravity lessened!

Yes!

"Fuck yes!"

He hoped he'd saved them. For Bare and for Tess and for Luck and for whomever else was left. He gripped another circuit board and pulled. The explosion happened so fast he didn't even know it had happened.

Outside the blizzard started to lessen.

671

Sam woke up dead.

This is what death felt like apparently, he thought as he looked up at the white ceiling. He knew he was dead because he couldn't move. Which was certainly annoying. Heaven was boring. More of that stucco ceiling that gave him a headache and drove him to counting. Maybe this was hell. They'd only have a ceiling as stupid as this in hell.

"He's up!"

Tess?

"Tess?"

"Sam! Sam you're up," Tess said as she put her front paws up on the bed. He wasn't nearly as scared as the last time this had happened. Her burns had healed, and some of the hair was even starting to grow back. She looked good.

"Am I dead again?"

"Not quite," Brick said.

Sam tried to turn his head, but it was difficult.

"What?"

"You've been out for a while," Hartley said as she put her arm around Brick. Cute. They were a thing now.

"SAM!"

Bare's voice.

"If I didn't think I'd break you I'd give you such a big squeeze right now!"

"Did I do it?"

"Ya did it buddy!"

"Yay," Sam said weakly. The pain was kicking in.

"Where are we?"

"Chicago," said Hartley.

"Is Luck ok?"

"She's alive and well thanks to you."

"What happened?"

"We're not sure. When we saw the rocket didn't explode we took a few cars out and went looking for you. Found you tucked into a giant pile of snow. No idea how it got there, but it looked like a relatively soft landing. Or at least, you know, not an atomic explosion one anyway," Brick explained.

"We thought you were dead when we pulled you out of there. Broke about every possible bone in your body. You're lucky I'm a brilliant doctor," Hartley said.

That would explain why Sam couldn't move. Hopefully this was just temporary.

"We also," Hartley leaned in close to whisper to Sam, "I also took care of that little syphilis problem you had. So, you know, you're welcome."

"It's just so good to see you awake! I thought you were all dead and stuff!" Bare said, a big grin plastered across his stupid, friendly bear mug.

"You too buddy. What about Misty?"

"I'm here," she said, quietly as usual.

"Thank you for saving us," said a voice Sam didn't recognize. Slightly soft and slightly Southern as well.

"Who?"

"I'm Trevor, Misty's husband. We haven't met," Trevor leaned over. He had a mustache. It looked pretty goofy, but he also had a friendly face, "I'd shake your hand, but…"

Sam looked down and took in his entire plaster coated body. Yikes.

"Sam?"

Luck's voice. His heart fluttered like it was in the breeze. Luck punched Sam's stomach, and he could feel that. Apparently he hadn't broken anything down there.

"Ooof," Sam said.

"That's for going and doing something so fucking stupid," Luck said before kissing him on the cheek, "And that's for being so fucking stupid too."

She pointed at Hartley.

"Do not even tell me to watch my language right now either."

Even through the cast, Sam blushed.

"So Chicago?"

"Safe and sound."

"And you?"

"Yeah."

"What about us?"

"Sure."

"What?"

"Yeah, you get out of that cast, and I'll let you take me out on a date. I'm not paying though. I want to be *wooed*."

So in the aftermath of Smith, the people of Chicago were hungry for leadership, and Brick fell right into place. They had a focus on education though, to try to make sure that these people didn't fall into the hands of some psycho like Smith again.

Bare and Tess worked to bring in more animals to the community, and the people and animals, with Luck and Sam's help of course, were beginning to work together. It was actually pretty cool. It had a post-apocalyptic Garden of Eden kind of feel to it. And from reports from the outside, it seemed like the animals had stopped just killing themselves. Sam had done it. He didn't know how, but he'd done it. He had stopped a goddamn atomic bomb. He was a hero. Or at least he wasn't a bad guy, which was just as good. And now they could all get back to living. Actually living, not just surviving. 'Take that stupid apocalypse,' Sam liked to think.

Since Sam's limp was pretty substantial still, and it was still pretty wintery outside, they decided to have their date indoors. She came over to Sam's new apartment. It was rustic themed and comfortable. Luck wore a brightly colored dress that along with her smile lit up the room of mostly muted browns or sepia tones. He cooked Luck a meal of real beef steak (the cow had died of natural causes) and his world famous mashed potatoes. The steak was perfectly seasoned, and expertly grilled on a small electric grill, or at least he thought it was.

They sat at a small table, an old red-checkered tablecloth draped over the wood, a view of five pine trees planted in a row in the small backyard out the picture windows. One of them was red and every time the Chicago wind hit her, she would shed some of her needles into the melting snow. Sam would have to do something about that when he was fully recovered.

Over dinner she told him the story of how she had been raised by dogs in Hong Kong, and how she didn't really remember anything before the crew found her. She told him this as she laughed and took huge bites of the steak, chewing sloppily with one side of her teeth.

Sam didn't have to believe her story, he just liked to see her talk, watch her eat. Be around her. He thought about all the time he had spent alone and how comfortable he thought he had been. Tentatively he put his hand on her leg, and when she didn't swat it away, when she in fact scooted forward so he wouldn't have to stretch, everything that had happened, everything he'd done seemed to not matter, and, with spittle and steak peppering his face, Sam closed his eyes and smiled.

As Luck might have said, 'not fucking bad.'

About the Author

Lex Larson is a New York based Writer and Illustrator. *A Red Pine Sunday* is his first novel. He is an alumni of NYU's Dramatic Writing program and also just one heck of a guy.